T0367598

Setting Your Course

How to Navigate Your Life's Journey

DR. GREG BOURGOND

iUniverse LLC
Bloomington

SETTING YOUR COURSE
HOW TO NAVIGATE YOUR LIFE'S JOURNEY

iUniverse books may be ordered through booksellers or by contacting:

iUniverse
1663 Liberty Drive
Bloomington, IN 47403
www.iuniverse.com
1-800-Authors (1-800-288-4677)

ISBN: 978-1-4917-2347-0 (sc)
ISBN: 978-1-4917-2348-7 (hc)
ISBN: 978-1-4917-2349-4 (e)

Library of Congress Control Number: 2014902049

Printed in the United States of America.

iUniverse rev. date: 3/28/2014

This book is dedicated to my wife, Debby, the greatest gift I have ever received. Through joys and sorrows, triumphs and trials, victories and defeats, and successes and failures, she has given me the platform to dance on. Her unwavering faith, unquestioned loyalty, unconditional love, and steadfast support have given me the courage and endurance to climb many mountains, explore new territory, and navigate unfamiliar terrain. Her wise counsel and innate wisdom have kept me from going off course. I have never known anyone who so embodies the fruit of the Spirit as she does. Thank you for believing in me and helping me stay on track and finish well.

Contents

Foreword

In my leadership classes at Fuller Theological Seminary, I often use these two quotes: "The difference between leaders and followers is perspective," and "The difference between leaders and better leaders is better perspective." Greg Bourgond exemplifies a deep understanding of both these statements. This book, *Setting Your Course*, is replete with leadership perspectives that can make a significant difference in a leader's life. Greg wants to help leaders become better leaders. He explains these perspectives by using three metaphors: the compass, the map, and the guide. Let me highlight these concepts by touching on just a few quotes from each part of the book.

Part I: The Compass

"We are God's very own. He knows us because He created us according to His design and wants us to live in accordance with that design. *When we choose to live in accordance with that design, we will find meaning and significance.* When we choose to live apart from that design, we will reap meaninglessness and insignificance."[1] When a person grasps God's design for their life he or she begins to live a more focused life.

"Being proactive about our journey will ensure that we arrive at a destination of our choosing. Understanding the landscape and what to expect on the journey helps prevent unforeseen obstacles that can impede the journey or terminate it altogether."[2] To avoid being blindsided, a leader must understand the landscape—the lifetime journey—and have useful expectations that help prevent unforeseen obstacles. Being proactive means having perspectives that allow choices furthering God's development of the leader.

---

1   Chapter 1, "Our Foundation," 32.
2   Chapter 6, "Our Pathway," 91.

Part II: The Map

"Now that the compass is in place, the next step is to define the map for the journey. Each of us has a unique map designed by God for us to follow."[3] If a leader seeks to know and follow God, a sense of destiny is important.

"God develops leaders over a lifetime. We have a part in the process. Cooperation with God will lead to growth in character, competence, and congruence."[4] Knowing how God shapes a leader enhances *proactive cooperation* with God's development for that leader.

"A personal timeline is a big-picture overview of your life, a chronological map of your development highlighting the critical incidents and circumstances God used to develop your spiritual character and purpose."[5] An important tool for gaining leadership perspective is a personal timeline that accounts for God's shaping of a leader's life.

Part III: The Guide

"We need to have a lifetime perspective on life, work, and ministry. Effective leaders view present actions from a lifetime perspective."[6] Finishing perspectives—characteristics of those who finish well, enhancements for those who finish well, and barriers that prevent good finishes—can all help leaders recognize God's present-shaping activities in order to benefit from them and move toward a good finish.

"Few people finish well. Those who do got timely help along the way from other individuals who significantly enhanced their development. Clinton's research indicates that people who finish well have had from ten to fifteen significant mentors in their life."[7] With three entire chapters devoted to mentoring, space alone indicates just how important being mentored and mentoring others is to the positive shaping of a leader.

In fact, let me close this foreword with a recommendation: as you read

---

3   Chapter 7, "Our Journey," 110.
4   Chapter 9, "Our Trajectory," 122.
5   Chapter 9, "Our Trajectory," 139.
6   Chapter 11, "Our Shaping," 171.
7   Chapter 12, "Our Story," 171.

this powerful book about leadership, do it with an older mentor who can clarify and thus reemphasize the importance of the many helpful ideas contained here.

Dr. J. Robert (Bobby) Clinton

Preface

Genesis

In the process of fulfilling my life purpose, I have helped hundreds of men and women realize their God-ordained potential and destiny. Most have participated in small groups that I have led or that have been led by others I have trained. Many I have mentored personally. I have written extensively on the subjects addressed in this book. My journey as a teacher, speaker, consultant, minister, businessman, military officer, mentor, and ministry leader has provided hundreds of opportunities to address and apply the topics and issues contained in the following chapters.

Having completed the exercises recommended in this book, I have come to clarity regarding my life's work. My life purpose is to influence leaders directly and indirectly to live all-out for Christ: to facilitate a process for determining how God has wired them; to help them align their lives according to God's plan; to encourage them to become proactive partners in fulfilling God's purposes and redemptive activity; and to exhort them to leave a worthwhile legacy in the lives of others.

My committed passion is to help men and women realize their God-given potential through Christ and develop to the fullest their God-given gifts, abilities, and capacities for godly leadership from the inside out and within legitimate limitations, such as temperament, aptitude, and maturity.

I have personally walked alongside men and women to help them engage their unique design. I have witnessed the life transformation brought about when they applied the principles in this book. In just about every encounter I've had with them, these men and women have expressed a longing for a closer relationship with their Creator, a desire to live more significant and meaningful lives, to live life more intentionally, and to give their lives over to something of eternal consequence.

For many seeking a more focused life, knowing how to convert a dream or desire to reality has remained an elusive skill. I have dedicated more than forty years to helping people find practical ways to do just that. The results have been astounding. Recently I gathered twelve men and their spouses to celebrate the completion of a two-year developmental journey. We met over a delicious dinner and shared what God had done during our time together.

They spent the first stage of the journey establishing an internal compass to help them live a life centered on the transformational truth of God's Word, tuning their beliefs, values, perceptual attitudes, and motives to the heart of God. They formulated personal alignment plans and executed strategic plans of implementation. During the second stage of the journey, they discovered their unique wiring in terms of biblical purpose, life purpose, committed passion, critical supportive role characteristics, and unique methodologies—their toolkit and ultimate contribution to God's redemptive purposes. A personal life mandate was developed encompassing these elements. The result projected a trajectory for their lives that will help them engage their God-inspired journey until He calls them home.

Once we completed our meal, I described what had transpired over the time we spent together. I told the gathering that before God can work effectively *through* us, He must first work surgically *in* us. Once our beliefs, values, attitudes, and motives are in alignment with God's commands, precepts, and principles, we are ready to engage His purposes for us—purposes that were determined before we ever came to be. When we live our lives in accordance with His design for us, we are fulfilled.

The graduates then shared their perspectives about the experience, lessons they learned and have applied, and their intentions going forward. Their comments concluded with a public declaration of their life purpose and committed passion and their ultimate contribution—the legacy they hope to leave when God beckons them home. After the last graduate spoke, the spouses spontaneously stood and gave a resounding round of applause. Several emotionally remarked how fortunate they were to have husbands who wished to live a life focused on intentionally honoring God.

In addition to helping others calibrate their heart to the heart of God and providing a means to determine their distinct trajectory, I have mentored many people, helping them build into their lives sustaining accountability and the momentum to finish well. I have encouraged some not only to be mentored, but also to mentor others.

Although I have spent years creating resources to help people develop their spiritual compass, map, and guide, until now I've never put them together as a single resource. However, I have received many requests to do just that. So, after decades of experience leading others to find their compass, navigate their map, and seek out guides who would help them finish well, I decided it was time to put these concepts and findings together in one book.

Purpose

The purpose of the book is to help men and women set their courses, find focus for their lives, engage God's journeys for them, and finish their journeys well. The book is divided into three parts, preceded by a prologue and followed by an epilogue. Many of the chapters provide thoughtful questions that will help you prepare executable plans. You also will be directed to additional resources and appendices to help you. Each part—the compass, the map, and the guide—provides directions for how to prepare a deliberate plan of action. A form for each plan is provided. Once all three plans are completed, you will have a *Focused Life Plan* to implement so that you will finish well.

The prologue presents the scenario of a wide-awake dream in which the dreamer is led to a heavenly throne where he finds out what is in store for him and his part in that future. The epilogue provides a summary and serves to put the entire journey together into a comprehensive whole—a focused life driven by a calibrated heart, defined by a unique and personal life trajectory, and aided by guidance from and accountability to others who will help us realize our calling.

Part 1—"The Compass"—explains the importance of orienting our lives in accordance with established compass points. Once we understand how to use the compass, plot our course, find our bearings, and determine the direction we will take to fulfill our destiny, we are ready for the exciting journey that lies ahead. We'll examine our beliefs, values, attitudes, and motives under the microscope of God's Word, and I'll present procedures to better align them and outline corrective and preventive measures for finishing well. The field of transformational change is the heart: a transformed heart leads to transformed behavior. Directions on how to develop a *Personal Alignment Plan* will complete this section. Part 1 is about God working *in* you so that He can work *through* you.

Part 2—"The Map"—defines the trajectory we are to follow based on how God has wired us. This section will help a man or woman move from a scattered approach to living to a laser-like focus. Beginning with an all-out commitment to Him, a focused life is dedicated exclusively to carrying out God's unique purposes by identifying specific focal issues: biblical purpose, life purpose, committed passion, major role, unique methodology, and ultimate contribution. Thus life's activities are prioritized around these focal issues, resulting in a satisfying life of being and doing. Directions on how to develop a *Personal Life Mandate* complete this section. Part 2 is about God working His redemptive purposes in the world *through* you.

Part 3—"The Guide"—stresses the importance of being mentored and mentoring others. Those who have finished well have had multiple mentors in their lives—intensive, occasional, and passive mentors who have guided them along their unique trajectory. I address living a legacy worth leaving in the lives of others, and I provide guidance on how to finish well. You will be taught how to find a mentor to address your developmental needs and how to determine what type of mentor you are and how to mentor others. Accountability guidelines are also addressed in this section, which ends with directions on how to develop a *Personal Mentoring Strategy*. Part 3 is about God working *in* and *through* us with the support of others working *with* us.

Throughout this book you will be given the opportunity to think through responses to key questions introduced by the phrase *Personal Assessment*. You will be encouraged to ponder thought-provoking questions that will help you come to clarity about your uniqueness and God's intended focus for your life. Your responses will prepare you to develop the three plans.

I encourage you to read this book carefully in its entirety. The real payoff comes when you proactively apply what you've learned from answering the questions posed throughout the book, prepare the plans recommended at the end of each part, and execute the specifics of each plan in a disciplined and dedicated fashion. I also encourage you to conduct an annual personal audit to evaluate your progress and revise your plans accordingly.

Acknowledgments

We can't finish well without the influence and support of and accountability to others God brings into our lives. I am indebted to so many men and women who have intersected my path over time. To be sure, I run the risk of leaving out many who deserve to be acknowledged for the way they have informed and shaped my thinking about focused living.

Passive mentors who have influenced my being and doing include Vance Havner, A. W. Tozer, D. Martyn Lloyd Jones, G. Campbell Martin, J. I. Packer, Dallas Willard, Charles Colson, Henry Cloud, Brother Lawrence, Augustine, Tim Keller, C. S. Lewis, Paul E. Little, John MacArthur, Alister McGrath, John Ortberg, John R. W. Stott, Rick Warren, Moses, Joshua, Caleb, Elijah, Samuel, Isaiah, Jeremiah, Daniel, King David, Jonathan, Solomon, Peter, John, James, and Paul.

Contemporary influences on my thoughts and actions, people to whom I am eternally indebted, are identified below.

J. Robert Clinton, professor emeritus, Fuller Theological Seminary

No other person has so profoundly shaped my thinking about personal and spiritual development as Bobby Clinton. You will see his DNA throughout this book. He has mentored me formally in person, nonformally at a distance, and informally through the materials he has produced. Bobby's Leadership Emergence Theory is the backbone of this book. I am forever grateful.

Neil T. Anderson, author and teacher on spiritual freedom

God used Neil as a catalyst for my initial thoughts on spiritual formation and maturation. Neil was instrumental in helping me understand that what we do does not determine who we are, but that who we are in Christ should determine what we do.

Erwin McManus, lead pastor, Mosaic

Erwin has taught me to dream, to see life as story, and to exercise creativity and innovation. I consider it a privilege to know him as my friend. He has a way of seeing who you really are and who you can become. He is all about discovery and unleashing people to fulfill their unique destiny.

Gary Gonzales, senior associate pastor, Overlake Christian Church

Gary has been my closest friend for more than forty years. He is the epitome of integrity and authenticity. He models godliness, professionalism, focused living, and ministerial effectiveness. God has used him repeatedly to keep me on track. His friendship has been a source of strength for me.

Terry Walling, president of Leader Breakthru

Terry, a peer mentor, is passionate about helping leaders finish well. His advice and wisdom have helped me become a better teacher and mentor to others who long to make a greater contribution to Kingdom purposes and values.

Randy Reese, president of Vantage Point 3

Randy, a peer mentor, lives and breathes personal development of ministry leaders. He models what he teaches. His focus on helping others discover their unique design has helped me understand the multidimensional aspects of focused living.

Sam Rima, executive pastor, 10th Church

Sam has been a great friend to me over the years, offering practical advice, timely humor, deep spirituality, and mature biblical insight. He helped me break out of my Western cocoon and see a much larger world where God lives and acts in unique ways.

John Cionca, executive director of Ministry Transitions

John's friendship, godly counsel, innate wisdom, and personal support have buoyed me on numerous occasions. His disarming humor, practical bent, and ministry expertise have kept me from falling off the ledge many times.

Paul Brushaber, senior pastor, Christ Community Church

This book would never have been written had it not been for Paul's graciousness; I am the executive pastor of the church he leads. He gave me an entire month off to write this book in Ireland, and he also gave me the platform upon which to preach and teach the principles and processes described herein.

Introduction

Many of us meander through life from one event to the next, living in the present with little thought about the future. We react to situations and circumstances rather than proactively addressing them based on informed strategies of engagement. Life happens to us. We give scant attention to what informs our actions, and as a result, our decisions lack cohesion, coherence, and consistency. Absent any unifying theme to direct our actions, we live incongruent lives filled with a mosaic of conflicting influences.

Our responses to life's crises produce behaviors that make little sense and reveal almost no integration. Our decisions reflect little constancy. Most of us are just trying to make it through the day, week, or month. We live from one experience to the next, one emergency to the next. Our lives are not ordered in any discernible way; if they were plotted on a scatter diagram, it would show no clear directionality or focus.

Consciously or unconsciously, we allow competing authorities to guide our beliefs, values, perceptions, attitudes, motives, and behaviors. These competing authorities might include divergent ideologies, philosophies, and worldviews. Perhaps we listen to the voices of secular humanism, postmodernism, relativism, or pluralism. Or maybe we embrace atheism, materialism, naturalism, communism, new ageism, modernism, agnosticism, liberalism, conservatism, universalism, skepticism, socialism, pessimism, pantheism, pacifism, optimism, fascism, ecumenism, cynicism, multiculturalism, or any of the many "isms" vying for our allegiance. Our worldview is the lens through which we view life and makes sense of our observations about life. Every worldview has a prescribed set of foundational beliefs and core values.

We find ourselves being pushed into our future by these forces rather than being pulled by a clear sense of direction, and we end up living unfocused lives. Then, at some point along the journey, we stop to wonder how we got where we are. The causes to which we have given our lives cease to provide satisfaction or, more important, significance. We regret many of the decisions we made along the way and wish we had chosen more wisely. We realize that a current we should have avoided has been carrying us along. Remorsefully, we feel resigned to our fate, with little or no opportunity to make a change so late in the game—or so we think.

Maybe we are at the front end of our lives, longing to live differently than others who are much further down the road. We have seen the negative consequences when people we love or admire have chosen poorly, leaving in their wake broken promises, unfulfilled dreams, and shattered relationships. We don't want to make the same mistakes, and so we search for a better way—a preventive that will guarantee a better future. Not knowing where to turn, however, we absorb over time the very worldviews that got others into a mess in the first place. If only life came with a GPS system that would give us the direction we seek: turn here, follow this road, avoid these hazards, or take this alternate route.

In fact, each of us must begin our journey with even more fundamental questions: What's my destination, and how am I going to get there? What road signs should I pay attention to? Who will help me get where I want to go—and is where I want to go the right destination for me? Given my unique and personal wiring, what are my options? Which of the roads ahead is the best one for me?

In my book *A Rattling of Sabers*, I made the following comments that bear repeating:

One of my favorite books in the Bible is Ecclesiastes. Solomon, the author, is near the end of his life, having squandered the gift of wisdom given to him. He has tasted all the world has to offer but concludes it was all vanity. In Ecclesiastes, he records his journey as a caution for the rest of us.

The book is a powerful argument against the self-centered, unbridled pursuit of wealth unshared, pleasure for pleasure's sake, success instead of significance, materialism at the expense of biblical values, self-actualization instead of Bible-informed purposes, the constant search for intellectual understanding of the world around us when the truth is found at the feet of Christ, and a desire for worldly rather than godly wisdom. Solomon reminds us over and over again that life lived on the horizontal plane of worldly affairs, apart from a vertical, empowering relationship with our Creator through a personal relationship with His Son, Jesus Christ, is utterly meaningless—simply an aroma left in the lives of others long after we're gone from this earthly plane.

Have you ever felt that life is meaningless—especially when you listen to the news, see events on television, observe life as it passes you by, or watch politicians destroy each other for a perishable crown? We all question the meaning of life. And when failure comes, as it inevitably will, our hopes and dreams go down the drain and a sense of emptiness descends on us like a black cloud.

What's even more alarming is that when our dreams and hopes *have* been realized, after a short period of elation, that same emptiness works its way back into our lives. Once again we are compelled to climb another mountain, reaching the top only to find that ultimate satisfaction is fleeting and there is yet another mountain to conquer.

Apart from God, such activity is meaningless—vanity of vanities! We hunger for meaning but look for it in all the wrong places. Life viewed and lived by human reason alone, apart from a personal and vibrant relationship with God, is worthless, meaningless, and unsatisfying. The world promises riches, fame, and power but delivers only progressive death and life-draining despair. Satan is the grand master of bait and switch!

The road to satisfaction and significance is not in what we acquire, what we sensuously enjoy, what we achieve, or what power we possess, but in our relationship with God in Christ. Aligning ourselves with His purposes for our lives, aligning ourselves with how He has wired us, and involving ourselves in activities directed by His purposes and our divinely directed destiny are the only means to satisfaction and significance, to meaning and purpose.

There are only two choices before us:

• Live life apart from God—the result is a meaningless existence.
• Live life under God—the result is a meaningful existence.

True satisfaction is found in a life well lived in obedience to God's divine direction, life-giving commands, and timeless purposes for His world generally and His people specifically. We are "a chosen people, a royal priesthood, a holy nation, a people belonging to God, that you may declare the praises of him who called you out of darkness into his wonderful light."[8]

The greatest tragedy that you and I can ever face is getting to the end of our lives, looking back, and mournfully realizing what we could have done in the Lord and chosen not to, thus failing to reach God's designed potential for us. Instead, we settled for mediocrity, making our way there through compromise and conformity to the pattern of this world.

The Bible urges us to do just the opposite. We are to "offer our bodies as living sacrifices, holy and pleasing to God—this is our spiritual act of worship. Do not conform any longer to the pattern of this world, but be transformed by the renewing of our mind. Then you will be able to test and approve what God's will is—his good, pleasing, and perfect will."[9]

God created us to be lean birds in the air, not fat birds on the ground. I am afraid many of us have forgotten what it's like to fly high and free, guided only by the internal conviction and power of the Holy Spirit.

How do we ensure that we have the right strategy in place for our lives? What does God's strategy for our lives look like? God's Word gives us that strategy, a pattern for our lives. Obedience to that pattern will help us realize our full potential in Christ. Personal application will bring honor and glory to God.

God is very clear about His purposes for us. If we want to live a meaningful life, it must be aligned with His purposes. Each of us has a unique purpose to fulfill, a committed passion to embrace, a role to perform, unique methodologies—a personal toolkit—to employ, and an ultimate contribution to make. None of this is possible if we don't tune our hearts to the heart of God: His foundational truth, His values, His worldview, and His primary motives. None of this is attainable without the help and guidance of others, mentors who will hold us accountable to what really matters. In other words, we need a compass that is true, a map for the journey, and a guide that will help us get where God wants us to go.

Recently, an accomplished emergency room physician and researcher completed an eighteen-month process to calibrate his internal compass—the heart—and determine his unique trajectory for the future—the map. Up to that point he had defined his life's meaning and significance in

---

8   1 Pet. 2:9.

9   Rom. 12:1–2.

terms of his professional achievements. After looking at his life through the lens of God's Word, he completely reordered his priorities. His personal alignment plan and personal life mandate laid down the tracks he would run on going forward.

He now recognizes that his profession is not an end in itself but a means to a greater end. He is determined to leverage his professional expertise to help other doctors repurpose their lives to facilitate God's plans and help them understand their ultimate purpose and priorities. He now meets with consulting doctors who are committed to the same strategy; his hope is that these doctors will take doctors in residence under their wing and disciple them during the three years of residency. He has sold his home in the suburbs and relocated to a house in the city, closer to work, so he can better minister to other doctors.

Part 1: The Compass

The value of a compass is its ability to help us find our bearings in relationship to true north. A compass can be used for many purposes, from telling which way is north to following an unmarked path through the wilderness to finding the right direction to an object sighted in the distance. A compass orients us with our surroundings, helping us find our way over unfamiliar territory that may be obscured by objects such as trees or mountains.

Life is full of twists and turns—unplanned circumstances, events, and other obstructions that interfere with our progress. When life happens outside our plans and pressures mount, it is easy to become disoriented and lose our way, ending up at an unintended destination. And once we're there, it can be difficult to get back on course. We end up running in place or back in the same lost state as before. Our lives become all motion and no forward movement. Without a compass to guide us, we wander aimlessly through life, bouncing from one crisis to the next. When we reach the end of our journey, we are often exhausted, discouraged, and disappointed: we didn't end up where we had hoped to be at this point in life.

Given the inevitability of unplanned circumstances, events, and situations, we try to maintain balance by shifting our priorities, removing obstructions, recalculating, and repositioning ourselves. But living a balanced life is futile. Why? Because life does not happen to us in a balanced way. No time-management seminar will help us sustain a balanced life. True, assessment and evaluation are important; realigning priorities is crucial; removing obstructions is vital. However, reordering our lives to create balance can provide only temporary relief. Life will intrude on our plans, and we'll repeat the same time-management strategy to bring some semblance of stability back into our lives. That pattern of activity leaves us feeling frustrated and anxious, wondering when the next crisis will emerge and knock us off balance again.

If balance is futile, then how should we live? Christ gives us the answer. Jesus was driven by one prime objective: to do the will of His Father, who sent Him to finish His work.[10] Jesus was never in a hurry; He was never too early or too late.

> Now a man named Lazarus was sick. He was from Bethany, the village of Mary and her sister Martha. This Mary, whose brother Lazarus now lay sick, was the same one who poured perfume on the Lord and wiped his feet with her hair. So the sisters sent word to Jesus, "Lord, the one you love is sick." When he heard this, Jesus said, "This sickness will not end in death. No, it is for God's glory so that God's Son may be glorified through it." Jesus loved Martha and her sister and Lazarus. Yet when he heard that Lazarus was sick, he stayed where he was *two more days* [italics mine]... After he had said this, he went on to tell them, "Our friend Lazarus has fallen asleep; but I am going there to wake him up." His disciples replied, "Lord, if he sleeps, he will get better." Jesus had been speaking of his death, but his disciples thought he meant natural sleep. So then he told them plainly, "Lazarus is dead, and for your sake I am glad I was not there, so that you may believe. But let us go to him."[11]

Others expected Jesus to rush to Lazarus's side, but He waited for two days to go. Why? So others would believe. He arrived at the right time according to His Father's will. What do we learn from this? That

---

10 John 4:34.
11 John 11:1–6, 11–15.

living a balanced life is impossible. Jesus modeled a centered life, a life of equilibrium found at the core of His being. Part 1, "The Compass," will help you learn how to live a centered life in Christ, one that will provide equilibrium for your journey. Such a centered life will equip you for whatever comes your way—planned and unplanned. Life's troubles may rock you, but they will not topple you. You will enjoy stability and steadiness to sustain you through life's ups and downs.

Part 2: The Map

While traveling through Ireland recently, I found myself turning again and again to a paper map of the region. Even though I had a GPS system to guide me, I relied on a map to provide a wider perspective and to orient me. I was somewhat unfamiliar with the area, and the map helped me visualize the locations I intended to visit in relation to the larger context of the country. When you are on the ground trying to make your way to a planned destination, it is easy to get lost. Some people seem to have an internal sense of direction, but I was not blessed with this gift. So a map, an overview of the entire area, helps me find my way over unfamiliar territory.

A topographical map helps you navigate terrain that does not have roads, especially if it has changes in elevation. You may want to proceed directly to that hidden fishing spot along a winding river, but the map will tell you the best route around a mountain or swamp and let you know whether you will be climbing or descending along the way. One important caution: a map alone won't guarantee that you will find your way to that hilltop or that lake or that river. You will also need a compass.

Each of us has a unique terrain we must navigate. Our maps may share similar features, but the layouts may be entirely different. The locations of the features on our maps will no doubt be different, as will the type of features on our maps. On topographical maps, symbols are used to represent man-made features such as roads, trails, buildings, boundaries, railways, campgrounds, mines, dams, and recreation areas. There are also natural features like rivers, streams, lakes, wetlands, swamps, rapids, mountains, canyons, forested areas, cleared areas, orchards, and other landforms.

So it is with each life. The maps of our lives are filled with different features arranged according to God's preordained plan. Other features are man-made, some contributing to the surrounding environment and others bearing the imprint of personal disregard for it. By God's perfect will, you were born at a certain time in history with a certain set of features of varying capacity—intellect, temperament, body shape, aptitudes, emotions, and gender. You were born into a specific family, a specific country, and a specific culture. All of this was ordained by God regardless of the family of origin issues and environmental influences, positive or negative. Other features on our maps fall under the purview of God's permissive will, where our free will is exercised. These features are man-made, formed by the decisions we make and the events and circumstances we create, as well as cultural influences. Our maps are also impacted by features, both positive and negative, placed there by others.

Part 2, "The Map," will help you define the distinctive features of your life and the potential you've yet to realize. The "topographical" features will include your biblical purpose, life purpose, committed passion, role characteristics, unique gifts (natural abilities, acquired skills, and other personal tools), and ultimate contributions to God's redemptive purposes in the world. Part 2 will help you define your trajectory going forward within the boundaries of your individual map, and it will clarify your directionality and life focus.

Part 3: The Guide

When I took two of my grandsons and their father on a fishing expedition recently, I was smart enough to realize that I didn't know what I was doing and needed help. I wasn't an expert fisherman, and I didn't know the lake or the location of the walleye. Not wanting to appear dumb to my grandsons, I contracted a guide to lead us, give us advice, and help us catch fish. On a sunny morning he arrived where we had tied up our houseboat. He took us in his boat to a spot where he taught us how to rig our poles, what bait to use, how much line to let out, and how to respond to a bite. We followed his advice meticulously. Doing so netted us twenty-four walleye. Over the next two nights we enjoyed wonderful meals as we nestled safely in a secluded spot on one of the lake islands.

My mentor, J. Robert Clinton, professor emeritus at Fuller Seminary in Pasadena, California, has dedicated his life to determining how God develops leaders. He has conducted more than four thousand case studies in his research, and as he analyzed the lives of biblical, historical, and contemporary Christian leaders, he noted certain characteristics in those who finished well. One of those characteristics includes having many mentors over a lifetime: intensive mentors who helped build critical faith foundations, occasional mentors who helped with a particular need or struggle, and passive mentors who provided resources that fed the soul.

Successfully navigating the topography of your life requires a compass, a map, and a guide. The latter essential component, the guide, comprises trusted mentors who will help you reach your divine potential before God calls you home.

> The relationship between mentor and mentee may be formal or informal, scheduled or sporadic. The exchange of resources can take place over a long time or just once. Mentoring can also occur face-to-face or may happen over a great distance. Mentors link mentees to important resources, from financial resources to opportunities for ministry. Mentors empower mentees with encouragement and timely advice garnered through life.[12]

Part 3, "The Guide," will explain the importance of mentoring, introduce you to successful mentoring concepts, give you guidelines for effective mentoring, help you select an appropriate mentor, and provide you with advice on mentoring others within your sphere of influence. Finishing well—reaching the end of your life having been faithful to God's calling—should be the desire of your heart. Finishing well is about being more passionate about Christ and His mission as you fulfill your life purpose than you were at the beginning. It entails a life that experiences the depth of God's grace and love. It means living out your destiny and making your unique and ultimate contribution to the expansion of God's Kingdom.[13]

This book is a practical guide for developing an internal compass to find your way, creating a personal map to understand your unique

12   Terry Walling, *Mentoring Workbook* (Leader Breakthru), 8.
13   J. Robert Clinton, Leadership Emergence Theory.

contribution to God's purposes, and finding guides to help you navigate your designed trajectory so that you finish well. Included is a *Focused Life Plan Worksheet* that will help you develop a detailed plan: a compass, map, and guide. Examples of each of these elements are provided. By the time you finish the book and have completed the assignments along the way, you will be able to develop a complete focused life plan that will give you direction and inform the critical decisions of your life.

Prologue

In Acts 2:17–18, we read, "In the last days, God says, I will pour out my Spirit on all people. Your sons and daughters will prophesy, your young men will see visions, your old men will dream dreams. Even on my servants, both men and women, I will pour out my Spirit in those days, and they will prophesy."

I encourage you to read my wide-awake dream carefully, as you will see scriptural truth embedded in its content. The message it conveys speaks about our true home, our temporary outpost, and our primary mission.

The Wide-Awake Dream

The last rays of sunshine began to disappear over the horizon. I was in a reflective mood brought on by my disappointment at the death of a dream at the hands of fearful and unimaginative leaders—leaders who were unwilling to take a risk to see God move in mighty ways. As I struggled with my discouragement and despair about this lost opportunity to make a difference in the world, my mind wandered to another place.

I found myself standing in a long line in a great hall leading to a destination outside my field of vision. I sensed that this journey was a temporary situation—a necessary step before moving on to something else. Many other people were in front of me, and others began to fall in behind me. Still others were with us but very different from us. They were encased in brilliant light but distinguishable from each other; they had separate identities. Their demeanor and actions indicated that they were there to serve us. They rarely spoke as we moved along; they seemed to be more like companions for the journey ahead. Yet they showed a keen interest in us, listening intently to our conversation with an attitude of respect.

My curiosity was killing me. I asked the person ahead of me what the line was for.

"We are in line to receive our assignment," he said.

"What assignment?" I asked.

He responded, "Don't you recall what the ancient scriptures say? We are a new creation, not a better version of our previous selves. The old self is gone, replaced by a new self—a gift from God through Jesus, His Son. Because He ended the conflict between us and Him and put us back on friendly terms with Him—He calls this 'reconciliation'—we now have been given a message of reconciliation to others within our sphere of influence. In fact, we are now Christ's ambassadors, His spokespersons through which He makes His appeal.[14] Isn't that amazing?"

"Ambassadors?" I said. "What does that mean?"

As the line slowly moved toward a destination I still could not see, my new friend began to explain to me the significance of being an ambassador for Christ. He said, "At the moment of your conversion, you were transferred from your citizenship in this world to a new citizenship in heaven. You are no longer of this world. You are a representative, a citizen, of the Kingdom of God in this world until he calls us to our future home."[15]

"My home is not on earth?" I replied. "My true home is the Kingdom of God? I don't understand."

My new friend motioned to one of the brilliant beings close to us, who came to us quickly. When my friend asked him to explain our future home, he began in a gentle but authoritative voice to unravel the mystery.

---

14 2 Cor. 5:16–20.

15 Phil. 3:20–21.

"Heaven," he said, "is your future home but not your final home. Heaven is a place where you will wait for the time of Christ's return to the earth, your bodily resurrection, the final judgment, and the creation of the new heavens and new earth. The center of the new heavens and new earth is a city like no other called New Jerusalem—the place you will ultimately live together with God.[16] The New Jerusalem is the equivalent of fourteen hundred miles in length, width, and height. The ground level of the city will be nearly two million square miles—forty times bigger than England and fifteen thousand times bigger than London, ten times as big as France or Germany, and far larger than India—and that's just the ground level. This will be the future Kingdom of God. You will rule with Christ in this future kingdom. Your reward will be service in His Kingdom. What you have done on earth will determine what you will ultimately do on the new earth and in New Jerusalem. All will be revealed at the judgment seat of Christ, where believers will give an account of what they have done with what God has given them.[17] That judgment will determine where you will serve in God's future kingdom and what authority you will possess in that kingdom."

What a sobering thought: we must all appear before the judgment seat of Christ so that each of us may receive what is due us for the things we've done while in the body, whether good or bad.[18] Each of us will give an account of ourself to God.[19]

The being then said, "Although there is a future dimension of the Kingdom of God, there is also a present Kingdom of God to which you must return to fulfill your assignment until the ordained number of days for you is complete."

"My assignment? What assignment?" By now I'd realized he was an angel of God, a messenger sent to serve us.

"Until you are called back to your eternal home, you have a mission to complete," he replied. "You are ambassadors of a kingdom far away. That kingdom has been called the Kingdom of God and is mentioned sixty-six times in what you have come to know as the New Testament. It has also

---

16   Rev. 21–22.
17   1 Cor. 3:10–15.
18   2 Cor. 5:10.
19   Rom. 14:12.

been referred to as the kingdom of heaven, mentioned thirty-two times in the Book of Matthew alone. You are no longer of this world, even though you temporarily live in it; you're of another world. That other world is very different from this world. In fact, this world, your temporary, earthly existence, is under the dominion of an evil king. His name is Satan—the great opponent and adversary of our king, Jesus Christ. He is the prince of this earthly world: 'the tempter,'[20] 'Beelzebub,'[21] 'the wicked one,'[22] 'the ruler of this world,'[23] 'the god of this age,'[24] 'Belial,'[25] 'the prince of the power of the air,'[26] and 'the accuser of our brethren.'[27]

"Satan's influence in worldly affairs is also clearly revealed.[28] His various titles reflect his control of the world system. The Bible declares, 'The whole world lies under the sway of the wicked one.'[29]

"But you are no longer of this world. Instead, you have been adopted into the family of God. You are indeed new citizens of His Kingdom. His Kingdom operates under a different set of principles and values. At the moment of your conversion, you were given a new heart and a new spirit was put in you, God's Spirit. His Spirit will move you to follow His decrees not out of obligation but out of obedient love. You will be His people and He will be your God while you live there for a while.[30]

"His character, His values—'the fruit of the Spirit'—were implanted in the core of your being, which you call the heart. You received it as a seed, and it requires intentional and careful nurturing if it is to produce abundantly in your life. You are marked by this fruit, which manifests as love, joy, peace, patience, kindness, goodness, faithfulness, gentleness, and self-control. The degree to which this fruit is visible in your life reflects your citizenship in God's Kingdom."

---

20 1 Thess. 3:5.
21 Matt. 12:24.
22 Matt. 13:19, 38.
23 John 12:31.
24 2 Cor. 4:4.
25 2 Cor. 6:15.
26 Eph. 2:2.
27 Rev. 12:10.
28 John 12:31.
29 1 John 5:19.
30 Ezek. 36:26–29.

With that, the angel moved back to his position at the right of the line, which was still moving to a destination just ahead.

My mind was full of imagery from the angel's comments and spinning from the ramifications of his statements. As I tried to get my mind around the significance of his remarks, I became very aware of the fact that I was under new leadership, new management. I had a new identity, and my temporary home was a new colony.

My king and new commander was Jesus, who appeared to all people, teaching us to say no to ungodliness and worldly passions, and to live self-controlled, upright, godly lives in this present age while we wait for the blessed hope: the glorious appearance of our great God and Savior, Jesus Christ, who sacrificed Himself to redeem us from all wickedness and to purify for Himself a people that are His very own, eager to do what is good.[31]

My new citizenship was the Kingdom of God, both a future hope and a present reality. *This changes everything*, I thought. *I am an alien and stranger in this temporary, earthly place. While on earth I am to abstain from sinful desires that war against my soul. I am to live in such a way among the fallen that though they may accuse me of many things, they will see my good deeds and glorify the king I serve.*[32]

My mind quickly went to comments that I had read some time before but that weren't clear until now. I remembered the words of Alister McGrath, a Christian historian and theologian, said that we should think of ourselves, our churches, and our families as "colonies of heaven, as outposts of the real eternal city, who seek to keep its laws in the midst of alien territory." I recalled similar remarks from a favorite writer of mine, C. S. Lewis, famed author of *Mere Christianity* and *Chronicles of Narnia*, who as a devout Christian viewed the world as enemy territory, territory occupied by invading forces.

Building on this theme, McGrath wrote, "In the midst of this territory, as resistance groups are the communities of faith." He went on to write that "we must never be afraid to be different from the world around us. It is very easy for Christians to be depressed by the fact that the world scorns our values and standards. But the image of the colony sets this in its proper perspective. At Philippi the civilizing laws of Rome contrasted with the anarchy [a state of

---

31 Titus 2:11–14.
32 1 Pet. 2:11–12.

lawlessness or political disorder] of its hinterland [regions outside of Rome].
And so our moral vision—grounded in Scripture, sustained by faith, given
intellectual spine by Christian doctrine—stands as a civilizing influence in
the midst of a world that seems to have lost its moral way."

Okay, I thought. *I am not of this world; my citizenship is in the Kingdom
of God. So what makes this kingdom distinct from all other kingdoms?*

As we continued to move along in the line leading to somewhere, I was
intrigued by the idea that I was no longer of this world. I wondered what
my relationship was to this world in which I wandered. How should I carry
myself in this world? What was my relationship to and with this world?
Realizing that I belonged to the Kingdom of God, how should I engage
this world while I waited to be called to my new home? My friend in line
ahead of me must have been reading my mind. He said that I should not
conform any longer to the pattern of this world, but be transformed by the
renewing of my mind. Then I will be able to test and approve what God's
will is—His good, pleasing, and perfect will.[33]

He went on to say that I should "not love the world or anything in the
world. If anyone loves the world, the love of the Father is not in him. For
everything in the world—the cravings of sinful man, the lust of his eyes,
and the boasting of what he has and does—comes not from the Father
but from the world. The world and its desires pass away, but the man who
does the will of God lives forever."[34]

Then he asked me, "Don't you know that friendship with the world
is hatred toward God? Anyone who chooses to be a friend of the world
becomes an enemy of God."[35]

All right—I was an alien and stranger, and I was to live my life in such
a way that it boldly proclaimed the kingdom to which I now belonged. I
was to no longer live my life in accordance with the dictates of this world,
I had to be careful not to embrace this world, and I had to remember that
friendship with this world meant hatred of God.

"Okay, I get it," I said. "So what defines the Kingdom of God?"

My friend said, "Our declaration of independence is our acknowledgment
that we stand in bold relief against the backdrop of our culture, prepared

33 Rom. 12:2.
34 1 John 2:15–17.
35 James 4:4.

to defend the hope that is in us—the hope that we are separate from this world and the culture in which we exist. The only other option is to give in to our culture, becoming a willing partner in it rather than distinguishing ourselves from it. Dependence on God produces independence from the world. Independence from the world is only possible when we become dependent upon the King. Dependence on the world results in independence from God.

"The constitution of the Kingdom of God is the Ten Commandments; its amendments are the Beatitudes; its vision is the Sermon on the Mount. Our new identity is our Bill of Rights and finds its focus in who we are in Christ."

I have been bought with a price, and I belong to God.[36]
I have been chosen by God and adopted as His child.[37]
I have been redeemed and forgiven of all my sins.[38]
I have direct access to the throne of grace through Jesus Christ.[39]
I am free from condemnation.[40]
I have been established, anointed, and sealed by God.[41]
I am a citizen of heaven.[42]
I am born of God, and the evil one cannot touch me.[43]
I am a branch of Jesus Christ, the true vine, and a channel of His life.[44]
I have been chosen and appointed to bear fruit.[45]
I am God's temple.[46]
I am a minister of reconciliation for God.[47]
I can do all things through Christ, who strengthens me.[48]

---

36 1 Cor. 6:19–20.
37 Eph. 1:3–8.
38 Col. 1:13–14.
39 Heb. 4:14–16.
40 Rom. 8:1–2.
41 2 Cor. 1:21–22.
42 Phil. 3:20.
43 1 John 5:18.
44 John 15:5.
45 John 15:16.
46 1 Cor. 3:16.
47 2 Cor. 5:17–21.
48 Phil. 4:13.

I could now see what was ahead of me. It was a magnificent throne. As I approached the throne, my friend felt it necessary to whisper one more important truth to me: "The evidence of our allegiance to the Kingdom of God is demonstrated by the outwork of the fruit of the Spirit in our lives. The proof that we belong to the Kingdom of God is shown in the degree to which the fruit of the Spirit is real in our lives."

It all made sense to me. Nobody would care what I had to say or what I proclaimed to believe until they observed how I lived. If I lived a life of integrity and authenticity, they would, eventually, listen to what I had to say. My life had to give evidence of the fruit of God's Spirit—the character of God and the values of His Kingdom.

Does my life bear testimony of the fact that I belong to the Kingdom of God? Does my behavior represent the values of the Kingdom of God?

As I contemplated these questions, I realized that the Kingdom of God stood in opposition to the world. I recognized that my behavior had to reflect the character of my King. I was indeed an ambassador of His Kingdom. My questions became more specific:

Is God's character, are His values, observable in my life?

To what degree am I defined by love, joy, and peace—a direct reflection of the quality of my relationship with God?

As I interact with others, am I seen as patient, kind, and good—a direct reflection of my relationship with those who are within my sphere of influence?

Does my life give ample evidence of gentleness, faithfulness, and self-control—a direct reflection of my internal discipline, diligence, and devotion?

Do people see Jesus in me?

As I was lost in my thoughts, I was startled by a loud voice calling my name. Two beings in brilliant light stood by me, one on each side. They gently urged me forward into a presence of majesty and beauty. I knew instantly that I was standing before my Lord and Savior, Jesus Christ. I was speechless and dropped to my knees immediately, afraid to look into His eyes. I felt a gentle touch on my shoulder as I heard Him say, "Greg, you are a man after my heart. Stand to receive your assignment."

As I looked into His eyes, I felt the peace that passes all understanding flood my being. I felt unconditionally loved and accepted in a way I had never felt before. I felt the full extent of His forgiveness and mercy and grace. My eyes filled with tears of joy.

He said to me, "I ordained your existence for a unique purpose. You are not a mistake, a coincidence, or the product of fate. I have searched you and know you. I have known when you sat and when you rose; I have perceived your thoughts from afar. I have discerned your going out and your lying down; I am familiar with all your ways. Before any word was on your tongue, I knew it completely. I hemmed you in—behind and before; I laid my hand upon you. You cannot escape my Spirit; you cannot flee my presence. If you go up to the heavens, I will be there; if you make your bed in the depths, I will be there. If you rise on the wings of the dawn, if you settle on the far side of the sea, even there my hand will guide you, my right hand holding you fast. Darkness will not hide you from me. You see, I created your innermost being; I knitted you together in your mother's womb—you are fearfully and wonderfully made. My works are wonderful, you know that full well. Your name was not hidden from me when you were made in the secret place, when you were woven together in the depths of the earth. My eyes saw your unformed body. All the days ordained for you were written in my book before one of them came to be.[49]

"As a result, you are no longer a foreigner and an alien, but a fellow citizen with my people, a member of my household, which was built on the foundation of the apostles and prophets, with me as the chief cornerstone. In me the whole building is joined together and rises to become a holy temple in the Lord. And through me, you, too, will become a dwelling in which God lives by His Spirit.[50]

"I desire that you stand out from the world around you as an ambassador for me. I commission you to carry my message of reconciliation. You are my ambassador, and I will make my appeal through you in the place where I send you. For it is by grace you have been saved through faith. This not of your doing, not the product of your works, but a gift from the Father, so that no one can boast. For you are God's workmanship, created in me to do good works that the Father prepared in advance for you to do.[51]

"And when your journey in the earthly world is done and I call you home, may you say, as my servant Paul once said, 'For I am already being poured out like a drink offering, and the time has come for my departure.

---

49 Ps. 139:1–18.
50 Eph. 2:19–22.
51 Eph. 2:10.

I have fought the good fight, I have finished the race, I have kept the faith. Now there is in store for me the crown of righteousness, which the Lord, the righteous Judge, will award to me on that day—and not only to me, but also to all who have longed for his appearing.'"[52]

Suddenly I was back where I started, on my deck, but I was different, my journey clear. I was a minister of reconciliation in a foreign land. My allegiance was fixed, firmly devoted to Christ; my values focused, the fruit of His Spirit; my temporary outpost established, this fallen world; and my new, permanent home in sight, the Kingdom of God.

Personal Assessment

To whose kingdom do you belong?

Whose allegiance do you seek?

To what extent does your behavior reflect God's values and character?

To what degree are you fulfilling His assignment for you?

---

52 2 Tim. 4:6–8.

PART 1:
The Compass

Chapter 1: Our Foundation

Two things fill the mind with ever new and increasing admiration and awe ... the starry heavens above me and the moral law within me.

—*Immanuel Kant, philosopher*

Why does humankind feel guilt or remorse? Why do people have a sense of fairness or unfairness, justice or injustice, unselfishness or selfishness, courage or cowardice, right or wrong, distorted as they may be? To be sure, we add our shades of gray to these concepts, corrupting their purity through our self-interest. Nevertheless, how can anyone even compare these contrasting ideas without some internal standard by which to compare them? When we feel betrayed or cheated or lied to, something within us tells us a standard of behavior has been violated. When someone takes something that belongs to us without our permission, we are upset. Even a gang of thieves after a heist feels that their rights have been violated when they do not receive what they consider their "fair share." And when an innocent man is accused of or punished for something he didn't do, his sense of injustice is keen.

Each of us has a moral code ingrained within us, even though we do not always act in accordance with that code. C. S. Lewis, scholar and author, wrote, "First, human beings, all over the earth, have this curious idea that they ought to behave in a certain way, and really cannot get rid of it. Secondly, that they do not in fact behave in that way. They know the Law of Nature; they break it. These two facts are the foundation of all the clear thinking about ourselves and the universe we live in."[53] Lewis went on to write that human beings are "haunted by the idea of a sort of behavior they ought to practice, what you might call fair play, or decency, or morality, or the Law of Nature" and "that they did not in fact do so."[54]

Moral impurity and spiritual corruption are the result of incremental compromise through a slow erosion of standards, a growing carelessness about details, a gradual blurring of distinctions, and poor moral discipline. One commentator said that the safest road to hell is a gradual one: the gentle slope, soft underfoot, without sudden turns or milestones or signposts.

So where does this embedded sense of right and wrong come from? Lewis argues that it is not simply cultural, as it is universal:

> Some people say the idea of a Law of Nature or decent behavior known to all men is unsound, because different civilizations and different ages have quite different moralities. But this is not true. There have been differences between their moralities, but these have never amounted to anything like a total difference. If anyone will take the trouble to compare the moral teaching of, say, the ancient Egyptians, Babylonians, Hindus, Chinese, Greeks and Romans, what will really strike him will be how very like they are to each other and to our own.[55]

Back to the question: where does this implanted sense of right and wrong come from—what is its source? Simply put, it came from our Creator. God has communicated His existence, His nature, His moral standards, and His plan of salvation to us. *Nelson Bible Dictionary* clearly articulates this fact. The quote is rather long, but worth every word, as our foundation is based on its truths:[56]

> God is a personal Spirit distinct from the world; He is absolutely holy and is invisible to the view of physical, finite, sinful minds. Although people can never create truth about God, God has graciously unveiled and manifested Himself to

---

53 Lewis, *Mere Christianity* (San Francisco: Harper, 2001), 7.
54 Ibid., 16.
55 Ibid., 5.
56 *Nelson Bible Dictionary*, Conscience.

mankind. Other religions and philosophies result from the endless human quest for God; Christianity results from God's quest for lost mankind. God has made Himself known to all people everywhere in the marvels of nature and in the human conscience, which is able to distinguish right from wrong. Because this knowledge is universal and continuous, by it God has displayed His glory to everyone.[57] Some Christians think that only believers can see God's revelation in nature, but the apostle Paul said that unbelievers know truth about God: The unrighteous must have the truth to "suppress" it;[58] they "clearly see" it;[59] knowing God, they fail to worship Him as God;[60] they alter the truth;[61] they do not retain God in their knowledge;[62] and knowing the righteous judgment (moral law) of God, they disobey it.[63] The reason the ungodly are "inexcusable"[64] before God's righteous judgment is that they possessed but rejected the truth which God gave them. What can be known of God from nature? God's universal revelation makes it clear that God exists,[65] and that God, the Creator of the mountains, oceans, vegetation, animals, and mankind, is wise[66] and powerful.[67] People aware of their own moral responsibility, who know the difference between right and wrong conduct and who have a sense of guilt when they do wrong, reflect the requirements of God's moral law (the Ten Commandments) that is written on their hearts.[68] What is the result of divine revelation in nature? If anyone lived

---

57 Ps. 19:1–6.
58 Rom. 1:18.
59 Rom. 1:20.
60 Rom. 1:21.
61 Rom. 1:25.
62 Rom. 1:28.
63 Rom. 1:32.
64 Rom. 2:1.
65 Rom. 1:20.
66 Ps. 104:24.
67 Ps. 29, 93; Rom. 1:20.
68 Rom. 2:14–15.

up to that knowledge by loving and obeying God every day of his life, he would be right with God and would not need salvation. However, no one loves God with his whole being and his neighbors as himself. People worship and serve things in creation rather than the Creator.[69] The problem does not lie with the revelation, which like the Law is holy, just, and good;[70] the problem is with the sinfulness of human lives.[71] The best human being (other than Jesus Christ) comes short of the uprightness God requires. When Christians defend justice, honesty, and decency in schools, homes, neighborhoods, businesses, and governments, they do not impose their special beliefs upon others. They merely point to universal principles that all sinners know but suppress in their unrighteousness.[72] As valuable as general revelation is for justice, honesty, and decency in the world today, it is not enough. It must be completed by the good news of God's mercy and His gracious gift of perfect righteousness. Nature does not show God's plan for saving those who do wrong: that Jesus was the Son of God, that He died for our sins, and that He rose again from among the dead. The message of salvation was seen dimly throughout Old Testament sacrifices and ceremonies. It was seen more clearly as God redeemed the Israelites from enslavement in Egypt and as God disclosed to prophetic spokesmen the redemptive significance of His mighty acts of deliverance. The full and final revelation of God has occurred in Jesus Christ. "God, who at various times and in different ways spoke in times past to the fathers by the prophets, has in these last days spoken to us by His Son, whom He has appointed heir of all things, through whom also He made the worlds."[73] Christ has "declared" God to us personally.[74] To

---

69 Rom. 1:25.
70 Rom. 7:12.
71 Rom. 8:3.
72 Rom. 1:18.
73 Heb. 1:1–2.
74 John 1:18.

see Christ is to see the Father. Christ gave us the words which the Father gave Him.[75] At the cross Jesus revealed supremely God's self-giving love. There He died, "the just for the unjust, that He might bring us to God."[76] And the good news is not complete until we hear that He rose again triumphantly over sin, Satan, and the grave, and is alive forevermore. Christ chose apostles and trained them to teach the meaning of His death and resurrection, to build the church, and to write the New Testament Scriptures. We are to remember the words of these eyewitnesses to Christ's resurrection. The content of God's special revelation concerning salvation, given to specially gifted spokesmen and supremely revealed in Christ, is found in "the words which were spoken before by the holy prophets, and of the commandment of ... the apostles of the Lord and Savior."[77] "The Holy Scriptures is able to make you wise for salvation through faith which is in Christ Jesus."[78]

These truths provide the foundation upon which we stand. God formed our inward parts; He knitted us together in our mothers' wombs; He knew us before we were; He established the days we would live on this earth. It should give you great peace to know that you were in God's heart before you ever came to be.[79] Back to our question once again: where does our sense of right and wrong come from? God, our Father, injected and infused His moral code in our hearts; we were given a conscience. And while our conscience can, unfortunately, be corrupted, it cannot be erased. It can be suppressed, marred, warped, and distorted, but it cannot be destroyed.

God has revealed Himself to us through general and special revelation. Those who do not know Christ have no excuse. Those who claim to know Christ also are without excuse. Finding our way, understanding our divine trajectory, and realizing our created potential all begin with the knowledge that God exists, that He cares for us, that He has provided a way for us to know Him through His Son, and that He established plans for us before

---

75   John 17:8.
76   1 Pet. 3:18.
77   2 Pet. 3:2.
78   2 Tim. 3:15.
79   Ps. 139:1–18.

we were born. We are not a mistake, a happenstance, a coincidence, or a product of fate. We are God's very own. He knows us because He created us according to His design and wants us to live in accordance with that design. When we choose to live in accordance with that design, we will find meaning and significance. When we choose to live apart from that design, we will reap meaninglessness and insignificance.

One of my favorite authors is J. I. Packer, a Bible teacher and world-class theologian. In my book *A Rattling of Sabers*, I quote Packer regarding God's design and what it means to be created in God's image. His remarks add depth to our discussion of humans' innate sense of right and wrong:[80]

> When God made man, He communicated to him qualities corresponding to His moral attributes. This is what the Bible means when it tells us that God made man (meaning both men and women) in His own image—namely, that God made man (and woman) a free spiritual being, a responsible moral agent with powers of choice and action, able to commune with Him and respond to Him, and by nature good, truthful, holy, upright: in a word, godly. The moral qualities which belonged to the divine image were lost at the Fall; God's image in man has been universally defaced, for all mankind has in one way or another lapsed into ungodliness. But the Bible tells us that now, in fulfillment of His plan of redemption, God is at work in Christian believers to repair His ruined image by communicating these qualities to them afresh. This is what Scripture means when it says that Christians are being renewed in the image of Christ[81] and of God.[82]

Packer offers a vivid description of the severe consequences if we violate God's natural order:[83]

> We are familiar with the thought that our bodies are like machines, needing the right routine of food, rest, and exercise

80 J. I. Packer, *Knowing God* (Downers Grove: Inter Varsity Press, 1973), 89–90.
81 2 Cor. 3:18.
82 Col. 3:10.
83 Packer, 102–3.

if they are to run efficiently, and liable, if filled up with the wrong fuel—alcohol, drugs, poison—to lose their power of healthy functioning and ultimately to "seize up" entirely in physical death. What we are perhaps slower to grasp is that God wishes us to think of our souls in a similar way. As rational persons, we were made to bear God's moral image—that is, our souls were made to "run" on the practice of worship, law-keeping, truthfulness, honesty, discipline, self-control, and service to God and others. If we abandon these practices, not only do we incur guilt before God; we also progressively destroy our souls. Conscience atrophies, the sense of shame dries up, one's capacity for truthfulness, loyalty, and honesty is eaten away, one's character disintegrates. One not only becomes desperately miserable; one is steadily being de-humanized.

Our foundation, our North Star that orients us, embodies the following truths:

- God exists and is active in our lives.
- We were in the heart of God before we ever came to be.
- We were created for a purpose and to facilitate God's purposes.[84]
- God is generally revealed in the things He has created.
- God is specially revealed in His Son, the Holy Spirit, and the Bible.
- Humans bear the image of God, and within that image is our conscience.
- God's moral nature and code is embedded in all beings.
- The image of God and our sense of morality are marred by sin.
- The solution for this dilemma is the person and work of Christ.
- We are to live in accordance with His design.
- He desires that we reach our full potential in and through Him.
- Our human destiny is eternal life with Him or eternal separation from Him.

---

84 Eph. 2:10.

Cardinal Points

Every orienting compass has four cardinal points: north, south, east, and west. If we are to find our way on our journey, we must keep before us the correct orientation.

North Cardinal Point: Jesus Christ

Abiding, remaining, and continuing in Christ is crucial. In John 15, we are told about the importance of abiding, remaining, and continuing in Christ:

> I am the true vine, and my Father is the gardener. He cuts off every branch in me that bears no fruit, while every branch that does bear fruit he prunes so that it will be even more fruitful. You are already clean because of the word I have spoken to you. Remain in me, and I will remain in you. No branch can bear fruit by itself; it must remain in the vine. Neither can you bear fruit unless you remain in me. I am the vine; you are the branches. If a man remains in me and I in him, he will bear much fruit; apart from me you can do nothing. If anyone does not remain in me, he is like a branch that is thrown away and withers; such branches are picked up, thrown into the fire, and burned. If you remain in me and my words remain in you, ask whatever you wish, and it will be given you. This is to my Father's glory, that you bear much fruit, showing yourselves to be my disciples. As the Father has loved me, so have I loved you. Now remain in my love. If you obey my commands, you will remain in my love, just as I have obeyed my Father's commands and remain in his love.[85]

In the verses that follow, God admonishes us to love others as He loves us, even if it means laying down our lives for them. He chose us and appointed us to go and bear lasting fruit. Doing so may not garner the adulation and appreciation of the beneficiaries of such unconditional love. But if the world hates us, we should keep in mind that it hated Him first. When we came to Christ, we released our passport to this

---

85   John 15:1–10.

world and received a passport to His Kingdom, of which we are now citizens. We no longer belong to this world, for God has chosen us out of this world. The fact that we don't embrace the ways of this world will not be appreciated by those who live by its dictates; if they persecuted Christ, they will persecute us as well. We who claim His name and are not afraid to acknowledge our allegiance to Him will be scorned by those who deny Him. In fact, because of the way we live, the beliefs we hold, the kingdom values we embrace, the biblical worldview we adhere to, and the motives that drive us, we will remind the world how far it has slipped from His standards. But we are not to lose hope, for His truth will prevail. We've been given a counselor, the Spirit of truth, who will empower us and guide us on the journey. The power of the lives we live will be a testament to Him.[86]

East Cardinal Point: The Holy Spirit

The Holy Spirit is vital to our journey. Many of us are unaware of His critical role in our formation. He provides energy, inspiration, strength, clarity, intercession, spiritual gifts, spiritual fruit, and empowerment.

The third person of the Trinity was active and present at creation.[87] In the Old Testament He is revealed as the origin of supernatural abilities,[88] the giver of artistic skill,[89] the source of power and strength,[90] the inspiration of prophesy,[91] the equipper of God's messengers,[92] and the cleanser of the heart for holy living.[93]

In salvation He regenerates the believer,[94] dwelling within[95] and sanctifying him.[96] He inspired the writing of scripture.[97] His present

---

86 John 15:11–27.
87 Gen. 1:2.
88 Gen. 41:38.
89 Exod. 31:2–5.
90 Judg. 3:9–10.
91 1 Sam. 19:20, 23.
92 Mic. 3:8.
93 Ezek. 36:25–29.
94 Titus 3:5.
95 Rom. 8:9–11.
96 2 Thess. 2:13.
97 2 Tim. 3:16; 2 Pet. 1:21.

ministry to us includes declaring the truth about Christ.[98] He endows us with the power for Gospel proclamation,[99] pouring out God's love in our hearts,[100] interceding for us,[101] imparting spiritual gifts for ministry,[102] enabling the fruit of holy living,[103] and strengthening our inner beings.[104]

We need the help of the Holy Spirit to navigate an ever-darkening world; to find our way around dangerous obstacles; to give us the strength to endure and persevere; to remind us of the truth that sets us free; to intercede with the Father on our behalf; and to cultivate the fruit of love, joy, peace, patience, kindness, goodness, faithfulness, gentleness, and self-control in our lives. This fruit of the Spirit given to each believer at conversion comes as a seed needing cultivation. This fruit represents the character of Christ and the family values of our heavenly Father—the DNA that is embedded in every follower of Christ, marking him or her as a member of God's family.

South Cardinal Point: The Bible

Submarines are designed to dive to great depths. But because pressure increases with depth, the strength of the submarine's hull and the type of metal used in its construction determines how deep it can go. If the submarine exceeds that depth, the hull can no longer sustain the pressure and implodes. If the hull is compromised in any way, the submarine's integrity is critically jeopardized.

In similar fashion, the pressures of life can implode our spiritual well-being if the integrity of our heart is compromised. The Bible helps build the core of our being. God uses the Bible as a chisel to shape us into the image of Christ, as water to quench our parched souls, as a scalpel to remove our sinful disease, as oil to soothe the bruises we receive, and as fuel to give us spiritual energy. In order to counter and resist the pressures of life or the worldliness that presses in on us at every turn, we need internal strength. Without it, we will implode.

---

98 John 16:13–14.
99 Acts 1:8.
100 Rom. 5:5.
101 Rom. 8:26.
102 1 Cor. 12:4–11.
103 Gal. 5:22–23.
104 Eph. 3:16.

How is strength formed in believers? How can we counter the daily pressures that compromise the integrity of our hearts? In the Book of Joshua we are reminded of the importance of scripture in our lives: "Do not let this Book of the Law depart from your mouth; meditate on it day and night, so that you may be careful to do everything written in it. Then you will be prosperous and successful."[105]

Mastering a solid grasp of God's Word, the Bible, requires hearing, reading, studying, memorizing, and meditating on scripture. Picture a stairway where the bottom step is hearing the Word of God, the second step is reading the Bible, the third step is studying the Bible, the fourth step is memorizing scripture, and the final step is meditating on scripture. Each successive step draws you deeper and closer to God and gives you more strength for the journey.

- hearing[106]
- reading[107]
- studying[108]
- memorizing[109]
- meditating[110]

Hearing

Many Christians only *hear* the Word in a sermon, a video, or a book; others take the next step and *read* the Bible, regularly or occasionally. That is where most Christians stop. But you can't depend on such retained knowledge as strength for your spiritual journey; it cannot sustain the rigors of the trip. After all, most of what we hear is quickly forgotten. Think of the last sermon you heard. Can you recall its details?

The Internet gives us ample opportunities to hear the Word of God from gifted preachers and teachers. Your own church may have a website where sermons are posted. Audio versions of the Bible are widely available. Regardless of the context, whenever you listen to a sermon or a lesson,

---

105 Josh. 1:8.
106 Rom. 10:17.
107 Rev. 1:3.
108 Acts 17:11.
109 Ps. 119:9–11.
110 Ps. 1:2–3.

always have a notebook and write down insights gleaned, lessons learned, and scripture explained. Retention goes way up when you listen in order to hear God's voice in your life and record what He is saying to you.

Reading

When we read the Bible we often do so as a matter of course, with no strategy in mind. We do not go to the Bible with intentionality. Reading the Bible with intentionality means asking God to reveal His being and character to us, to give us insight into building a deeper relationship with Him, to help us learn more about Him: His purposes, His plans, His values, and so forth. After all, the Bible is God's letter to us, revealing who He is, His love for us, His expectations of us, and His activity in the world around us. Knowing *of* God is more important than knowing *about* God; developing a relationship with Him is more important than mastering facts about Him. As you read the Bible, I would encourage you to keep a journal of what God tells you or what you learn.

Going to the Bible with intentionality should be preceded by prayer. Ask God to give you eyes to see what He wants you to see, hear what He wants you to hear, and do what He wants you to do. The following questions will help you focus on what you might glean from the Bible each time you pick it up. Perhaps you might select one question for your devotion each day.

- Is there *something about God* I should know?
- Is there *something about Christ* I should learn?
- Is there an *example* I should follow?
- Is there a *sin* I should avoid?
- Is there a *promise* I should claim?
- Is there a *prayer* I should repeat?
- Is there a *command* I should obey?
- Is there a *condition* I should meet?
- Is there a *verse* I should memorize?
- Is there an *error* I should observe or avoid?
- Is there a *challenge* I should face?
- Is there a *service* I should perform?
- Is there a *person* I should help?

Studying

This step in grasping God's word includes the study of the Bible. I recommend a simple, three-step process: observation, interpretation, and application. Paraphrased Bibles such as The Living Bible and The Message are fine for general reading and devotions, but word-for-word (New American Stand Bible, English Standard Version) or thought-for-thought (New International Version, New Revised Standard Version) translations are better for study.

Too many of us jump right to the "application" step without understanding what a passage actually says and means. Bible study is like detective work. When a crime is committed, a detective surveys the crime scene and makes *observations* about what he or she sees. At this point he or she is not interpreting what he or she sees; he or she is just making focused observations to discover any and all clues. He or she is trained to see things an uninformed observer would likely miss. The evidence is gathered and transported to the lab, where it is analyzed using the latest technology and methods. The job of the lab is to *interpret* what the evidence reveals: What does each piece of evidence indicate? How do the pieces of evidence fit together? And what conclusions can be reached when the analysis is complete? The lab technician may have to go over the evidence more than once to ascertain its significance. Finally, the detective puts his or her observations alongside the analyzed evidence to arrive at possible *applications*, posing further, informed questions to help him or her reconstruct the crime and solve the case.

In similar fashion we should begin any study of scripture with a simple, unemotional *observation*. What does the passage say? Resist the temptation to jump to application. The basic idea of observation is awareness—it is training the eye to see and the mind to grasp what is there. You are seeking to answer the following questions: *What do I see? What are the clues? What are the facts?* Several techniques for making good observations are located in **Appendix B: Observation.**

Once you've made objective observations, you are ready to move to *interpretation*. What does the passage mean? When you're interpreting a passage, your objective is to determine what the original author meant at the time that he wrote it. Here is where, as the interpreter, you bombard the text with questions such as "What did these details mean to the people to whom they were given?" "Why did the author say this?" "What's the main idea the author wants to get across?" Interpretation answers the following general questions: *What is the context? What did the passage mean then? What does it mean today?*

In a crime lab, certain rules are followed when evidence is handled and analyzed. Similarly, in scriptural study, rules of interpretation must be followed to ensure accurate interpretation. **Appendix B: Interpretation** covers some of these basic rules and suggests a process for applying them.[111]

Once observation and interpretation are complete, you are ready for *application*, which seeks to answer two primary questions: *How does this passage apply in general? How does this passage apply to me specifically?* See **Appendix B: Application** for suggested techniques.

Those who finish well, according to J. Robert Clinton's research, are lifelong learners. As he neared his martyrdom, the apostle Paul asked his protégé for two things he needed while in prison awaiting his fate—his cloak and his scrolls, especially his parchments.[112] He was a learner right up to the last day of his earthly life.

Memorizing

Nothing can be brought to mind unless it has been stored in the memory. "Your capacity to remember is a God-given gift. You may think you have a poor memory, but the truth is, you have millions of ideas, truths, facts, and figures memorized. You remember what is important to you. If God's Word is important, you will take the time to remember it."[113]

In the Spiritual Training Series published by Saddleback Church in California, Rick Warren, the senior pastor, gives helpful insight and advice on memorizing scripture and identifies five reasons why doing so is important:

- Jesus Christ modeled it for you. Jesus repeatedly quoted

---

111 For those who want a deeper understanding of biblical interpretation processes, I would recommend two resources: (1) Robert H. Stein, *A Basic Guide to Interpreting the Bible*; and (2) Walter A. Henrichsen and Gayle Jackson, *Studying, Interpreting, and Applying the Bible*.

112 2 Tim. 4:13.

113 Rick Warren, *Spiritual Trainer Series: Memorizing Scripture* (Lake Forest: Saddleback Church, 2003), 2–3.

scripture. For example, when Satan tempted Him to sin, Jesus defeated the temptations by reciting scripture.[114]

- It teaches you to think with the mind of Christ. When God's Word is in your mind, it will compel you to think and respond as Christ would.[115]
- It helps you overcome temptation and sin—and it is the best help available because it is the inspired Word of God![116]
- It equips you to offer solid biblical advice to others. The Holy Spirit will bring to your mind verses that will meet a person's particular needs (spiritual, emotional, physical, and relational).[117]
- It creates in you a greater ease in sharing your faith. When you know "by heart" verses that present God's plan of salvation, you can more comfortably share your faith in Jesus Christ with nonbelievers.[118]

Warren goes on to suggest a process for memorizing scripture: Read the verse in its context. Read it out loud. Memorize it phrase by phrase. Write it on a note card, the text on one side and the reference on the other. Review it regularly.

Meditating

A man approached a speaker and said, "You Christians are all brainwashed." The speaker replied, "I think we are all brainwashed to a degree. The important thing is that we Christians choose what we want to wash our brains with." Meditation is a lost art for many Christians, but the practice needs to be cultivated again. Meditation is the bridge to personal application of general biblical principles.

J. I. Packer offers a great definition of Christian meditation.

> Meditation is the activity of calling to mind, and thinking over, and dwelling on, and applying to oneself, the various things that one knows about the works and ways and purposes

---

114 Matt. 4:4.
115 Rom. 12:2.
116 Ps. 119:11.
117 Prov. 13:14.
118 1 Pet. 3:15.

and promises of God. It is the activity of holy thought, consciously performed in the presence of God, under the eye of God, by the help of God, as a means of communion with God. Its purpose is to clear one's mental and spiritual vision of God, and to let its truth make its full and proper impact on one's mind and heart. Meditation is the regular filling of your mind with the thoughts of God and godly thoughts. Finally brothers, whatever is true, whatever is noble, whatever is right, whatever is pure, whatever is lovely, whatever is admirable— if anything is excellent or praiseworthy—think about such things.[119]

Why meditate? The Word of God encourages us to do so. We are to meditate on His Word day and night.[120] Our meditation is pleasing to the Lord.[121] Our meditation makes us aware of how we demonstrate our love for Him through obedience to His Word.[122] Our meditation helps us focus on what is important to God.[123] Our meditation gives us an eternal perspective.[124]

What can we expect from meditation? Renowned Christian theologian Dietrich Bonhoeffer suggests that "we want to rise from meditation different from what we were when we sat down to do it. We want to meet Christ in His Word. His fellowship, His help, and His direction for the day through His Word—that is His aim." Richard Foster, recognized expert in the practice of spiritual disciplines, says the goal of meditation is to create a sense of balance in our lives, an ability to rest and take time to enjoy beauty, an ability to pace ourselves. Meditation should produce knowledge *of* God, not knowledge *about* God. Over time, our meditation will transform our character; God's presence will become increasingly real to us as our relationship with Him deepens. Our demeanor will reflect the glory of God as we consciously and unconsciously manifest His excellence in our lives.

119 Phil. 4:8.
120 Ps. 1:2.
121 Ps. 19:14.
122 Josh. 1:8.
123 Phil. 4:8.
124 Col. 3:2.

In summary, if you want to have a solid grasp of the Bible, you must hear, read, study, memorize, and meditate upon it.

West Cardinal Point: Spiritual Disciplines[125]

The following story illustrates the cooperative nature of realizing renewal. God does His part, and we must do ours.

> A farmer can sit around and pray for a good harvest, but if he does not prepare the field, plant the seed, and water the crop, it will not come. Equally foolish is the farmer who thinks because he does his part in these tasks that harvest is assured. It takes God through rain, sunshine, and proper weather patterns to bring the crop to maturity. The farmer works in cooperation with the principles of sowing and reaping, seed time and harvest revealed in God's Word. God is still sovereign, for the rain, sun, and proper weather patterns must come from Him.

We can cultivate our faith by the practice of spiritual disciplines. The practices themselves are not the objective; they are a means to a greater end, a greater awareness of God and a deepening of our relationship with Him. The disciplines foster a change of heart and make us more aware of His presence. They bring us back to God and help shape us into what God wants us to be. Spiritual disciplines are a means to a greater end, the continuance of a personal, healthy, ongoing relationship with Christ, not a panacea for corrupt and sinful behavior. In his book *The Spirit of the Disciplines* Dallas Willard writes, "The disciplines are activities of the mind and body purposefully undertaken, to bring our personality and total being into effective cooperation with the divine order."[126]

Practices like prayer, fasting, worship, and meditation, in cooperation with God's grace and the empowerment of the Holy Spirit, will help us develop godly lives. Paul reminds us to "have nothing to do with godless

---

125 For more information consult *The Spirit of the Disciplines* by Dallas Willard or *The Celebration of Discipline* by Richard Foster.

126 Dallas Willard, *Spirit of the Disciplines* (London: Hodder & Stoughton, 1996), 68.

myths and old wives' tales; rather, train yourself to be godly. For physical training is of some value, but godliness has value for all things, holding promise for both the present life and the life to come."[127] Richard Foster informs us that "God has given us the disciplines of the spiritual life as a means of receiving His grace. The disciplines allow us to place ourselves before God so that He can transform us."[128]

There are several benefits to practicing spiritual disciplines: They help keep our hearts turned toward God, heighten our awareness and love of God, keep our relationship with God in good working order, facilitate spiritual growth, and guide us to see our Father's heart more clearly. They can lead us to a closer walk with Christ, can change our perceptual attitudes about the world around us, liberate us from fear and self-interest, and give us the focus to determine the real priorities in life.[129]

Willard identifies two categories of disciplines: abstinence and engagement. Disciplines of abstinence[130] include solitude, silence, fasting, frugality, chastity, secrecy, and sacrifice. Disciplines of engagement[131] include study, worship, celebration, service, prayer, fellowship, confession, and submission.[132]

Foster lists the disciplines using three categories: inward, outward, and corporate. Inward disciplines include meditation, prayer, fasting, and study. Outward disciplines include simplicity, solitude, submission, and service. And corporate disciplines include confession, worship, guidance, and celebration.[133]

Spiritual Disciplines and Renewal

Through spiritual disciplines we can renew areas of our lives where we have been backsliding. How do you know when renewal is necessary? *The*

---

127 1 Tim. 4:7–9

128 Richard J. Foster, *Celebration of Discipline* (London: Hodder & Stoughton, 1989), 6.

129 *Renewal Manual—A Guide for Personal Spiritual Renewal* (Laguna Hills, CA: Asia Pacific Education Office, 1998), http://ctaoc.com/courses/PersonalSpiritualRenewal.pdf.

130 1 Pet. 2:11.

131 Mark 2:11.

132 Willard, *Spirit of the Disciplines*, 158.

133 Foster, *Celebration of Discipline*, 14ff, 78ff, 142ff.

Renewal Manual: A Guide for Personal Spiritual Renewal identifies twenty signs that renewal is needed:

- When prayer ceases to be a vital part of your life.
- When the quest for biblical truth ceases and you become content with the knowledge you have already acquired.
- When thoughts about eternal things cease to be regular and/or important.
- When you pardon your own sin with self-righteousness and by saying, "The Lord knows I am just dust," or "That is the way I am."
- When pointed spiritual discussions are an embarrassment.
- When other things like recreation, sports, and entertainment become first in your life.
- When sin can be indulged in without protest by your conscience.
- When aspirations of Christ-like holiness are no longer dominant in your life.
- When the acquisition of money and goods becomes dominant in your thinking.
- When you can hear the Lord's name taken in vain, spiritual concerns mocked, and eternal issues flippantly treated and not be moved to indignation and action.
- When worship becomes weariness.
- When breaches of unity in the fellowship are of no concern to you.
- When the slightest excuse seems sufficient to keep you from Christian service.
- When your fleshly senses are out of control.
- When you adjust happily to the world's lifestyle.
- When your lack of spiritual power no longer concerns you.
- When your church has fallen into spiritual decline.
- When the moral, political, spiritual, and economic conditions of the world and your nation are of no concern to you.
- When your heart is hard.
- When you have lost your spiritual strength and do not even realize it.

Personal Assessment

If you were to take a personal audit of your need for renewal, which of these indicators would be true of you?

How would you evaluate your spiritual health at this moment?

How would you evaluate your relationship with Christ?

nonexistent _____

distant _____

stagnant _____

warm _____

growing _____

vibrant _____

Chapter 2: Our Orientation

Two orientations are critical for our journey ahead: godliness and being Bible-centered. A priority for developing and nurturing godliness in our lives will give us a laser beam focus on our primary objective on the horizon. Being Bible-centered will help us get there and not be distracted by the world around us.

—J. Robert Clinton

Godliness[134]

We know to *whom* our lives should be oriented: Jesus Christ. But to *what* should our lives be oriented? What is the point on the horizon toward which we should be aiming? What is the primary objective we should be seeking? On what should we focus our efforts, empowered by the Spirit of God? What is the bull's-eye we should aim for?

In the second chapter of the Book of Titus, we find our answer: a succinct, rich, and profound passage that encompasses everything the

---

134 1 Tim. 4:7–8; 2 Pet. 1:5–7; Titus 2:11–14.

Gospel intended for believers. In a word, what God wants from us is godliness.

> For the grace of God that brings salvation has appeared to all men. It teaches us to say "No" to ungodliness and worldly passions, and to live self-controlled, upright and godly lives in this present age, while we wait for the blessed hope—the glorious appearing of our great God and Savior, Jesus Christ, who gave himself for us to redeem us from all wickedness and to purify for himself a people that are his very own, eager to do what is good.[135]

Our orientation should be *godliness*—an unfamiliar term to most people. What is godliness? One biblical resource defines it as "piety or reverence toward God. Godliness means more than religious profession and a godly conduct; it also means the reality and power of a vital union with God."[136] Another resource suggests godliness "supposes knowledge, veneration, affection, dependence, submission, gratitude, and obedience."[137] It speaks of a life marked by reverence for God and committed to holiness. Of note is the importance of truth as it relates to godliness. Knowledge *of* the truth, as opposed to knowledge only *about* the truth, leads to godliness.[138]

In the broad sense, godliness means practical Christian piety, which includes holiness, goodness, devotion, and reverence to God. It finds its basis in a proper knowledge of God,[139] its outwork in a life yielded to God through Jesus Christ,[140] and its final goal as a greater consciousness of God. It includes similar traits like righteousness, faith, love, patience, and meekness.[141] It is the sum total of Christian values and duties.[142]

We also learn from scripture that God hears godly people who do His

---

135 Titus 2:11–14.
136 *Nelson's Bible Dictionary*, Godliness.
137 *McClintock and Strong Encyclopedia*, Godliness.
138 Titus 1:1.
139 1 John 5:18.
140 Rom. 12:1.
141 2 Pet. 1:6.
142 *Wycliffe Bible Encyclopedia*; *New Unger's Bible Dictionary,* Godliness.

will.[143] As followers of Christ we are to live peaceful, quiet lives marked by godliness and holiness.[144] We are commanded to train ourselves in godliness because it has value and holds promise, now and in the life to come.[145] Godliness with contentment is of high value in God's eyes.[146]

In addition to fighting the good fight of faith, we are to pursue godliness.[147] Scripture tells us that there will be terrible times in the last days, and people will be anything but godly in their behavior. They may have a godly appearance, but their lives will give true evidence of powerlessness.[148] They may talk a good story; they may put on airs for all to see. But the substance of who they are will become apparent soon enough. Their professions of faith will not match their confessions lived out. In those last days, and even now, if we choose to live a godly life we will be persecuted.[149] Look at the public figures who have run for political office or been nominated for government positions and were shunted aside because they openly declared their commitment to their faith.

In the second letter from Peter we are told that God has given Christ's followers everything they need to live godly lives.[150] Godliness also makes Peter's list of biblical qualities essential for effectiveness and productivity in our knowledge of Christ; those who don't possess godliness, in addition to other key qualities he mentions, are blind and ignorant.[151] Finally, Peter urges us to live holy and godly lives while we wait for God's final judgment of the world. We are not to be stagnant in our faith.[152]

Titus 2:11–14 is the bull's-eye for which we should aim. Or, to use other metaphors, it provides the beacon by which we steer our lives, the compass by which we find our way, the map by which we plan our journey, the scale by which we weigh our lives, the gyro by which we pinpoint our location, the balance by which we determine our equilibrium, the ruler

---

143 John 9:31–32.
144 1 Tim. 2:1–2.
145 1 Tim. 4:7–8.
146 1 Tim. 6:6.
147 1 Tim. 6:11–13.
148 2 Tim. 3:1–5.
149 2 Tim. 3:12–13.
150 2 Pet. 1:3–4.
151 2 Pet. 1:5–9.
152 2 Pet. 3:11–13.

by which we measure our walk, the tuning fork by which we calibrate our lives, and the buoy by which we navigate the treacherous waters of our existence.

In this powerful passage we find the beginning, ongoing, and completed Gospel as it plays out in our lives. The Gospel, in the person of Jesus Christ, brings salvation. The Gospel He preaches and the life He lived is a model for us in that it teaches us to live differently than the world around us—to say no to ungodliness and worldly passions and to live self-controlled, upright, and godly lives now, in the present age, while we wait for the blessed hope: the glorious appearing of our great God and Savior, Jesus Christ. The fact that He is God in the flesh sets Him apart from all others who clamor for the worship and allegiance of mankind.

While pursuing my undergraduate degree in a secular institution, I took a class in religious philosophy. The instructor invited us to the home of a psychiatrist who was a follower of an Indian guru named Sai Baba. In his testimonial about Sai Baba, the psychiatrist said that the guru was Jesus, Buddha, and Moses all wrapped up into one. I was incredulous and asked how this man, Sai Baba, could live with such opposing forces within him. When I was asked to explain, I said that Buddha didn't believe in God, Moses was a follower of God, and Jesus was God in the flesh. (I was told I just didn't understand.) The power of the Gospel is its message that Jesus is God and fully capable of saving mankind from its natural tendency toward self-destruction of flesh and soul.

God does not want us to live in terror or exist as hermits, separated from the world around us. No, we are to live our beliefs boldly and powerfully. No one will want to hear what we have to say about our faith until they observe how we live as a result of our faith. Credibility comes with a life lived in congruity with what we declare we believe.

The following passage from Corinthians reminds us that as we live our lives, we are not to forget the giver of life, who has predetermined our roles in His redemptive plan and purposes. We are not to sit idly by, whiling away our time, waiting to go home to be with Him. No, we are to do what is good and show the world what a redeemed sinner looks and acts like. After all, we are not only members of God's family; we are His representatives, His ambassadors, His messengers of reconciliation.

Therefore, if anyone is in Christ, he is a new creation; the old has gone, the new has come! All this is from God, who reconciled us to himself through Christ and gave us the ministry of reconciliation: that God was reconciling the world to himself in Christ, not counting men's sins against them. And he has committed to us the message of reconciliation. We are therefore Christ's ambassadors, as though God were making his appeal through us. We implore you on Christ's behalf: Be reconciled to God. God made him who had no sin to be sin for us, so that in him we might become the righteousness of God.[153]

A life of godliness requires four essential things: (1) focused, intentional action;[154] (2) disciplined pursuit;[155] (3) transformed living;[156] and (4) reliance on God's promises.[157]

Bible-Centeredness

The Bible is our inspired[158] source of wisdom and counsel, our rule of faith and practice, our repository of truth and values, and our moral compass. The Word of God is living and active, sharper than any two-edged sword, penetrating the deepest recesses of our souls and persons, and it stands as an authority over the thoughts and attitudes of our hearts.[159] The Bible has a position of authority because it is the inspired Word of God, profitable for teaching, reproof, correction, and training so that we can be adequately equipped for every good work.[160]

As followers of Christ, each of us must decide what will inform, condition, and influence what we believe and value, how we view and understand the world around us, and what should legitimately compel us

---

153 2 Cor. 5:17–21.
154 James 2:14–26.
155 1 Tim. 6:11–16.
156 2 Pet. 3:11–13.
157 2 Pet. 1:3–9.
158 2 Pet. 1:19–21.
159 Heb. 4:12.
160 2 Tim. 3:16–17.

to act. Whether or not we want to admit it, we are primarily by-products of our environment: our family dynamics, friends, educational institutions, society, government, culture, and social interactions. Unless we are proactive and decide what will be given the privileged vantage point of authority for us, we will simply be swayed by whatever prevailing philosophy or ideology best suits our purposes. On a more subtle level, we will absorb the beliefs, values, and worldviews of others, often without even realizing it.

So, what is it to be—tradition, heritage, reason, experience, some "-ism" like postmodernism or secular humanism, or a compelling ideology or philosophy? If you want a centered life, if you want to contribute to God's redemptive purposes in the world, if you want to reach your full, God-given potential, if you want to live a legacy worth leaving in the lives of others, if you want your life to matter for eternal purposes, then choose God's Word, the Bible, and model your life after Christ.

All of us lead sometimes. Any time you take an initiative that will influence others and change circumstances, events, or people for some purpose, you are leading. When you make decisions regarding your children, you are leading. When you take charge of a project, no matter how small, you are leading. When you persuade others to take a different direction, you are leading. In the biblical context, J. Robert Clinton defines a leader as a person with a God-given capacity (spiritual gifts, natural talents, and acquired skills) and a God-given responsibility (a burden from God to influence others for Him, with accountability to Him for the people being influenced) to influence a specific group of God's people (directly and indirectly) to further His purposes (this requires God-given vision—the leader recognizes God's external direction, while the followers recognize the need to bringing about His vision).

Whether you know you are a leader or you are a reluctant leader or you don't believe you are a leader at all (think again), I offer five reasons why you need a solid biblical foundation:

Because we are invited to serve in God's mission …
"Therefore, go and make disciples of all nations, baptizing them in the name of the Father and of the Son and of the Holy Spirit, and teaching them to obey everything I have commanded you."[161]

---

161 Matt. 28:19–20.

Because a biblical foundation is different …
"Now we have received not the spirit of the world, but the Spirit that is from God, so that we may understand the gifts bestowed on us by God. And we speak of these things in words not taught by human wisdom but taught by the Spirit, interpreting spiritual things to those who are spiritual."[162]

Because we are shaped by biblical truths …
"For the word of God is living and active. Sharper than any double-edged sword, it penetrates even to dividing soul and spirit, joints and marrow; it judges the thoughts and attitudes of the heart."[163]

Because scripture can inform, inspire, and direct …
"All Scripture is inspired by God and is useful for teaching, for reproof, for correction, and for training in righteousness, so that everyone who belongs to God may be proficient, equipped for every good work."[164]

Because there is a movement of God within us …
"For we are what he has made us, created in Christ Jesus for good works, which God prepared beforehand, to be our way of life."[165]

When you are Bible-centered, you rely on the Bible as your single most important source of wisdom, guidance, and practice. You recognize that it has the power to transform you and make you more Christ-like.[166] There are only two roads: If you choose to be independent from God, you will surely be dependent on the world. If you choose to be dependent on God, you will become independent from the world and cease to be driven by its negative influence over you. The Bible is God's truth. It tells us that if we hold to (submit to and obey) Christ's teachings, we will be His disciples. Only then will we know the truth, the truth that sets us free.[167]

Clinton describes a Bible-centered leader as a leader "whose leadership is informed by the Bible, and who has been personally shaped by Biblical

---

162 1 Cor. 2:12–13.
163 Heb. 4:12.
164 2 Tim. 3:16–17.
165 Eph. 2:10.
166 2 Cor. 3:18.
167 John 8:31–32.

leadership values, who has grasped the intent of Scriptural books and their content in such a way as to apply them to current situations and who uses the Bible in [life and] ministry so as to impact followers."

Gaining Solid Footing

Neil Anderson, author, professor, ministry practitioner, and founder of Freedom in Christ Ministries, connects the dots for us: "We need a firm grip on God's Word before we will experience much success at practical Christianity. We need to understand who we are as a result of who God is and what He has done. A productive Christian behavior system is the byproduct of a solid Christian belief system, not the other way around." God-honoring behavior is the result of having a firm grasp of God's Word.

How does one develop a strong grasp of God's Word and thereby gain solid footing for the journey ahead? Clinton offers a strategy for becoming Bible-centered that consists of four components: the notion of individualized core items, the equipping formula, practical levels of communication, and paradigm values.[168]

Core Items

Clinton notes that as Bible-centered followers of Christ, we usually have favorite books of or passages from the Bible—what he calls "core items"— that God has used mightily in our lives to spur our growth, solve our problems, or otherwise meet us. It is these books or special passages that form the basis for much of what we share with others. In other words, these books, passages, and verses mean something to us personally. They repeatedly feed our soul, clarify our understanding, provide direction and motivation, and result in fundamental change.

We have an active interest in these core items and repeatedly use them privately in our devotional lives and publicly in our ministries. Our list of core items will expand over time, but we discover most of them within ten to fifteen years after we decide to follow Christ and become serious about our faith.

In Clinton's strategy, core items include a core set and a core selection.

---

168 Clinton, *Having a Ministry*. Used by permission of the author.

A core set, he says, "is a collection of very important Bible books, usually five to twenty, which are or have been extremely meaningful to you in your own life and for which you feel a burden from God to use with great power over and over in your ministry in the years to come."

What is your core set? Why are these particular books so important to you?

A core selection, according to Clinton "refers to important passages, key biographical characters, special psalms, special parables, special values or key topics that are or have been extremely meaningful to you in your own life and for which you feel a burden from God to use with great power over and over in your ministry in the years to come."

What is your core selection? Why are these items so important to you?

Equipping Formula

The equipping formula has four components: devotional input, core work, familiarity reading, and situational study.

Devotional Input means a disciplined and regular quiet time in which you use the Bible to feed your soul and grow in your intimacy with God and His ways. This time should be spent alone before God and with God. The objective of devotional input is to hear from God and feel His touch. A committed follower of Christ should be able hear from and feel the touch of God through his or her core items.

Basic Steps for a Quiet Time
Make sure you have the right heart attitude.[169] Let God speak to you, and speak to Him. Share with others what happens in your quiet time.

What method do you use for quiet time?

Seven-Question Method
What is the subject of the passage? Where and when does it take place? What does it teach me about God? What does it teach me about leadership, if anything? What warning is there for me to heed or example for me to

---

169 Prov. 3:3–4; Matt. 5:6; Ps. 119:18, 34; John 7:17.

follow? What promise is there for me to claim or command for me to follow? What is the most meaningful verse to me?

The One-Thought Method

Prepare your heart for quiet time by praying a short paraphrase of Psalm 119:18—for instance, "Oh Lord, show me one truth from yourself today." Trust God to answer this prayer. Believe He will be active in your very thought processes. Choose a short portion of scripture and read it several times, jotting down the thoughts that come to you as you read. Identify the most prominent thought (the one you're most impressed with, the one that best fits your circumstances, the one that repeatedly comes back to mind … or simply choose one). Turn this thought into prayer and tell it to God.[170]

Other Thought Questions

- What is the overall theme of the book I am reading?
- What is the historical background to the situations it describes?
- Who wrote the book?
- Who was its intended audience?
- Is there any discernible literary structure to the book/passage?
- What is the meaning of particular words?
- What is the meaning of particular words in the context of the text?
- How do other versions of the Bible interpret the same passage?
- What is the book, passage, or verse saying to me personally?
- What might the book, passage, verse mean for my ministry?

Core Work is the yearly study of one or more of your core items in order to advance your knowledge of them, and the design of communication events to apply the results of your studies. The focus of core work can be biblical books, passages, psalms, parables, people, values, or topics.

---

170 *Having a Ministry That Lasts* outlines basic steps for having quiet time (page 84) and suggests quiet-time strategies for devotional input from your core books (the Seven-Question Method and One-Thought Method, pages 86–93).

What core item have you done core work on? What one unique insight did you derive from the study?[171]

Familiarity Reading means reading scripture in order to remember it better and discover new core items. It also facilitates greater general knowledge of the Bible apart from an intimate knowledge of core items. Reading the Bible on a regular basis will build a basic knowledge of the Bible as a whole. For new leaders—and new Christians, for that matter—Clinton suggests seven to ten readings of the whole Bible to start with.

Which books of the Bible are you most/least familiar with? When is the last time you read through the Bible in its entirety?[172]

Situational Study refers to a leader's special study of the Bible in response to a specific situation or for the purposes of ministry in general. Much of what is preached today is based on situational study. But unless situational study is regularly augmented by comprehensive, expository study, the resultant preaching will lose cohesiveness and relevance.

How much of your preaching or teaching is derived primarily from situational study as compared to expository study? How has this impacted your knowledge and application of the Bible?[173]

Levels of Communication

According to Clinton, a Bible-centered follower of Christ "ought to master his or her core books and other miscellaneous core materials always with a view to using these studies for impact communication." You should master core materials not just for your personal development, but also so you can use them for maximum impact on those whom God has called you to serve, your sphere of ministry influence.

---

171 *Having a Ministry That Lasts* includes detailed information on how to identify your core items (pages 96–98). It also describes how to plan core work (pages 113–14).

172 *Having a Ministry That Lasts* provides guidance for familiarity reading of the Bible (pages 115–17).

173 *Having a Ministry That Lasts* provides guidance for situational study (pages 118–19).

As part of your plan for mastering a core item, arrange to present the key idea in four kinds of communication settings:

- a three- to five-minute informal presentation
- a ten- to fifteen-minute devotional-like presentation
- a twenty- to thirty-minute sermon-like presentation
- a one- to two-hour workshop-like presentation

When selecting important ideas from core material, look for the following types of passages:

- those naturally emphasized by the core material
- those that moved you
- those you see needed in a certain situation
- those that challenge people to be a part of God's work, surrender their lives, grow, etc.
- those that help people grow, especially those that develop leaders
- those that communicate best[174]

Finally, Clinton advocates the use of what he calls the "slot/filler technique for designing a communication event." This technique includes five slots and can be used with all levels of communication (minimum, expanded minimum, limited public presentation, maximum public form).

The five slots include an attention getter, a lead-in, an obligatory or main slot (the heart of the presentation), follow-up, and closure.[175]

Effective communication in this manner includes developing a three- to five-minute presentation on one of your core items that includes all five slots of Clinton's slot/filler technique for designing a communication event.

Paradigm Values

Six key values underlie Clinton's "Life Long Bible Mastery Paradigm."[176]

---

174 Guidelines for this technique may be found in *Having a Ministry That Lasts*, page 221.

175 Guidelines for this technique may be found in *Having a Ministry That Lasts*, pages 225–26.

176 More detailed information can be found in Appendix A of *Having a Ministry That Lasts*.

Value 1: You should be free to be yourself and not have to live up to someone else's standards, especially regarding your study and use of the Bible in life and ministry. God has uniquely created you and will develop you along lines that flow out of who you are and what He has created you for.

Value 2: You should seek primarily to build on your strengths and secondarily to improve your weaknesses.

Value 3: You should have goals that are challenging yet reachable.

Value 4: You should build on your past studies, advancing them at every new opportunity.

Value 5: You should master your core books and selections with a goal of using these studies for impact communication.

Value 6: Especially if you are concerned with developing others, you should be able to pass on your skills, knowledge, and models to others who can use them with the same level of effectiveness.

Personal Assessment

On a scale of 1 to 5, 5 being 'fully realized' and 1 being 'not realized at all,' how would you assess your present status of godliness?

What are your favorite books in the Bible?

What are your favorite chapters in the Bible?

What are your favorite passages in the Bible?

What are your favorite verses in the Bible?

Chapter 3: Our Core

When I think of God I hear a song. It's a song that moves me. It has a melody and it has a groove. It has a certain rhythm.

—*Nooma: Rhythm 011*

The author of "Rhythm" has a poetic way of picturing the beauty of God's existence as a song and describing how we are to live in congruence with that song. He concludes with a provocative question:

> People have heard this song for thousands and thousands of years across continents and cultures and time periods. People have heard the song and they've found it captivating, and they've wanted to hear more. Now there've always been people who say there is no song and who deny the music. But the song keeps playing. And so, Jesus came to show us how to live in tune with the song … that He's the way and truth and the life … Jesus is like God in taking on flesh and blood, and so

in his generosity and His compassion that's what God's like. And in his telling the truth, that's what God's like. In His love and forgiveness and sacrifice—that's what God's like. That's who God is. That's how the song goes. The song is playing all around us all the time. The song is playing everywhere, it's written on our hearts, and everybody is playing the song. The question isn't whether or not you're playing a song. The question is, are you in tune?[177]

A Centered Life

As we discussed earlier in this book, attempting to live a balanced life is futile, because life happens between plans. Christ modeled a centered life driven by doing the will of His Father. What does a centered life look like for a Christian? In my book *A Rattling of Sabers*, I made the case for a centered life and how it should be lived. I do not intend to replicate that discussion here; if the reader wants more details, I would recommend reading the book. I will, however, briefly cover some of that information to provide a context for what follows.

The Bible refers to the locus for living a centered life as "the heart." Bible scholars are nearly unanimous about what scripture means when it refers to the heart. The word *heart* or one of its derivatives is found more than eight hundred times in the Bible, with approximately 80 percent of those references in the Old Testament and 20 percent in the New Testament.

Vine's Expository Dictionary of Biblical Words is very helpful to us at this point. It tells us that the New Testament describes the heart as the "seat of physical life, joy, desires, affections, perceptions, thoughts and motives, understanding, reasoning powers; imagination; conscience; intentions; purpose; the will; and faith." It is the seat of morality—that dimension of life related to right conduct, including virtuous character, honorable intentions, and right actions.

Vine's tells us that the Old Testament view of the heart "includes the emotions, the reason, and the will. The heart stands for the inner being of man. As such, it is the fountain of all one does. All thoughts, desires,

---

177 Rob Bell, *Nooma 011: Rhythm* (2005).

words, and actions flow from deep within the person. Yet one cannot fully understand his or her heart."

Nelson's Illustrated Bible Dictionary adds to this definition by explaining that the heart is "the inner self that thinks, feels, and decides. In the Bible the word heart has a much broader meaning than it does to the modern mind. The heart is that which is central to (a person). Nearly all the references to the heart in the Bible refer to some aspect of human personality. Finally, heart often means someone's true character or personality. Purity or evil; sincerity or hardness; and maturity or rebelliousness—all these describe the heart or true character of individuals."

What about the mind? The mind is the control center of the heart. It is the gateway to our heart and the gatekeeper of our soul. The mind decides what will pass through to the heart; apathy and complacency compromise its integrity.

Here's another way to look at the mind: it acts as the operating software for the hard drive of the heart.

The mind can be dulled. The smallest compromises originating in our mind can lead to the hardening of our heart—to ignorance and darkened understanding, to separation from a godliness, to lessened sensitivity to sin, to a life based on sensuality.

In essence, the heart is our inner being, the core of who we are, the unvarnished receptacle of our being, the irreducible minimum. It is the place from which the impetus for our actions arises. It is the repository of what we truly trust in, rely on, and cling to. It is the filter through which we process all life's decisions. It is the lens through which we make judgments about the world around us. It is what moves us to action. It is worth guarding; it must be guarded.

A perusal of scripture yields five primary concepts related to the heart: out of the heart comes evil,[178] God is concerned about the hearts of humanity,[179] God desires a pure heart and pure motives,[180] the enemy

178 Gen. 6:5, 8:21; Mark 7:21–23; Matt. 12:35; Heb. 3:12; Luke 6:45; Rom. 3:23.
179 1 Sam. 16:7; Rom. 10:9–10; Pss. 51:10, 86:11–12; 1 Cor. 3:3; Heb. 8:10; Acts 13:22.
180 Ps. 24:4; 1 Kings 3:6, 9; Ezek. 36:26; 2 Cor. 9:7; Eph. 6:5–6; Heb. 4:12; Prov. 4:23; 2 Pet. 3:1; Titus 2:11–14.

doesn't want our hearts to be transformed,[181] and God wants our hearts to be transformed.[182]

The Bible tells us that we are to think about whatever is excellent and praiseworthy; that we are predestined to be conformed to the image of Christ; that we are being transformed into His likeness one step at a time; that God wants our behavior to be Christ-like; that He has given us everything we need to live a godly life; that we can understand and experientially know Christ; and that we are not alone or powerless, as He has given us His Spirit to be with us. If our lives are to bring honor and glory to the Father, our hearts must be tuned to Him. To change our behavior, we must have a change of heart. If we are to live a centered life in Christ, our heart must reflect His character.

In summary, the heart is the real battlefield where defeat or victory is attained. God looks at our hearts and evaluates us based on what He finds there. The enemy also knows that whoever wins and controls our hearts also guides our behavior. The enemy wants to bring us back to the failures of our past; God wants to bring us to the victories of our future. The struggle is in the present. But it isn't fought by equal adversaries. God is supreme; the enemy is not. Our behavior can galvanize, enhance, embolden, animate, electrify, incite, fire up, stimulate, rouse, spur on, bolster, and reinforce what is already in the heart. Our minds choose how we will respond.

Behavior simply strikes a resonant chord with what already is inside us. Our hearts, stimulated by situations, incidents, or circumstances, determine our behavior. Our behavior may appear to determine what is in our hearts, but it merely strikes a responsive note with what is already stored there.

While behavior can solidify what is stored in our hearts, kind of like a feedback loop, it does not happen in a vacuum. It is activated by the heart and put into play by the mind. Our susceptibility to behavioral influences is determined by how much access those influences have to our hearts. Passivity or lack of vigilance can make our hearts vulnerable to outside influences.

---

181 Matt. 13:15, 19; Eph. 4:27; Rom. 1:21; Eph. 4:17–19; 1 Pet. 5:8; John 8:44.

182 Phil. 4:8; Rom. 8:29; 2 Cor. 3:18; Eph. 4:13, 15; 2 Pet. 1:3–4; Jer. 9:24; John 14:16, 17.

If the convictions within our hearts are not strongly held, and if we do not allow the Spirit of God to control, inform, and condition our hearts, then they can and will be shaped by other influences—friends, circumstances, the world, even Satan himself.

The point is to be so controlled and influenced by the Spirit of God that we have the mind and character of Christ in our hearts. Our resulting behavior will be Christ-like and bring glory to God. To change our behavior, we must have a change of heart.

Satan and his minions want to corrupt our hearts; God wants us to have pure hearts. The battle rages, and you and I have the deciding vote. Who is going to win this struggle, Satan or God? We tip the scales. We decide with our minds who and what will influence our hearts. We determine what will control our behavior. One sure way to have the enemy win the struggle is to do nothing at all, because passivity is the oil on the slippery slope of destruction. Our lack of concern or proactive involvement speeds up the decay of our soul. As Edmund Burke, an eighteenth-century Irish statesman, said, "The only thing necessary for the triumph of evil is for good men to do nothing."

From God's point of view, character matters! The Bible is clear—behavior (or performance) is essentially a reflection of the health of the heart. And character is a portrait or snapshot of what's in the heart. In other words, what is stored in the heart determines and conditions behavior. More will be said later about the components of the heart.

To live a centered life is to have a heart that reflects the heart of Christ, that sets Christ on the throne, and that recognizes Christ as master, mediator, and messiah. Living a centered life means that Jesus is our authority for faith and practice—that He informs, conditions, and establishes our beliefs, values, attitudes, and motives. Living a centered life means that we owe our allegiance to Him alone, that we are under new management, and that our expression of love for Him is validated by our unquestioned obedience to Him. In Christ we find our congruence, coherence, consistency, convergence, and completeness. Following Christ is not like a partaking of a smorgasbord, where you go along the line and pick what you want and leave the rest. He is all of it or none of it. He is Lord of all or He is not Lord at all. When we come to Christ, it must be with an attitude of complete surrender, holding nothing back. He is not just our Savior; He is our Lord.

Receiving versus Accepting

Have you *accepted* Jesus or have you *received* Jesus? What's the difference?

First, nowhere does the Bible state or suggest that we "accept" Jesus. For one thing, who is accepting whom? "Accepting" Jesus implies that we are the final arbiters, that we are the ones deciding whether the opportunity merits our consideration, rises to the level of serious attention, makes a compelling case. It implies, in other words, that we are the authorities who matter in this situation. How arrogant of us. More accurately, we receive God's provision of salvation—something He determined in advance that He would extend to us as a gift, something we cannot earn but can only receive.[183]

Second, coming to Christ is not an installment plan where your receive Jesus as Savior, garnering all the attendant benefits, and then, sometime later, receive Him as Lord, submitting to the fact that you are now under new management. This is not a two-stage event. When we receive Christ, we are receiving Him for all we know Him to be at that moment: as Savior, with the attendant benefits, and as Lord, with the attendant obligations and responsibilities.[184] Have you *received* Jesus?

Receiving Him as Savior in one instance and Lord at some other time down the road when we are ready to cede control of our lives to Him is not biblical. It has been said that the Japanese never truly surrendered until they surrendered their sword to General Douglas MacArthur. Many of us want the benefits of salvation but not the obligations or responsibilities that it requires. We want to hold on to the sword of control and independence rather than surrendering it on bended knee in submission to the majesty, sovereignty, and authority of Christ in our lives. Surrendering the sword of control and independence facilitates God's ongoing spiritual renewal of our lives.

Third, upon receipt of His gift requiring acknowledgment of His Son as Savior and Lord, we also receive the following at the very instant of conversion:

---

183 Matt. 10:15.
184 Rom. 10:9–10; Eph. 1:4; Gal. 3:14; 1 Thess. 5:9–10.

- a new nature[185]
- adoption[186]
- joint heirship with Christ[187]
- new citizenship[188]
- membership in God's household[189]
- justification[190]
- adoption[191]
- regeneration[192]
- forgiveness and redemption[193]
- a new heart[194]
- fruit of the Spirit in seed form[195]
- the indwelling of the Holy Spirit[196]

In your own experience of conversion, you may have accepted Christ as Savior and Lord. Please be assured that God knows our hearts and judges the sincerity of our convictions, regardless of semantics. Because of the distinction I am drawing between *receiving* and *accepting*, do not assume that *accepting* Christ is somehow inferior to *receiving* Him. I am merely trying to help you understand the attitude I believe we should have when we commit our lives to Christ. I would argue that *receiving* Christ recognizes that salvation is a gift from the Giver of Life.

Have you taken the time to review the great gift God has given us and what He imparts to us at the moment of conversion? All this comes by simply receiving Jesus as Savior and Lord.

---

185 Eph. 4:22–24.
186 Rom. 8:13–15.
187 Eph. 8:16–17.
188 Phil. 3:20.
189 Eph. 2:19–22.
190 Rom. 3:21–24.
191 Eph. 1:5–6.
192 Eph. 2:1–6.
193 Eph. 1:7–8.
194 Ezek. 36:26.
195 Gal. 5:22–24.
196 Eph. 1:13–14.

Bold Relief

As I write this book, my wife and I are enjoying an extended stay in Ireland. At this moment we are appreciating the quiet and serenity of a little cottage outside Cong Village in the west of Ireland. For the first half of our visit we stayed in a condo in Roundstone, a sleepy little fishing village on the country's western shore. There were numerous paintings and other objects hanging on the wall, including a two-dimensional painting alongside a three-dimensional work of art, a carving with variously raised features. This form of art is called a relief, among other things.

It used to be quite comfortable to have one foot in the purposes of the world and one foot in the purposes of God. No more. The gap between them is too large. As committed followers of Jesus Christ, we are being asked to stand in bold relief against the backdrop of our culture and defend the hope that lives inside us.[197] Our only other option is to give in, to fold back into our culture, becoming transparent within it and indistinguishable apart from it. There is, at this point, nothing in earthly life that would draw anyone to the foot of God's Son's cross. The choice is yours: where will you plant your feet?

What stands out about you? Is it your walk with Jesus? What do people observe about you? Even those who don't know Christ can tell if you are a person of faith. If I were able to follow you for a few weeks and you didn't know I was there, I wouldn't have to listen to what you said to determine your walk. I would just have to watch how you lived. When the few weeks were over, I would be able to tell you with some degree of accuracy what you truly believed and what you truly valued. A life well lived speaks more loudly than any well-articulated argument for what we say we believe and value.

Living in bold relief means there is constancy to our life, congruence to our existence, an internal compass of morality that reveals a discernible pattern of commitment to a code of behavior. Living this way means that we will buck our culture from time to time. We will stand against the prevailing winds. We will take unpopular positions.

---

197 1 Pet. 3:15.

Hills to Die On …

In some instances we will have to declare the hills we will die on. In other situations we must decide the hills we will bleed on. In yet other circumstances we will decide the hill isn't worth climbing. Even though anxiety will weigh heavily upon us, we will know the proper time and course of action for each.[198]

We can't die on every hill, we can't bleed on every hill, and there may be many more hills that aren't worth climbing at all. That doesn't mean the issue before us is not important; it simply means that it is not a hill God wants us to ascend. The hills to die on should be few. The hills to bleed on should be God's hills and not our own. And the hills not worth climbing may be someone else's hill to die or bleed on. For example, I have chosen four hills to die on.

- Faith in the Gospel[199]
- Family responsibility[200]
- Focus on a life purpose[201]
- Fidelity to the Bible[202]

Hills to Bleed On …

At a certain time in my life, I came to the realization that I was bleeding on too many hills—and they were my hills, not God's hills. I realized that many of the issues weren't worth bleeding over, at least for me, and I had to make some changes.

My hills may not be your hills. That's okay. Every person has to decide which hills he or she will die on, bleed on, or not climb at all. Take on too many hills, and people will dismiss what you stand for because every issue seems to be a hill you'll die or bleed on.

Hills to die on probably won't involve sacrificing your life, but they might mean sacrificing a promotion, a career decision, a friendship, an association, or some worthwhile pursuit for the sake of what God wants to do in you and through you.

---

198 Eccles. 8:6.
199 Titus 2:11–14.
200 1 Tim. 5:8.
201 Eph. 2:8–10.
202 2 Tim. 3:16–17.

I know a man who was growing in the Lord, and as a result, his priorities changed. Instead of giving his life over to achievement and success, he rethought what really mattered in his life and to his family. When given the opportunity to pursue a career move that would mean more money, much more money, and realize a longtime dream to succeed in his chosen profession, he was faced with an integrity check.

An integrity check is a test God uses to evaluate our hearts and the consistency of our inner convictions with our outward actions. It can come by way of temptation, conflict, persecution, or a challenge to follow through on some commitment we've made earlier. It's not that God doesn't know how we'll respond. Rather, *we* must know how we'll respond. God allows such checks to stiffen our spiritual backbone. Sometimes we pass the test; other times we fail. In either case we learn something about ourselves.

Back to my friend: he turned down the promotion he had sought and worked toward. Why? Because he had seen what God was doing in and through him and how it was affecting his family, and he decided that it was not worth abandoning for the sake of money and prestige.

Hills Not Worth Climbing …

In my journey I have come to realize that many of the hills I thought were important enough to make a stand on were not the hills God appointed for me. In fact, He wasn't asking me to climb them at all. These hills were someone else's to climb, to bleed on, or to die on, but they weren't mine.

If you've contemplated an issue but determined it is not a hill to die on, bleed on, or climb at all, that does not mean the issue is not important. Maybe it's very important, and God already has someone else lined up to take it on. Perhaps it doesn't fall within your sphere of influence, although it may be within your circle of concern. As you grow in Christ generally and as a leader specifically, your sphere of influence also grows. As you mature in Christ, your influence reach expands proportionately. Sin can diminish your reach.

Influence Reach

Influence reach refers to the influence we wield in three different domains: direct, indirect, and organizational.

Direct influence indicates a measure of people being influenced by the real presence of a leader, usually in focused, structured situations where feedback between follower and leader is possible and necessary. This type of influence carries a high level of accountability to God. It extends to those immediately under the authority and responsibility of the leader and is generally restricted to those in front of or face-to-face with or otherwise in close proximity to the leader. Situations involving direct influence might include mentoring individuals, leading a small group, preaching to a congregation, teaching a seminar or workshop, or speaking at a conference.

Indirect influence indicates a measure of people being influenced by the non-time-bound, miscellaneous impact a leader makes through other people, through media, or through writing. With this type of influence, feedback between the leader and those influenced is difficult, if not impossible, and accountability is primarily for the content of influential ideas. Examples of indirect influence might include serving on a committee, advisory board, or executive board that makes decisions for a larger group; writing for an unseen audience; having a radio ministry; or recording messages preached and uploaded to a website for general access.

Organizational influence indicates a measure of people being influenced by a person in organizational leadership via direct, indirect, or organizational power. Examples of this kind of influence might include being a policy formulator, corporate board member, department head, or business leader, and leveraging that authority to help facilitate God's redemptive purposes in people.

When leaders mature and their intensity, passion, and ministerial focus crystallize—that is, when they move from "shotgun" to "laser beam"— their direct influence grows linearly, while their indirect influence grows exponentially. In other words, their extensiveness (quantity, or the number of people they influence), comprehensiveness (scope, or the increasing variety of subjects they are able to address), and intensiveness (depth, or their ability to move those being influenced to deeper understanding, commitment, and action) grows linearly in the direct domain, while those same measures grow exponentially in the indirect domain. When a leader penetrates the life and heart of a follower more extensively, comprehensively, and intensively, that follower and those with whom he or she interacts are affected accordingly.

Circles of Concern and Influence

We operate within two circles—the circle of concern and the circle of influence. Within the *Circle of Concern* are issues we are concerned about but have little to no control over. For instance, we might be concerned about political or economic issues in Washington, a judge's ruling on an issue that touches us, a decision being made by someone regarding our personal circumstances, world poverty, global warming, or any host of matters that we consider important. We may have some limited influence on these matters, but for all practical purposes they are out of our reach to do anything about them. In these cases, we have essentially one option— prayer. Once we have prayed about these matters, we must release them to the Lord and move on to those issues we can control.

Within the *Circle of Influence* are issues we have some degree of control over; our direct input or interaction will determine their outcome. People, events, and circumstances can be changed by our involvement, direct or indirect. We might choose to address the specific issue head-on, or we can have a hand in factors that in turn may impact the situation (e.g., a note to a friend or authority may cause her or him to respond to a set of circumstances over which she or he has some influence).

Each of us has a finite amount of energy at our disposal (emotional, spiritual, and physical); the amount differs for each person. Our circle of influence can expand as we grow emotionally, spiritually, and intellectually, and it can also diminish as a result of our bad decisions and/or sins.

If we expend our limited energy on matters over which we have little influence or control, the amount of energy remaining will be reduced. Then when we turn our attention to issues within our sphere of influence, we will find that the circle of influence has shrunk while our circle of concern has grown. Spending our finite energy in this sphere will only increase our anxiety and stress because we can do little to change the outcome.

Focusing our finite energy primarily on issues within our circle of influence and praying about issues within our circle of concern (and releasing these issues to the Lord) will reduce the circle of concern to a more manageable size and therefore cause less anxiety and stress in our lives. This is a far more constructive activity—focusing on what we can change and leaving to God those issues we cannot change to any significant degree.

So focus on your circle of influence—and pray about your circle of concern.

Personal Assessment

What hills are you prepared to die on?

What hills are worth bleeding on?

What hills are not worth climbing at all?

What influence can you exert for facilitating God's redemptive purposes in and for others?

Where do you wield direct, indirect, and organizational influence?

What issues rightfully fall within your circle of influence?

What issues rightfully belong in your circle of concern?

The Sponge

Every follower of Christ must determine his or her spiritual rhythm. By way of illustration, visualize a sponge in a shallow bowl. If you pour water over the sponge, it will absorb the water until it's saturated; after that, the water will simply spill over it. Now visualize wringing out the sponge. Pretty soon there will be no more water to wring out; after that, if you continue to wring it, the sponge will become dry and over time may simply break down or crumble in your hands.

What can be learned from this illustration? Many Christians I know listen to every sermon preached in their church or on the Internet. They regularly attend workshops, seminars, every event that can fill their spiritual sponge. And over time, their sponge becomes saturated. I always know when it happens because I hear them say something to this effect: "I'm leaving this church. I'm not being fed anymore. I am not getting the deep teaching I need."

Many Christians I know jump at every opportunity to serve. Some can't even sit through a sermon without getting up to help with something. They are constantly volunteering, in or outside of church, constantly wringing out their spiritual sponge. When their sponge becomes dry and brittle, I hear something like this: "I'm leaving this church. People don't appreciate what I do here. I'm going somewhere else, where my gifts of service will be appreciated. I'm just taken for granted here."

We are called to a rhythm of nurture and service. Our spiritual rhythm is to fill up our spiritual sponge through nurturing activities such as worship, prayer, study, reflection, fellowship, and personal application to our lives. Our spiritual rhythm is also to wring out what we have learned into other people's lives through service and outreach. Fill it up, wring it out, fill it up, and wring it out. There will be no more room for what fills our sponge if we don't wring out what we have learned for the benefit of others, building up the body in the process.

Personal Assessment

What activities are available to fill up your sponge?

What activities are available to wring out your sponge?

List all nurture and service activities in which you are currently involved.

Dr. Greg Bourgond

Which ones make the best use of your time and spiritual gifts?

Which ones are redundant?

To arrive at a healthy spiritual rhythm, which activities should you eliminate and which should you retain?

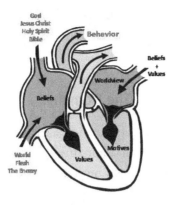

Chapter 4: Our Heart[203]

Above all else, guard your heart, for everything you do flows from it.
—Proverbs 4:23

The terrain where spiritual victory or defeat is determined is our heart. The heart comprises four domains: beliefs, values, attitudes, and motives. Collectively, these four locations are the ground on which spiritual victory or defeat is decided, where the struggle for our souls is won or lost.

In scripture, both the Old and New Testaments, terms for the heart are best understood in a metaphorical sense—that is, figurative, symbolic, or allegorical. Gary Carpenter's concordance study of the Hebrew and Greek words for *heart* suggests that the term "refers to the true self, the whole inner man, or to the specific aspects that make up the inner man."[204]

I find it helpful to envision the landscape of the heart as four specific areas. Each has its unique challenges—its strengths and weaknesses, its dangers and threats, its skirmishes and pitched battles, its place of

---

203 Some of what is contained here, albeit in revised form, can be found in my book *A Rattling of Sabers* (2012). For purposes of structural integrity, primacy of concepts, and congruence with the intent and scope of this book, I have chosen to excerpt sections here.

204 Gary Carpenter, *What the Bible Says about the Heart* (Joplin: College Press, 1990), 19.

significance in an individual's spiritual well-being—and each area impacts the others. The enemy fights in all four areas; we must be prepared to confront him in all four.

The Domains

As I reviewed and analyzed verses and passages referring to the heart, I began to recognize four primary domains, or areas of engagement: beliefs, values, attitudes (worldview), and motives.

Beliefs: Our Foundation[205]

Beliefs are not merely facts we affirm; they are the foundation for all our behavior. The Greek word for *believe* means what we trust in, rely on, and cling to. Our beliefs are more than verbal affirmations; they are what we really believe at our deepest core—so much so that they are a part of our being. They determine our values, affect our attitudes, and influence our motives. They ultimately determine how we react in a given situation.

A word of caution is necessary at this point: what we verbally affirm as our beliefs may have little relationship to how we behave. What we say we are does not always align with who we really are. Talk is cheap, as the saying goes.

We have become very good at rhetoric that has little or no relationship to who we are at the core of our being. We use skillful verbiage to hold others at a distance, because if they get too close and observe our behavior over time, they will discover what frauds we are.

So the verbal statements we make are not proof-perfect. If our behavior were observed over time, without regard for what we said about ourselves in the process, a pattern would soon emerge that would give us a clearer picture of who we really are and what we really believe. Behavior observed over time will reflect the core of our being.

Hebrew scholars attest to the fact that real faith is belief in action. They see no separation between one's beliefs and one's actions: more specifically, a belief doesn't become an ingrained belief until it's acted upon.[206] Repeated

---

205 Prov. 6:20–23; John 8:31–32; James 2:14–26; 1 John 2:3–6; 1 John 3:18–19; 1 John 5:2–5; 1 John 5:9–12; 1 Pet. 2:9; 1 Pet. 3:15–16.
206 James 2:14–26.

application of one's beliefs indicates what one really believes. If there is disconnect between the two, between one's beliefs and one's actions, then they are not really beliefs, but simply affirmations or aspirations.

A biblical belief system might include the Ten Commandments as well as precepts and principles like these: love others as yourself, we are created in the image of God, man is sinful, human nature is corrupt, God loves us, life is meaningless apart from God, salvation is the only means to wholeness, God has plans for our lives, man's chief purpose is to demonstrate God's excellence in all that we do, human life is to be cherished, widows and orphans are to be taken care of, Christ is the only means of salvation.

Corrupted or distorted beliefs might include the following: truth is relative, my body is my own, there is no God, there are no absolutes, power is success, all lifestyles are to be accepted, performance is all that matters, and the end justifies the means.

Values: Our Filter[207]

Values are the principles we live by, the hills we will die on. They comprise our moral system, and they are the filter through which our lives are processed and our decisions are made. We don't make a decision without referring to our value system, even if we cannot articulate those values. We hold our values in high esteem and find it hard to understand why others may not share those values. Related terms would include *morals, virtues, ethics, principles, rules, standards,* and *norms.* A value becomes a virtue when it is an ingrained habit we apply without really thinking much about it.

Examples of biblically informed values might include centered living, devotion to God, family first, loyalty, justice, mercy, honesty, fairness, hard work, punctuality, self-discipline, courage, submission to the authority of God's Word, and personal integrity.

Examples of corrupted values might include acts or habits like self-satisfaction, cunning, euthanasia, and deception; and beliefs like any form of sex is permissible, one race is superior to others, "If it feels good do it," pornography is art, tolerance first and always, and cheating is okay.

---

207 Prov. 4:7; Jer. 9:23–24; Phil. 4:8; Heb. 8:10; Gal. 5:22–24; 2 Pet. 1:3; 2 Pet. 1:5–9.

Attitudes: Our Lens[208]

What we think—our perceptions and our worldview—is the lens through which we view and understand the world around us. Each of us has a set of perceptual attitudes that help shape our outlook on life. If beliefs are the foundation for our behavior, and values are the filter through which we process our decisions, then attitudes are the lens through which we observe life around us. Our perceptions about life are shaped by our attitudes. Our system of attitudes is also called our worldview. The term *worldview* refers to any ideology, philosophy, theology, movement, or religion that provides an overarching approach to understanding God, the world, and man's relationship to God and the world.

Our set worldview determines how we perceive and interpret our observations of the world around us. In *The Myth of Certainty*, Dan Taylor explains that "every person has a way of making sense out of the world. We have a compulsion for ordering and explaining our experiences. We belong to communities of belief which help shape, whether we are conscious of it or not, our views of the world and our actions in it ... Most people thoughtlessly adopt an inherited world view, or one absorbed from their surroundings. Even those who explicitly work one out often operate in daily life by a different, less conscious system than the one they carefully construct."

How we interpret events, draw conclusions about what we read, evaluate what we observe, assess what we hear, and process arguments depends on our worldview at the time. Examples of biblically informed worldviews might include the Beatitudes (Matt. 5:3–12) as well as the following concepts: God is involved in history, humans bear God's imprint, something good can be found in every human being, all things work together for good, there is one supreme God, all creation is divinely inspired, the world is corrupted by sin, and all life is sacred.

Examples of corrupted or distorted worldviews might include white supremacy; humanism (man is the final authority); postmodernism (there is no absolute truth); racism; pro-choice; a sense of entitlement; a predatory mentality (strength rules); pluralism (all views, values, and practices are

---

208 Matt. 5:3–12; Eph. 4:22–24; Phil. 2:5–8; James 3:14–16; Heb. 4:12.

equally correct and acceptable); the belief that "the world is my oyster"; relativism (situational ethics); and hedonism (pleasure is preeminent).

Motives: Our Stimulus[209]

Motives are what stimulate our activity, mobilize us to act, and inspire our behavior. Daniel McGuire, a biblical scholar, suggests that "motive gives essential and constitutive meaning to human action." A motive is anything that causes a person to act. It might take the form of a need or desire, an impulse or inducement, a goad, or something else that "spurs us on." It can be seen as a driving force arising from our predispositions, biases, or habitual inclinations.

Motives compel us to take action and may arise from an external stimulus such as an opportunity, circumstance, or event. They provide the bridge from thoughts (temptation) to action (behavior). Some people, for instance, are motivated by greed or jealousy. Others are motivated by love or desire. Still others might be motivated by idealism or self-interest.

Examples of biblically informed motives might be unconditional love, commitment to God, a personal vow, Christ-centered desires, commitment to a certain value, devotion, diligence, love of others, or self-preservation in the face of danger. Examples of distorted or corrupted values might include greed, lust, self-gratification, gluttony, hatred, anger, pride, or a desire for domination or conquest.

Unconditional love has always been the greatest motive for behavior that brings glory to God.[210]

Composition of the Heart

Beliefs, values, attitudes, and motives stimulated by situations, incidents, or circumstances determine behavior. Our behavior may appear to determine our beliefs, values, attitudes, and motives, but in fact it merely strikes a responsive and resonant chord with what is already stored in our hearts. Behavior simply reinforces our existing beliefs, values, attitudes and motives.

Behavior can act as galvanizing influence on the heart. Behavior can

---

209 John 13:34–35; 1 Cor. 4:5; 1 Cor. 13:4–8; 1 John 2:3–6; James 4:3.
210 1 Pet. 1:22; 1 Cor. 13:4–6; 1 John 3:16–18.

solidify what is stored in our hearts, kind of like a feedback loop to the heart. Behavior, however, does not happen in a vacuum. It is activated by the interaction of our beliefs, values, attitudes, and motives in the heart. Susceptibility to behavioral influences is determined by the degree of accessibility to the heart. Our passivity or unguardedness can make our hearts vulnerable to outside influences.

If our beliefs, values, attitudes, and motives are not strongly held, and if we do not allow the Spirit of God to control them then they can and will be shaped by other influences including friends, circumstances, the world, and Satan himself.

The point is to be so controlled and influenced by the Spirit of God as to have the mind of Christ in our beliefs, values, attitudes, and motives so that our character is Christ-like and our behavior brings glory to God. To change behavior, we must have a change of heart.

In other words, to change our behavior we must have a change in our beliefs, values, attitudes, and motives. Behavior that brings glory to God is based on these factors that must be influenced by the Spirit.

The Components

There is a relationship among the four components of the heart. Although it is depicted as a straightforward cause-and-effect model, it is more like a feedback loop. Using the blood circulation in the heart as metaphor, we can visualize the flow: beliefs to values to worldview to motives to behavior.

Our central beliefs are formed by certain influences—the world,[211] the flesh,[212] the enemy,[213] or God.[214] It matters what you allow to occupy the privileged vantage point of authority over your beliefs—or, for that matter, over your values, attitudes, and motives. The behavior produced as a result of the interaction between these components will be directly related to what stands as an authority over them. It matters what belief system we embrace. Our beliefs provide the foundation for our values, our worldview, and our motives.

---

211 1 John 2:15–17; 1 Pet. 2:11.
212 Mark 7:20–23.
213 1 Pet. 5:8–9.
214 Titus 2:11–14.

The Connection

Our central beliefs *establish* our core values. Our core values *inform* our perceptual attitudes, our worldview. Our worldview *conditions* our motives, and our motives *energize* our behavior. Our behavior *reflects* what is stored in our hearts.

Through my research I've concluded that there is an interdependent relationship among the "chambers" of the heart. Beliefs—our central, foundational, and operational beliefs, what we trust in, rely on, and cling to—determine all else that follows: our values, our perceptual attitudes, our motives, and ultimately our behavior.

Our central beliefs *establish* our values. Every value we esteem and act upon rests on a belief or system of beliefs. One belief can breed many values, just as many beliefs can coalesce to establish a specific value. For instance, several verses in the Bible deal with our relationship to the world, variously stressing nonconformity,[215] aliens and strangers,[216] allegiance,[217] and true citizenship.[218] Taken together they could yield a value like "Be in the world but not of the world" or "I will be governed by the Kingdom of God."

Our core values *inform* our perceptual attitudes, our worldview. Our every major or moral decision is made based on a value we hold. Every decisions passes through the filter of our values. Values differ from beliefs in that they must be acted upon if they are indeed true values. Perhaps one of your core values is people ("My capacity to influence is based on relationships more than expertise") or being rather than doing ("It is easier to do, but it is more important to be") or family ("My wife and kids are my significant ministry").

Our values compel us to respond to integrity checks,[219] word checks,[220]

---

215 Rom. 12:2.

216 1 Pet. 2:11–12.

217 1 John 2:15–17; James 4:4.

218 Phil. 3:20–21.

219 God uses an *integrity check* to evaluate the heart and the consistency of inner convictions with outward actions. Examples: temptation, conflict, persecution, values check, follow-through.

220 A *word check* tests the capacity to hear from God through His Word and apply insights to life situations. Examples: personal and ministry guidance, submission, lordship, direction.

obedience checks,[221] faith challenges,[222] and isolation,[223] among other "process items" God uses to shape us. We are given a family set of values when we receive Christ as Savior and Lord and become members of God's family. Those values are the fruit of the Spirit[224] and must be cultivated. God also places in our hearts other values by which our lives are to be defined and our characters formed.

Our perceptual attitudes about life form our worldview, our view of reality. Our worldview *conditions* our motives. In fact, our worldview primarily comprises our foundational beliefs plus our core values. How we see the world and make sense of what we see is determined by the worldview we hold, and an ideology or philosophy then animates our worldview. We Christians have but one worldview, a biblical one, and God's general revelation (creation, nature, and conscience) and special revelation (Jesus Christ, the Holy Spirit, and the Bible) stand as the ideology or philosophy that animates our biblical worldview. Every worldview consists of perceptions about ultimate reality, humankind, the major dilemma humankind faces, a solution to that dilemma, and an ultimate destiny for humankind.

In its simplest form, a biblical worldview acknowledges that God created the universe, including our world and the people who live in it. He created every human being in His image; therefore we are important to Him and He cares about our well-being. The greatest destructive power in the world and the major dilemma we face is sin, which mars that image. God provided a way out from under the weight of our sin through the life, death, and resurrection of Christ, who restores God's image in us so we can facilitate His life-giving, redemptive purposes in the world. Our ultimate destiny will be either eternal life with Him or utter and complete separation from Him.

---

221 *Obedience checks* are circumstances where God calls for obedience despite confusion and apparent contradiction. Examples: perseverance, a clarity-of-life situation, new opportunities, a test of submission.

222 A *faith challenge* tests our willingness to take steps of faith and grow in our capacity to trust God. Examples: ministry crossroads, decisions, new directions, a lack of growth, a plateau.

223 *Isolation* is the setting aside of an individual from normal involvements to hear from God in a deeper way. Examples: sickness, new education, self-renewal, spiritual retreat or reflection, solitude.

224 Gal. 5:22–24.

So what does it mean to be created in the image of God? J. I. Packer, the world-renowned theologian and author of the best seller *Knowing God*, offers helpful counsel on this point.[225] For the sake of emphasis I include his statement cited earlier in the book.

> When God made man, he communicated to him qualities corresponding to His moral attributes. This is what the Bible means when it tells us that God made man (meaning both men and women) in His own image—namely, that God made man (and woman) a free spiritual being, a responsible moral agent with powers of choice and action, able to commune with Him and respond to Him, and by nature good, truthful, holy, upright (Eccl 7:29): in a word, godly. The moral qualities which belonged to the divine image were lost at the Fall; God's image in man has been universally defaced, for all mankind has in one way or another lapsed into ungodliness. But the Bible tells us that now, in fulfillment of His plan of redemption, God is at work in Christian believers to repair His ruined image by communicating these qualities to them afresh. This is what Scripture means when it says that Christians are being renewed in the image of Christ[226] and of God.[227]

We are designed to live in accordance with God's design—and if we don't, there are consequences. What would happen if you filled your car's gas tank with sugar water? Your engine would seize up. What would happen if you filled it with diesel fuel? It would run for a while but ultimately quit: the plugs would gum up and refuse to fire.

When I was mentoring several men from a church in which I was an associate pastor, we spent a week in Montana, fishing for trout. After dinner one evening I decided to wash the dishes but couldn't find soap for the cabin's dishwasher. However I did find a box of Tide, and so, figuring soap was soap, I poured some in, set the wash cycle, and went outside for a while. To my utter surprise, I came in to find soapsuds knee-deep

---

225 Packer, *Knowing God* (Downers Grove: Inter Varsity Press, 1973), 89–90.
226 2 Cor. 3:18.
227 Col. 3:10.

throughout the kitchen and slowly making their way into the other rooms. I learned the hard way that dishwashers aren't made for laundry detergent.

J. I. Packer is again instructive about God's design:[228] Once again, I include his statement cited earlier in the book.

> We are familiar with the thought that our bodies are like machines, needing the right routine of food, rest, and exercise if they are to run efficiently, and liable, if filled up with the wrong fuel—alcohol, drugs, poison—to lose their power of healthy functioning and ultimately to "seize up" entirely in physical death. What we are perhaps slower to grasp is that God wishes us to think of our souls in a similar way. As rational persons, we were made to bear God's moral image—that is, our souls were made to "run" on the practice of worship, law-keeping, truthfulness, honesty, discipline, self-control, and service to God and others. If we abandon these practices, not only do we incur guilt before God; we also progressively destroy our souls. Conscience atrophies, the sense of shame dries up, one's capacity for truthfulness, loyalty, and honesty is eaten away, one's character disintegrates. One not only becomes desperately miserable; one is steadily being dehumanized.

When we violate God's designed purposes we can expect less-than-favorable results.

Our worldview *conditions* our motives. It will move us to some catalytic motive resulting in predictable behavior. Motives can be base or blessed, bad or good, devious or honorable, diabolical or transformational. Our motives depend on the beliefs we hold, the values we embrace, and the worldviews we have.

Christians should be primarily motivated by unconditional love—genuine concern for the well-being and welfare of other individuals as exemplified by our overt actions on their behalf, regardless of whether they deserve it or not, and whether they are lovable or not.[229] Such love is action-oriented, not emotionally based. Acts of love of this kind should be exercised as acts of worship to God, the recipient simply being the

---

228 Packer, *Knowing God*, 102–3.
229 1 Cor. 13:4–8.

beneficiary of the fruits of those actions. Other motives might be a sense of mission or service, servanthood, understanding, godliness, holiness, or Christ-likeness.

Our motives *energize* our behavior. They compel us to act given a catalyst like a circumstance, situation, event, or person that stirs us to respond. Our motives, combusted by our beliefs, values, and worldview, underlie our actions and the manner in which we engage the world around us. The behavior that results reflects the condition of our hearts—our beliefs, values, attitudes, and motives. Our behavior mirrors our hearts and merely resonates with what is already stored there. Behavior can certainly bring to life what is there, awakening our dormancy and enlivening these sources, but behavior cannot create what is in our heart.

Our behavior, then, is a by-product of what is in our hearts, so you can understand why Christ pays attention to our heart[230] and why the heart needs to be protected and guarded.[231]

Personal Assessment

What are your central beliefs?
What foundational beliefs do you hold?[232]
  What operational beliefs do you act on?[233]
  What behaviors are evidence of their validity?
  What would your loved ones say are your central beliefs?

What are your core values?
What is the current status of the fruit of the Spirit in your life?
  What personal values has God impressed upon you and are the ones from which you make your key decisions?
  What recent decisions have you made or actions have you taken that give unmistakable testimony as to their importance in your life?

---

230 1 Sam. 16:1–7.
231 Prov. 4:23.
232 See definition of *foundational* beliefs on page 74.
233 See definition of *operational* beliefs on page 74.

What constitutes your worldview?

> *In your own words, how would you describe a biblical worldview?*
> *How does your current worldview compare to a biblical worldview?*
> *What would those who know you describe your worldview?*

What motivates *you to act?*

> *Within the last three months, what primary motives compelled you to act?*
> *To what degree do you demonstrate unconditional love for your spouse, children, relatives, friends, acquaintances, associates?*
> *What motives should you possess and act upon?*

Select a dominant behavior of yours and trace it back to the motive that brought it to life to begin with, the attitude that gave rise to the motive, the value or values that informed the attitudes, and the belief that established the value.

Select a biblical operational belief and derive a value from it. How does that value shape your attitudes or worldview? What motive naturally flows from that value? What behavior can others see that reflects your beliefs, values, worldview, and motives?

Chapter 5: Our Positioning

The revolution of Jesus is in the first place and continuously a revolution of the human heart or spirit. His is a revolution of character, which proceeds by changing people from the inside through ongoing personal relationships to God in Christ and to one another. It is one that changes their ideas, beliefs, feelings and habits of choice. It penetrates to the deepest layers of their soul.

—Dallas Willard

Back to our compass.

We have identified our cardinal directions: north, south, east, and west. Orienting compasses display these cardinal directions. The compass dial is also divided into 360 degrees. North is 0 degrees, east is 90 degrees, south is 180 degrees, and west is 270 degrees. For our purposes, north is *Jesus Christ*, east the *Holy Spirit*, south the *Bible*, and west *spiritual disciplines*.

Orienting compasses also indicate what are called ordinal or primary intercardinal directions: northeast (NE) at 45 degrees, southeast (SE) at 135 degrees, southwest (SW) at 225 degrees, and southeast (SE) at 315 degrees. To continue the illustration, northeast is our *beliefs*, southeast is our *values*, southwest is our *worldview*, and southeast is our *motives*. Having a clear understanding of and commitment to these compass points will ensure that our lives are properly oriented for any journey we take, planned and unplanned.

Orientation

Professor Dumbledore counsels his young protégé, Harry Potter, "It's not our abilities that show us who we are; it's the choices we make." Our choices are the by-product of our central operational beliefs, our core values, our perceptual attitudes we have about life, and the primary motives that compel us to act. Our behavior—the pattern of our lived-out life—reflects the interplay between our beliefs, our values, our worldview, and our motives. The health of our hearts is determined by the interaction of these ordinal directions.

Every choice we make of any consequence is based on a value we hold, whether we are conscious of it or not. Every decision we make is processed through the filter of our value system, whether we can articulate those values or not. The only exceptions to this rule are babies who have not reached the age of reason, people who are severely mentally handicapped or insane, and individuals who are under the influence of drugs or alcohol.

The concept of multiculturalism suggests there is value in every culture and that no culture is better than another. The Bible stresses one culture,[234] the Kingdom of God. We are now citizens of heaven,[235] and our allegiance is to our king, Jesus Christ. We are under a new constitution, a new code of ethics.

In his article "Doctrine and Ethics," theologian Alister McGrath encourages Christians to see ourselves as a "city upon a hill" (to use a biblical image) or a local form of community. He also describes us as "citizens of heaven." Finally, he quotes another scholar who suggests we are living in a "new Dark Age."[236]

---

234 1 Cor. 12:12–13.
235 Phil. 3:20–21.
236 Alister E. McGrath, "Doctrine and Ethics," *Journal of the Evangelical Theological Society* 34, no. 2 (June 1991): 145–56.

City upon a Hill

In his first metaphor of a "city upon a hill," McGrath sees Christians as a city set apart from the world around us. "Within that community there is a distinctive way of thinking and acting that is nourished by the Gospel, sustained by the grace of God, and oriented toward the glory of God. It does not matter if those outside the community fail to understand or share this vision; the important thing is that the vision presented to them is kept alive. By joining this community of faith, they may come to understand its hopes, beliefs, and values."

Citizens of Heaven

The second metaphor—Christians as citizens of heaven—is taken from Philippians 3:20–21. McGrath remarks that the image is "that of a colony, an image familiar to the Philippians, Philippi then being a Roman colony. It was an outpost of Rome on foreign territory. Its people kept the laws of the homeland, they spoke its language, and they longed for the day when they could return home to the motherland." Do you see the comparison and correlation for us today?

McGrath further stresses that we should think of ourselves, our churches, and our families as "colonies of heaven, as outposts of the real eternal city, who seek to keep its laws in the midst of alien territory." He refers to C. S. Lewis's similar depiction. Lewis, in his written reflections on the Christian life, sees the world "as enemy territory, territory occupied by invading forces. In the midst of this territory as resistance groups are the communities of faith." McGrath goes on to say that "we must never be afraid to be different from the world around us. It is very easy for Christians to be depressed by the fact that the world scorns our values and standards. But the image of the colony sets this in its proper perspective. At Philippi the civilizing laws of Rome contrasted with the anarchy (a state of lawlessness or political disorder) of its hinterland (regions outside of Rome). And so our moral vision—grounded in Scripture, sustained by faith, given intellectual spine by Christian doctrine—stands as a civilizing influence in the midst of a world that seems to have lost its moral way." Sound familiar?

New Dark Age

The third metaphor—the new Dark Age—provides an apt description of our society today. In *After Virtue*, Alasdair MacIntryre, senior research professor at the University of Notre Dame, compares modern culture to the Dark Ages, making the following comment:

> A crucial turning point in that earlier history occurred when men and women of good will turned aside from the task of shoring up the Roman imperium and ceased to identify the continuation of civility and moral community with the maintenance of the imperium. What they set themselves to achieve instead—often not recognizing fully what they were doing—was the construction of new forms of community within which the moral life could be sustained so that both morality and civility might survive the coming ages of barbarism and darkness. If my account of our moral condition is correct, we ought also to conclude that for some time now we too have reached that turning point. What matters at this stage is the construction of local forms of community within which civility and the intellectual and moral life can be sustained through the new dark ages which are already upon us. And if the tradition of the virtues was able to survive the horrors of the last dark ages, we are not entirely without ground for hope. This time however the barbarians are not waiting beyond the frontiers; they have already been governing us for quite some time. And it is our lack of consciousness of this that constitutes part of our predicament.[237]

So what does this metaphor mean for us today? The old Dark Ages were marked by people's fear of the unknown and their reliance upon the learned for interpreting the world around them. Knowledge and wisdom resided with the aristocracy and the Church. Individual study of God's Word was left to the so-called scholars with agendas. Interpretation was under the sole purview of these authorities; the common man and woman

---

237 Alasdair MacIntryre, *After Virtue* (Notre Dame: University of Notre Dame Press, 2007), 263.

relied upon others for truth. The reformation broke that bondage. Luther's rebellion essentially gave the scriptures back to the people.

MacIntryre suggests we are in a new dark age. Life in the fast lane and susceptibility to the tyranny of urgency has compelled many of us to rely on new authorities for knowledge and wisdom. These subject-matter experts can be found on newscasts, talk shows, newsstands, and some pulpits. Because of our hectic lifestyles, we turn to sound bites from popular celebrities inside and outside the church for "truth." I agree with MacIntryre—we are living in the new dark ages. When the organizing center of our beliefs, values, worldview, and motives shifts from the Bible to a pluralistic syncretism and amalgamation of philosophies and ideologies, it isn't long before we lose our way and fall into factions and special interest groups fitting our preconceived notions and whims.

The Bible tells us that we are to "watch our lives and doctrine closely" (1 Tim. 4:16). "Preach the Word; be prepared in season and out of season; correct, rebuke and encourage—with great patience and careful instruction. For the time will come [and I believe is upon us now] when men will not put up with sound doctrine. Instead, to suit their own desires, they will gather around them a great number of teachers to say what their itching ears want to hear. They will turn their ears away from the truth and turn aside to myths. But you, keep your head in all situations, endure hardship, do the work of an evangelist, discharge all the duties of your ministry" (2 Tim. 4:2–5).

The Environment

In a September 2002 address to a United Nations prayer breakfast, Ravi Zacharias, a noted Christian philosopher, summarized the thought trends by decade and provided insight into some of the issues involved. This backdrop helps us understand how we arrived at our current crossroads regarding our beliefs and values, and which ones take precedence over others.

In the 1950s, kids lost their innocence. They were liberated from their parents by cars, well-paying jobs, and lyrics and music that gave rise to a new term, "the generation gap."

In the 1960s, kids lost their authority. It was a decade of protests. Church, state, and parents were all called into question and found wanting. Their authority was rejected, yet nothing ever replaced it.

In the 1970s, kids lost their love. It was the decade of nihilism, dominated by hyphenated words beginning with "self"—self-image, self-esteem, self-assertion. It made for a lonely world. Kids learned everything there was to know about love, and few adults had the nerve to tell them that there was indeed a difference.

In the 1980s, kids lost their hope. Stripped of innocence, authority, and love, and plagued by the horror of nuclear nightmare, large and growing numbers of this generation stopped believing in the future.

In the 1990s, we lost our ability to reason. The power of critical thinking has gone from induction to deduction, and very few are able to think clearly anymore. I have often said the challenge of the truth-speaker today is this: how do you reach a generation that listens with its eyes and thinks with its feelings?

To this list I would add the following …

In the 2000s, we are losing our moral and spiritual moorings. We are encouraged to tolerate everything. Compromise and political correctness is the rule of the day. Christianity is depicted as an intolerant faith. We are urged to be for everything and against nothing. Syncretism and pluralism are diluting and corrupting our theological, spiritual, and moral distinctiveness.

In the 2010s, we see the ascendency of human rights extended to alternative lifestyles. We see the marginalization of Christianity in all its forms and the promotion of other world religions as having more merit. We see moral equivalency drawn between the right to abortion and the rights of nature and animals. We see "dominance relativism"—a "your truth ends where my nose begins" mentality—and the push to accept and affirm any expression of individual preference and advocacy.

Chaos ensues when our moral foundations are corrupted or eliminated altogether. Mahatma Gandhi famously identified seven conditions that lead to chaos: wealth without work, pleasure without conscience, knowledge without character, commerce without morality, science without humanity, worship without sacrifice, and politics without principle.

Intercardinal Points

The intercardinal points on a compass—northeast, southeast, southwest, and northwest—lie in between the cardinal points of north, east, south, and west. If north is 000°, northeast is 045°, east is 090°, southeast is 135°, south is 180°, southwest is 225°, west is 270°, and northwest is 315°, with north again at 360°/000°.

Again, viewing our compass metaphorically, we'll see that north is Jesus Christ, east is the Holy Spirit, south is the Bible, and west is spiritual disciplines. Northeast is beliefs, southeast is values, southwest is worldview, and northwest is motives.

Northeast: Beliefs

Beliefs are important because they claim to describe the way things are. They assert that they declare the truth about reality.—Alister McGrath

What you believe is critical to your journey. In "Doctrine and Ethics," Alister McGrath helps us understand why:

> Beliefs are not just ideas that are absorbed by our minds and that have no further effect upon us. They affect what we do and what we feel. They influence our hopes and fears. They determine the way we behave. A Japanese fighter pilot of the second world war might believe that destroying the enemies of his emperor ensured his immediate entry into paradise—and, as many American navy personnel discovered to their cost, this belief expressed itself in quite definite actions. Such pilots had no hesitation in launching suicide attacks on American warships. Doctrines are ideas—but they are more than mere ideas. They are the foundation of our understanding of the world and our place within it.[238]

---

238 Ibid., 87.

According to *Merriam-Webster Dictionary*, ethics is the discipline dealing with what is good and bad and with moral duty and obligation; a set of moral principles or values; a theory or system of moral values; the principles of conduct governing an individual or a group; a guiding philosophy; the study of human conduct and values. The foundation of our ethics should be the truth found in scripture. In "Doctrine and Ethics," McGrath establishes the importance of right beliefs:

> Thinking people need to construct and inhabit mental worlds. They need to be able to discern some degree of ordering within their experience, to make sense of the riddles and enigmas. They need to be able to structure human existence in the world, to allow it to possess meaning and purpose, to allow decisions to be made concerning the future of their existence. In order for anyone—Christian, atheist, Marxist, Muslim—to make informed moral decisions, it is necessary to have a set of values concerning human life. Those values are determined by beliefs, and those beliefs are stated as doctrines. Christian doctrine thus provides a fundamental framework for Christian living.[239]

Our beliefs provide a solid foundation for our journey. Beliefs matter. Many believers espouse a belief system that is not at all reflected in the way they behave. They may declare a certain belief system, but their lives bear little testimony to their proclamations. They may, in fact, act opposite of what they say they believe. The clear evidence of what people declare as their beliefs is a life lived in correlation with those beliefs.

In Hebrews 13:7–8, we read, "Remember your leaders, who spoke the word of God to you. Consider the outcome of their way of life and imitate their faith. Jesus Christ is the same yesterday and today and forever." Notice what we are to pay attention to: we are told to consider the outcome of the lives of those who have influenced us. We are to imitate their faith. What is the one irreducible minimum? Consistency!

Words are cheap unless they are backed up by a life that represents their assertion. Other people can deconstruct your proclamation of faith;

---

239 Ibid., 84.

they can dismiss what you have to say because it is your truth and not theirs; they can disregard your arguments for your beliefs. But they cannot deconstruct, dismiss, or disregard a life lived in bold relief—one that is consistent with what you believe, congruent with the faith you embrace, committed to a life of godliness, and consecrated to the God who gives you life and purpose. For you see, regardless of who is observing you, enemies or friends, they all can sense the impact of a life devoted to "whatever is true, whatever is noble, whatever is right, whatever is pure, whatever is lovely, whatever is admirable; if anything is excellent or praiseworthy, think about such things."[240]

Two qualities are essential for the journey: integrity and authenticity. Integrity suggests you are the same person in tribulation as you are in victory, the same in the shadows as you are in the light. Authenticity means you are that same way all the time. It defines you in every situation, as recognized by observers of your life along the way.

John Maxwell has written extensively on leadership. In my opinion, his definition of *integrity* is best: "Integrity binds our person together and fosters a spirit of contentment within us. It will not allow our lips to violate our hearts. When integrity is the referee, we will be consistent; our beliefs will be mirrored by our conduct. There will be no discrepancy between what we appear to be and what our family knows we are, whether in times of prosperity or adversity. Integrity allows us to predetermine what we will be regardless of circumstances, persons involved, or the places of our testing."

For the believer, the definition of authenticity is modeled in Christ. Authenticity, then, means conforming to the original, Jesus Christ, and reproducing those features that reflect His character. The person who does this leaves little doubt to whom he belongs, because he bears the imprint of the Master.

Our beliefs establish our values. What we truly believe at our core— what we trust in, rely on, and cling to at our core—will determine the integrity and authenticity of our values, our perceptual attitudes, our motivation, and ultimately our behavior.

---

240 Phil. 4:8.

Southeast: Values

The world's values are pleasures, possessions, and prestige. Here's our choice: the way of the world or the way of the Word, the way of culture or the way of Christ.—Bob Merritt

I have defined a value as the hill we are prepared to die on, the principle we intend to live by, and the filter through which we process our decisions. A value is something held in high regard, an idea we hold to be important. Values govern the way we behave, communicate, and interact with others. Put another way, values are the basis for our motivation and behavior. The values to which we are committed motivate us to act in a certain way.

Beliefs, on the other hand, are judgments we hold about ourselves and the world around us. A belief is something we regard as true. The beliefs we trust in, rely on, and cling to at our core establish the values we hold. Our beliefs may be foundational and/or operational in focus.

Foundational beliefs provide the stable platform of our existence. They are absolute truths that establish our relationship with our Creator and His created world. An example of a foundational belief is that God created the heavens and the earth or that Jesus is God.[241] Foundational beliefs give us confidence, hope, and orientation for our journey. They establish the fact that we are connected to our Creator, and they answer fundamental questions about our existence, identity, purpose, and destiny. They have to do with our beingness.

Operational beliefs are also absolute truths, but they are actionable— they compel us to do something. An example of an operational belief is "I am to love my neighbor as myself" or "I am to abstain from immorality."[242] Operational beliefs require a response and provide a general guideline for our behavior and actions. They provide the basis for our values—the filter through which we process our decisions, the hills we are prepared to die on, the principles we intend to live out in our daily lives. They have to do with our doingness.

No value stands in suspended animation; every value rests on a belief or system of beliefs that gives it life. Values strongly held compel us to act

---

241 Gen. 1:1; John 1:1–4, 14.
242 Matt. 22:39; 1 Thess. 4:3–8.

in certain ways. In Hebrew philosophy, a belief is not a belief until it is acted upon. As one writer put it, beliefs literally shape our map of reality.

Our beliefs and values shape our attitudes and opinions. Beliefs and values are closely related and interdependent; in fact, they are inseparable. Our closely held beliefs inform the values we hold. Beliefs give our life experiences meaning and provide a context for our values. Values represent our aims, desires, and goals. Our beliefs and values shape the way we view God, ourselves, and the world around us.

For instance, if I truly believe that every human being is created in the image of God, which is certainly scriptural,[243] such a belief could give rise to a value or values that will compel me to act in certain ways, given the proper motivation to do so. Our motives are triggered by circumstances, events, or people that impress us with a need to act. Values arising from a belief that every human being is created in the image of God might include the following.

- Regardless of ethnicity or creed, every person has value.
- Everyone is equal in God's eyes.
- Every person has redeemable qualities.
- Everyone has value.

Confronted by a situation or circumstance that brings our belief and attending value into play, we might act by ministering to marginalized people, finding something redeemable in someone others have abandoned, taking time to help the downtrodden, or stopping to listen to the problems of others even when it is inconvenient. The interplay between our belief and values might induce us to feed the poor, give shelter to the homeless, provide medical assistance to the diseased, visit a retirement home, or work as a volunteer in an assisted-living facility.

Southwest: Worldview

A person's worldview is their perception of reality. The problem is we interpret everything we hear and see through the grid of our own education and experiences. Wisdom is seeing life from God's perspective. It is part of our sanctifying process to renew our minds to a biblical worldview seen from God's

---

243 Gen. 1:26–27, 9:6.

perspective, which includes both the world we see and the spiritual world we don't see with our physical eyes.—Neil T. Anderson

Our beliefs plus our values equal our worldview, the set of perceptual attitudes we have about our world and from which we make sense of it. Every worldview comprises a set of core beliefs and values that become reality for the person holding that view. Every worldview has answers to the nature of ultimate reality,[244] the nature of humankind,[245] the basic human dilemma,[246] the solution to the human dilemma,[247] and our human destiny.[248]

Many worldviews vie for our allegiance.[249] But it is a biblical worldview that should warrant our allegiance.[250] We should see the world as God sees it. The biblical worldview stands above all others in that it represents the world as God designed it to be. A biblical worldview should provide the

---

244 What is your belief about divine intelligence? Is the world we live in all there is to reality? Is there a higher intelligence out there? Does God exist? If so, how is He related to humans?

245 What is your understanding about humanity? What makes us human? What makes us distinct from other living things? Are human animals of a higher order or the divine image of God?

246 What is the basic fundamental problem of mankind? What is the most significant issue that prevents us from reaching our full potential? What holds us back from reaching perfection? What prevents us from rising above our situation or circumstances?

247 What is the solution to the basic human dilemma? How can the problem of mankind be resolved? What force or forces can be brought to bear to solve our dilemma? What is the answer to our dilemma?

248 Where will you go when you die? Is there existence after death? Is there more than one destination after death? If there is a place of "bliss," how do we attain it?

249 Agnosticism, atheism, existentialism, humanism, naturalism, nihilism, pantheism, polytheism, relativism, theism, deism, etc. For more information on these consult FEVA Ministries Inc. The text is in part a summary of *The Universe Next Door* by James Sire. The illustrations are based on the "2 Ways to Live" tract published by Matthias Media. For definitions of other worldviews, see *A Rattling of Sabers* by Dr. Greg Bourgond, pages 169–70.

250 God exists and is active in our lives. Humans bear the image of God. The image of God is marred by sin. The solution to our human dilemma is the person and work of Christ. Our human destiny is eternal life or eternal damnation.

lens through which we observe the world, make sense of our observations, and navigate the world in which we temporarily live.

Scott McKnight identifies the following corrupt worldviews.

- individualism—the story that "I" am the center of the universe
- consumerism—the story that I am what I own
- nationalism—the story that my nation is God's nation
- moral relativism—the story that we can't know what is universally good
- scientific naturalism—the story that all that matters is matter
- New Age—the story that we are gods
- postmodern tribalism—the story that all that matters is what my small group thinks
- salvation by therapy—the story that I can come to my full human potential[251]

Key beliefs of a biblical worldview include the following: All human beings carry the image of God in their person. This image, marred by sin, makes us creatures capable of reason, love, and God-consciousness. It also explains why we are moral creatures. Universal moral laws exist and are ordained by God. The chief purpose of man is to glorify God and enjoy Him forever. Sin alienates us from God and enslaves us. All human beings long for purpose, progress, and permanence. Human beings have a need for forgiveness and redemption. Christ's redemptive work is the basis of human salvation. Receiving Christ as Savior and Lord brings a new birth, a new heart, a new relationship with God, and a new power to live. The Christian has God's nature and Spirit within and is called to live a particular kind of life in obedience to God. The Bible is the Christian's ultimate authority for faith and practice. Physical death is not the end of our existence. What we do in life echoes in eternity.

Northwest: Motives

Therefore judge nothing before the appointed time; wait till the Lord comes. He will bring to light what is hidden in darkness and will expose the motives of men's hearts. At that time each will receive his praise from God.—1 Cor. 4:5

---

251 Scot McKnight, *King Jesus Gospel* (Grand Rapids: Zondervan, 2011), 157.

Any good detective tries to ascertain the motive behind a crime. Doing so will help him or her find the perpetrator. What motivates you? What stirs you to take action? What pushes you to respond? What demands that you act? Our motives frame our response and catalyze us to act in whatever circumstances and events present themselves to us.

Our motives, the energy that causes us to move from thought to action, are conditioned by our worldview, informed by our values, and established by our beliefs. This amazing ecosystem propels us to act in certain ways when stimulated by a situation, circumstance, or event.

People are motivated by many motives: love, hate, greed, vengeance, self-centeredness, sexual gratification. gluttony, jealousy, pride, a sense of entitlement, superiority, anger, immorality, conquest, destruction, self-protection, conditional love, lust, materialism, possessiveness, hatred, meanness, control, domination, covetousness, racism, blind ambition, cruelty—all of which are destructive and corrosive.

Godly motives underpinned by biblical beliefs, values, and attitudes might include unconditional love, Christ-likeness, servanthood, mission-mindedness, eternal significance, worship, sacrifice, service, development, redemption, salvation, sanctification, purity, holiness, or godliness.

James tells us that faith without deeds is dead.[252] What good is it to think great thoughts, espouse great beliefs, promote great values, and encourage great attitudes if they don't result in great acts that demonstrate the love of Christ to a fallen world? In scripture we are told that God judges the motives of our hearts.[253] It is entirely possible to have the right motives but fail in the results. It is also true that the wrong motives can produce desirable results. In God's economy, it is the integrity of the motives that really matters.

Magnetic Influences

The only magnetic influence you want on a compass is the earth's magnetic field. But the needle of a compass responds to any local magnetic force, such as that generated by ferrous or electromagnetic materials. If you must rely on a compass, you should check ahead of time to make sure

---

252 James 2:14–26.
253 1 Cor. 4:5.

no watches, batteries, ice axes or poles, electrical equipment, power lines, GPS devices, cell phones, climbing equipment, or vehicles are affecting the accuracy of the compass.

As I said earlier, the beliefs and values we hold are informed, shaped, and conditioned by influences such as the world, the flesh, the enemy, or God. If we do not proactively decide which influence will have authority over our beliefs and values, we will be all over the map in terms of our choices, decisions, and actions.

The World

Let's look at each of these influences separately, beginning with the world. The world is under the dominion of Satan, who in scripture is called the "prince of this world"[254] and even the "god of this world."[255] His influence over world affairs is pervasive. Worldliness is living life on your own terms, apart from God and in accordance with conventional wisdom and worldly philosophy. This life is lived on a horizontal plane, devoid of a vertical relationship with God. When we embrace the world—its philosophies, ideologies, strategies, methods, and processes—without our values being informed, established, and conditioned by God and His Word, we are living a life of worldliness.

The Bible admonishes believers not to love the world or the things in the world. Rather, we are to view ourselves as aliens and strangers here. We are not to conform to the pattern of this world, or seek friendship with the world.[256] John MacArthur, noted preacher, teacher, and author, defines worldliness as "any preoccupation with or interest in the temporal system of life that places anything perishable before that which is eternal … it involves love for earthly things, esteem for earthly values, and preoccupation with earthly cares. Scripture plainly labels it sin—and sin of the worst stripe. It is a spiritual form of adultery that sets one against God Himself."[257]

Bible teacher Jerry Bridges describes the world this way: "The world … is characterized by the subtle and relentless pressure it brings to bear upon us to conform to its values and practices. It creeps up on us little by little.

---

254 John 12:31, 14:30, 16:11.
255 2 Cor. 4:4; Eph. 6:12.
256 1 Pet. 2:11–12; Rom. 12:2; 1 John 2:15–17; James 4:4.
257 John MacArthur, *Glory of Heaven* (Wheaton: Crossway, 2013), 48.

What was once unthinkable becomes thinkable, then doable, and finally acceptable to society at large. Sin becomes respectable, and so Christians are no more than five to ten years behind the world in embracing most sinful practices."[258] Theologian David Wells sees worldliness as "that system of values, in any given age, which … makes sin look normal and righteousness seem strange."[259]

In summary, the world is a system of conventional precepts and principles devoid of and eschewing God, and choosing instead to live life apart from His influence and seeing man as the sole arbiter of what is right and true. The "world" system sees man as capable of managing man; it is a philosophy and ideology that places man at the center of the universe, needing no one else to determine his fate. It is the arrogant belief system that man knows best.

The Flesh

In its references to the *flesh*, the Bible means the residual effects of sin in us. Before a person becomes a believer, he or she struggles with a sinful nature inherited from Adam. We are helpless against this sinful nature and subject to its power in our lives. But once a person comes to a saving knowledge of Jesus Christ, that sinful nature is replaced with a new, spiritual nature. The Christian is no longer helpless; the penalty of sin has been paid, and the power of sin has been broken. We are new creations in Christ.

However, we struggle with our predisposition to sin in certain areas, with sin strongholds within us, with bad habits learned and formed before we were saved, with the consequences of poor decisions in the past—these issues comprise what the Bible calls the "flesh." Through the power of the Holy Spirit, these last footholds of the enemy can be demolished. The process of demolishing these influences in our lives is called "sanctification," the progressive cleansing of remaining sin patterns in our lives.

The "flesh"[260] is the metaphorical repository of residual patterns toward sin that we developed while unsaved. The penalty for our sin was paid

---

258 Jerry Bridges, *The Discipline of Grace* (Wheaton: Tyndale House Publishers, 2006), 202–3.
259 David Wells, *Losing Our Virtue* (Grand Rapids: Eerdmans Publishing Company, 1999), 4.
260 Rom. 8:12–14; Mark 7:20–23.

at the cross. The power of sin was defeated in Christ, and its influence is mediated by the work of the Spirit. When we are in heaven, the very presence of sin will be eliminated forever. Yet many of us are still living as if we are chained to our old natures.

By way of illustration, Neil T. Anderson describes the "flesh" as follows.

When I was in the Navy, we called the captain of our ship "the Old Man." Our Old Man was tough and crusty and nobody liked him. He used to go out drinking with all his chiefs while belittling and harassing his junior officers and making life miserable for the rest of us. He was not a good example of a naval officer. So when our Old Man got transferred to another ship, we all rejoiced. It was a great day for our ship. Then we got a new skipper—a new Old Man. The old Old Man no longer had any authority over us; he was gone—completely out of the picture. But I was trained under that Old Man. So how do you think I related to the new Old Man? At first I responded to him just like I had been conditioned to respond to the old skipper. I tiptoed around him expecting him to bite my head off. That's how I had lived for two years around my first skipper.

But as I got to know the new skipper, I realized that he wasn't a crusty old tyrant like my old Old Man. He wasn't out to harass his crew; he was a good guy, really concerned about us. But I had been programmed for two years to react in a certain way when I saw a captain's braids. I didn't need to react that way any longer, but it took several months to recondition myself to the new skipper.

You also once served under a cruel, self-serving skipper: your old sinful self with its sinful nature. The admiral of that fleet is Satan himself, the prince of darkness. But by God's grace you have been transferred into Christ's kingdom.[261] You now have a new skipper: your new self which is infused with the divine

---

261 Col. 1:13.

nature of Jesus Christ, your new admiral. As a child of God, a saint, you are no longer under the authority of your old Old Man. He is dead, buried, gone forever. So why do you still react as if your old skipper were still in control of your behavior?

Why do you still react as if your old skipper were still in control of your behavior? Because while you served under it, your old self trained and conditioned your actions, reactions, emotional responses, thought patterns, memories, and habits in a part of your brain called "the flesh." The flesh is that tendency within each person to operate independently of God and to center his interest on himself. An unsaved person functions totally in the flesh,[262] worshipping and serving the creature rather than the Creator.[263] Such persons "live for themselves,"[264] even though many of their activities may appear to be motivated by selflessness and concern for others.

When you were born again, your old self died and your new self came to life, and you were made a partaker of Christ's divine nature. But your flesh remains. You brought to your Christian commitment a fully conditioned mind-set and lifestyle developed apart from God and centered on yourself. Since you were born physically alive but spiritually dead, you had neither the presence of God nor the knowledge of God's ways. So you learned to live your life independently of God. It is this learned independence that makes the flesh hostile toward God.

During the years you spent separated from God, your worldly experiences thoroughly programmed your brain with thought patterns, memory traces, responses, and habits which are alien to God. So even though your old self is gone, your flesh remains in opposition to God as a preprogrammed propensity for sin, which is living independently of God. Be aware that

262 Rom. 8:7–8.
263 Rom. 1:25.
264 2 Cor. 5:15.

you no longer have to obey that preprogrammed bent to live independently of God. You are a child of God, and you are free to put to death those fleshly deeds and obey Christ.[265]

What comes from within—our predispositions, biases, and predilections—causes us to sin. We can blame the world or accuse the devil, but in many instances the influences of our own internal corruption compete for our allegiance and behavior. "What comes out of a man is what makes him 'unclean.' For from within, out of men's hearts, come evil thoughts, sexual immorality, theft, murder, adultery, greed, malice, deceit, lewdness, envy, slander, arrogance, and folly. All these evils come from inside and make a man 'unclean.'"[266]

The Enemy

In our temptations, or competing for our beliefs and values, are the influences of the world, the flesh, and the devil—who, scripture says, prowls around like a roaring lion looking for someone to devour.[267] But many Christians give the devil too much credit for being the source of temptation and sin. They assign him God-like attributes and qualities, almost putting him on an equal footing with God.

First, Satan is a created being, not the Creator; as a created being, he has limits. God alone possesses the attributes of being all-knowing, all-powerful, and all-present. Second, if Satan were all-knowing, why would he have suggested to God that if God's protection of Job were removed, Job would turn his back on God? If Satan were all-knowing, he wouldn't have bothered. If he were all-knowing, he wouldn't have attempted to tempt Christ; he would have already known he would fail.

The more compelling questions for a believer can be summarized as follows: Can Satan or his demons know our thoughts and read our minds? Can Satan or his demons put thoughts and desires in our minds and hearts? Ron Jones of Titus Institute sheds light on these questions.[268]

---

265 Neil T. Anderson, *Victory Over the Darkness* (Ventura: Regal Book, 2000), 79–80.
266 Mark 7:20–23.
267 1 Pet. 5:8.
268 Ron Jones, *Can Satan Implant Thoughts into Our Minds or Read Our Minds?* 1999. http://www.titusinstitute.com/spiritualwarfare/thoughts.php.

In response to the first question, the Bible never says directly that Satan cannot know our thoughts or read our minds, but it never shows him doing it and implies that he can't. Satan and his demons would only be able to do this if this was an ability God created angels with. Remember, Satan and his demons are fallen angels. What defines their power and abilities is their angelic nature, not their evil nature. How they use their power and abilities has to do with their evil nature. It is not stated anywhere in Scripture that he is able to do things that other angels cannot do. So if Satan can do it, so can all angels. The Bible clearly shows that angels can wield tremendous power in the physical realm. They have struck people blind, shut the mouths of lions, (and) executed God's judgment.[269] But it says nothing about the mental realm. Even though angels exist in the spirit realm that does not necessarily mean they can read our minds. Even though demons can possess the bodies of unbelievers and even speak audibly through them (a physical manifestation), that does not necessarily mean that they possess their mind, only their physical bodies. There are "clues" in the book of Job that imply Satan cannot read the minds of humans.[270]

As for the question of whether Satan or his demons can put thoughts and desires in our minds and hearts, the answer is no. In reference to Job 2:1–10, Jones makes the following observations:

Notice that Satan only attacks Job externally. There is no mention of implanting thoughts or desires in Job's mind or heart. Why? Satan does not have the ability to do that. Again, implanting thoughts in a person's mind goes along with the ability to read his or her mind. If you can do one you can do the other. If you can't do one you can't do the other. Also, God never tells Job that his trials came from Satan nor is Job ever encouraged to identify the source. He is only encouraged to

---

269 Gen. 19; Dan. 6:22; 2 Kings 19:35.
270 Job 1:1–12.

trust the Lord. The focus is always on the Lord and His power to overcome.[271]

One more fact: since Satan is a created being, he cannot be in more than one place at a time. But he is very powerful and possesses a superior intellect. He has had centuries to observe mankind. From those informed observations he can make near-perfect predictions about how we will respond to certain situations and temptations. Therefore, he knows our limitations and weaknesses. In many cases, it is his followers or demons, those who fell with him, who tempt us, apart from the world or our flesh.

Satan and his demons use multiple strategies[272] to tempt us and torment us in the hope that our spiritual failure will discredit God and dissuade others from following Christ. His tactics include equivocation,[273] distortion,[274] sifting,[275] compromise,[276] delusion,[277] deprivation,[278] revenge,[279] outwitting,[280] masquerading,[281] a thorn in the flesh,[282] a struggle,[283] a confrontation,[284] worldliness,[285] infiltration,[286] deceit,[287] and overpowering or oppressing us.[288]

---

271 Ron Jones, *Can Satan Implant Thoughts into Our Minds or Read Our Minds?* 1999. http://www.titusinstitute.com/spiritualwarfare/thoughts.php.

272 John 8:44, 10:10; 1 John 5:19; Rev. 12:9.

273 Matt. 5:37.

274 Matt. 13:19.

275 Luke 22:31. "Sifting" refers to a process in biblical times where wheat was tossed in the air to allow the wind to separate the grain from the chaff. In this passage, Peter was going to be challenged to see if he had true faith that would withstand the testing of Satan.

276 Acts 5:3.

277 Acts 26:18.

278 1 Cor. 7:5.

279 2 Cor. 2:10.

280 2 Cor. 2:11.

281 2 Cor. 11:14.

282 2 Cor. 12:7.

283 Eph. 6:12.

284 Eph. 6:13, 16.

285 1 John 5:18–19.

286 Matt. 13:25, 39.

287 Acts 13:10.

288 1 Pet. 5:8.

In summary, we can be negatively influenced by the world, the flesh, and the devil, or positively influenced by God through Christ in the power of the Holy Spirit. The choice is ours.

Personal Assessment

To whom will you give your allegiance?

To whose authority will you submit?

What will stand as sole arbiter over your faith and practice?

What will establish, inform, and condition your beliefs and values?

How will you choose to view the world and make sense of it?

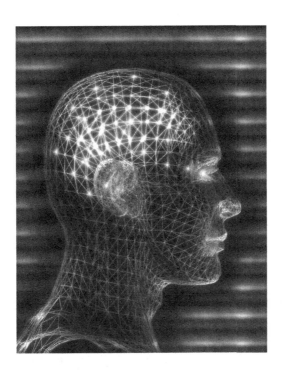

Chapter 6: Our Pathway

It's not our abilities that show us who we are; it's the choices we make.
—Professor Dumbledore

The pathway from sensory input to the *brain* and resultant behavior is a complex process that brings into play an array of faculties, including *mind, conscience, heart,* and *soul.* Making any moral decision involves an interaction among them. The brain receives sensory input and forms patterns of recognition; the mind assesses and comprehends the input; the conscience evaluates the moral implications of the input; the heart weighs the moral importance of the input and facilitates action based on that assessment; the soul or spirit, breathed into humans by God, infuses the input with eternal ramifications. The soul is the seat of all that makes us human and distinguishes us from animals.

The Brain

Sophisticated, purposeful control of behavior based on complex sensory input requires a brain capable of integrating information. The brain also exerts centralized control over the other organs of the body, generates patterns of muscle activity, and secretes body chemicals. Essentially, the brain is an information processing system. Sensory input from sight, hearing, taste, smell, and touch are received by the brain. Perception, motor control, memory storage, and learning are functions of the brain. As someone once put it, the brain and head provide us with a number of stock images for the mind and its functions.

When the brain receives sensory input, it processes that input, telling us what it means and how our body should respond. If the brain is injured, any further processing by the mind, conscience, and heart is impaired, corrupted, or stopped altogether. Mind-altering drugs and alcohol abuse create the same types of interference. Think of someone you know, or perhaps yourself, under the influence of drugs or alcohol: judgment is impaired, moral constraint is diminished, and the likelihood of engaging in destructive moral or physical activity increases in proportion to the level of impairment. Mental illness due to a chemical imbalance, physical defect, or injury produces the same loss of control.

The brain, then, is the repository of the mind, acting as the first receptor of stimuli coming from the external world or internal consciousness. The brain does the first analysis of the sensory data but makes no moral evaluation. The brain receives, orders the data into comprehensible patterns, compares the patterns with those already stored in memory, produces a recognizable framework for those patterns, determines bodily responses (e.g., the secretion of adrenaline or other chemicals), and in effect passes on this information to the mind. I realize this is a rather elementary description of a very complex organ scientists are still trying to figure out, but for our purposes it will be help illustrate the connection between the brain and the other faculties mentioned.

The Mind[289]

The mind is the part of us that thinks and reasons. It's the operating system for the brain, which is the hardware. Remember, the mind is the control center of the heart, the gateway to the heart, the gatekeeper of the soul. It is the mind that decides what will pass through to the heart. In the Bible, in particular the New Testament, the word *mind* is usually used in reference to the cognitive, rational, and purposive functions of a person. In many instances in scripture, *mind* is used interchangeably with *heart* and *soul*, and in some cases with the *spirit of man.*

More specifically, the mind is a gift from God, animated when He breathed His spirit into our lives at the Creation. The mind is where thought, emotion, and will or volition reside. The mind is where intellect and intellectual understanding are exercised and expressed. It is the seat of perception, memory, conception, abstraction, judgment, reasoning, comprehension beyond simple recognition, association, causation, imagination, comparison, classification, reflection, sense of direction, and discernment.

The mind possesses knowledge and wisdom,[290] and our innermost thoughts and secrets are found there.[291] The mind searches out wisdom and the scheme of things,[292] but it can also be fickle,[293] vacillate between different opinions,[294] be overshadowed by doubts,[295] be dulled,[296] and be blinded by the god of this age,[297] and it is subject to troubling thoughts and confusion.[298] The apostle Paul said the mind can resist the knowledge of God.

---

289 Several resources were consulted to provide information on the mind, including *Nelson's Illustrated Bible Dictionary*, the *Dictionary of Biblical Imagery*, *McClintock and Strong Encyclopedia*, and the *International Standard Bible Encyclopedia.*
290 Prov. 18:15, 22:17, 23:12; Eccles. 1:13, 1:17, 7:25, 8:16.
291 Judg. 16:17.
292 Eccles. 7:25.
293 1 Sam. 15:29.
294 1 Kings 18:21.
295 Luke 24:38.
296 2 Cor. 3:14.
297 2 Cor. 4:4.
298 Gen. 41:18.

The Hebrew Old Testament does not have one term that refers to the mind. In most instances it is translated as *heart*, a comprehensive term for the integrative center of a person's emotional, volitional, and intellectual life. The mind is the seat of reason and comprehension, as evidenced extensively in texts of scriptural wisdom. Solomon, for example, was given a "wise and discerning mind"[299] that enabled him to distinguish between right and wrong.

The mind is also the seat of intention and direction, as well as disposition, attitude, and inclination. According to biblical scholars, the mind is the faculty that makes choices and is responsible for a person's course of life. It plans, but ultimately God determines the way.[300] In scripture, the directing function of a person's life is often called *the heart and mind*.[301] The Bible also suggests that the mind can be perverse, obstinate, stubborn, and headstrong.[302] In some biblical translations, Revised Standard Version in particular, the text uses the word *mind* to indicate the cognitive, reasoning, and purposive parts of a human. The Bible also speaks of the renewing of the mind.[303] The Spirit of God helps Christians know the mind of Christ; as believers conform to His will, they are said to have the mind of Christ.

In summary, the mind processes the sensory input the brain receives. This processing covers a wide spectrum of activity involving thought, emotion, and will, yielding reason and direction. Besides our God-given aptitudes and intellect, the mind houses our emotions, personality, and temperament; and our powers of reason and cognition, perception, and imagination. Unless informed and conditioned by the heart, the mind is susceptible to the influences of the world, the flesh, and the devil. The mind can be swayed easily over time unless some authority presides over its operation.

---

299 1 Kings 3:12.
300 Prov. 16:9, 19:21.
301 1 Sam. 2:35; 1 Kings 8:48; 1 Chron. 22:19, 28:9; 2 Chron. 6:38.
302 Prov. 11:20, 12:8, 17:20, 23:23.
303 Rom. 12:2.

The Conscience

Dictionary.com defines the conscience as "the aptitude, faculty, intuition, or judgment of the intellect that distinguishes right from wrong. The complex of ethical and moral principles that controls or inhibits the actions or thoughts of an individual—the inner sense of what is right or wrong in one's conduct or motives impelling one toward right action: to follow the dictates of conscience."

In scripture we read, "Indeed, when Gentiles, who do not have the law, do by nature things required by the law, they are a law for themselves, even though they do not have the law, since they show that the requirements of the law are written on their hearts, their consciences also bearing witness, and their thoughts now accusing, now even defending them."[304] When God breathed His Spirit into man and created him in His image, He imparted a conscience to him. Biblical scholarship makes a clear case for the conscience.[305]

The conscience of an individual is the awareness that a proposed act is or is not conformable to one's ideal of right and manifesting itself in the feeling of obligation or duty. The OT usually expresses the idea as "having something on the heart."[306] Conscience is not so much a distinct faculty of the mind, like perception, memory, etc., as an exercise of the judgment and the power of feeling, as employed with reference to moral truth. It implies the moral sense "to discern good and evil"[307] and a feeling, more or less strong, of responsibility. Thus it will appear to be wrong to name conscience "the voice of God," although it is true that the testimony of conscience ·certainly rests on the foundation of a divine law in man, the

---

304 Rom. 2:14–16.

305 *New Unger's Bible Dictionary,* The Conscience; Pierce, *Conscience in New Testament*; Lillie, *New Testament Ethic*; McKenzie, *Guilt,* 21–54, 138–58; Niebuhr, *The Responsible Self*; Thielicke, *Theological Ethics,* 298–358; *Unger Bible Dictionary.* PC Study Bible, Version 5.2. 2008.

306 Gen. 20:5–6; 1 Sam. 25:31; Job 27:6.

307 Heb. 5:14.

existence of which, its claims and judgments, are removed from his subjective control.

If a man knows his doing to be in harmony with this law his conscience is good,[308] pure,[309] and void of offense. If what he does is evil, so also is his conscience, inasmuch as it is conscious of such evil;[310] it is defiled[311] when it is stained by evil deeds; or seared with a branding iron[312] when it is branded with its evil deeds, or cauterized, i.e., made insensible to all feeling. Paul lays down the law that a man should follow his own conscience, even though it is weak; otherwise moral personality would be destroyed.[313]

Nelson Bible Dictionary describes the conscience and its influence as follows: a person's inner awareness of conforming to the will of God or departing from it, resulting in either a sense of approval or condemnation. The term does not appear in the Old Testament but the concept does. David, for example, was smitten in his heart because of his lack of trust in the power of God.[314] But his guilt turned to joy when he sought the Lord's forgiveness.[315]

In the New Testament the term *conscience* is found most frequently in the writings of the Apostle Paul. Some people argue erroneously that conscience takes the place of the external law in the Old Testament. However, the conscience is not the ultimate standard of moral goodness.[316] Under both the old covenant and the new covenant the conscience must be formed by the will of God. The law given to Israel

---

308 Acts 23:1; 1 Tim. 1:5, 19; Heb. 13:18; 1 Pet. 3:16, 21.
309 1 Tim. 3:9; 2 Tim. 1:3.
310 Heb. 10:22.
311 Titus 1:15; 1 Cor. 8:7.
312 1 Tim. 4:2.
313 1 Cor. 8:10–13, 10:29.
314 2 Sam. 24:10.
315 Ps. 32.
316 1 Cor. 4:4.

was inscribed on the hearts of believers;[317] so the sensitized conscience is able to discern God's judgment against sin.[318]

The conscience of the believer has been cleansed by the work of Jesus Christ; it no longer accuses and condemns.[319] Believers are to work to maintain pure consciences. They also must be careful not to encourage others to act against their consciences. To act contrary to the urging of one's conscience is wrong, for actions that go against the conscience cannot arise out of faith.[320]

In summary, the conscience is that faculty of mind, that inborn sense of right and wrong, by which we judge the moral character of human conduct. It is common to all mankind but was perverted by the Fall.[321] Our conscience can be defiled[322] and seared.[323] A "conscience void of offense" is to be sought and cultivated.[324] The conscience is malleable and can be shaped by our experiences and our will and influenced by circumstances, events, and other people if not guarded and informed by the Word of God and the Holy Spirit.[325]

The Soul

The soul refers to our inner life, the seat of our emotions; the center of our personality; the seat of feelings, desires, affections, and aversions; and the entire nature of a person. We became living souls when God first breathed life into us.[326] Biblical writings describe the soul as the seat of emotions and desires, love, longing for God, rejoicing, knowing, and

---

317 Heb. 8:10, 10:16.
318 Rom. 2:14–15.
319 Heb. 9:14, 10:22.
320 1 Cor. 8, 10:23–33.
321 John 16:2; Acts 26:9; Rom. 2:15.
322 Titus 1:15.
323 1 Tim. 4:2.
324 Acts 24:16; Rom. 9:1; 2 Cor. 1:12; 1 Tim. 1:5, 19; 1 Pet. 3:21.
325 *Easton's Bible Dictionary*, Conscience.
326 Gen. 2:7.

memory.[327] The word *soul* is frequently used interchangeably with the biblical metaphor *heart*. The soul is designed by its Creator for everlasting life.[328]

One biblical resource puts it this way: "The 'spirit' is the out breathing of God into the creature, the life-principle derived from God. The 'soul' is man's individual possession, that which distinguishes one man from another and from inanimate nature … God's spirit made me, the soul called into being, and the breath of the Almighty animates me."[329] The soul is the core of our beingness, the animating principle originally derived from God Himself and breathed into us, creating a living being.[330] We are body, soul, and spirit.

It is the soul that is regenerated at conversion, renewed during sanctification, and glorified when we leave this earth for heaven. It is the soul that outlives the body and returns to its maker. It is the soul, so often referred to as the "heart," that enjoys eternal life or eternal damnation. It is the soul that separates us from animals and distinguishes us from all of creation, including angels. It is the soul that matters to God and therefore should matter to us. It is the soul we are to protect and guard from the evil one. It is the soul that is redeemed and revitalized and transformed through the work of the Holy Spirit and the person of Christ.

The Heart

Found more than eight hundred times in the Bible, the word *heart* (as defined earlier) refers to the inner being of a person, the core and essence of who we are; it is the unvarnished receptacle of our being, the irreducible minimum from which the impetus for our actions arises. It is the repository of what we truly trust in, rely on, and cling to. It is the filter through which we process all life's decisions. It is the lens through which we make judgments regarding our observations of the world around us. It is what

---

327 Deut. 12:20–21; Song of Sol. 1:7; Ps. 63:1; Eccles. 3:10–11; Pss. 86:4, 139:14; Lam. 3:20.
328 3 John 2; Heb. 13:17; James 1:21, 5:20; 1 Pet. 1:9.
329 *International Standard Bible Encyclopedia*, Soul.
330 Gen. 2:7.

moves us to action. It is worth guarding; it must be guarded. It is what makes us tick.

God looks at our hearts rather than our actions. Man might look at appearances, but God looks at the heart.[331] In many ways, our heart is our soul: It informs and conditions our conscience. It influences our mind, for good or bad. Scripture tells us that the wellsprings of our lives flow from the heart.[332]

Several versions of the Bible offer further clarity regarding "wellsprings": Watch over your heart with all diligence, for from it flow the springs of life (NASU). Keep thy heart with all diligence; for out of it are the issues of life (ASV). Keep and guard your heart with all vigilance and above all that you guard, for out of it flow the springs of life (AMP). Above all else, guard your affections. For they influence everything else in your life (TLB). Keep vigilant watch over your heart; that's where life starts (The Message). Guard your heart with all vigilance, for from it are the sources of life (NET). Above everything else, guard your heart. It is where your life comes from (NIrV). Guard your heart above all else, for it determines the course of your life (NLT). Above all else, guard your heart, for everything you do flows from it (TNIV).

Our true emotions flow from the heart—joy, fear, courage, despair, sadness, trust, and anger.[333] Regarding our free will, the heart not only thinks and feels, remembers and desires, but also chooses a course of action and stimulates our behavior.[334] Our heart is the seat of our conscience and can be wicked or good, honorable or dishonorable, courageous or cowardly, godly or ungodly, depending on our relationship with God through Christ in the power of the Holy Spirit.

The heart can be hardened when we make mini-compromises with our faith. If not checked, the hardening of our hearts can lead to ignorance of what we previously knew to be the truth, the darkening of understanding we once had, gradual separation from God and the things of God, the loss of sensitivity to what we once were acutely sensitive, and the giving over to sensuality—what only our senses can experience—and,

---

331 1 Sam. 16:1–7.
332 Prov. 4:23.
333 Exod. 4:14; Lev. 19:17; Deut. 1:28; Ps. 27:3; Deut. 28:65; Pss. 28:7, 29:3.
334 Mark 7:20–23.

ultimately, indulgence in every kind of impurity, with a continual lust for more.[335] "Hardness of heart evidences itself by light views of sin; partial acknowledgment and confession of it; pride and conceit; ingratitude; unconcern about the word and ordinances of God; inattention to divine providences; stifling convictions of conscience; shunning reproof; presumption, and general ignorance of divine things."[336]

But as Paul reminds us,

> You, however, did not come to know Christ that way. Surely you heard of him and were taught in him in accordance with the truth that is in Jesus. You were taught, with regard to your former way of life, to put off your old self, which is being corrupted by its deceitful desires; to be made new in the attitude of your minds; and to put on the new self, created to be like God in true righteousness and holiness. Therefore each of you must put off falsehood and speak truthfully to his neighbor, for we are all members of one body. In your anger do not sin. Do not let the sun go down while you are still angry, and do not give the devil a foothold. He who has been stealing must steal no longer, but must work, doing something useful with his own hands, that he may have something to share with those in need. Do not let any unwholesome talk come out of your mouths, but only what is helpful for building others up according to their needs, that it may benefit those who listen. And do not grieve the Holy Spirit of God, with whom you were sealed for the day of redemption. Get rid of all bitterness, rage and anger, brawling and slander, along with every form of malice. Be kind and compassionate to one another, forgiving each other, just as in Christ God forgave you.[337]

The brain, the mind, the conscience, and the heart act and react to one another, determining the health and well-being of the soul, which was first animated by the breath of God. According to scripture, the heart may think, understand, imagine, remember, speak to itself, or make decisions;

335 Eph. 4:17–19.
336 *Easton's Bible Dictionary*, Heart.
337 Eph. 4:20–32.

it may be wise, purposeful, intentional, mature, or rebellious.[338] The heart is the true character of an individual, and God knows the heart of each person.[339] The heart can be pure or evil.[340] It is the reservoir of the entire power of life, the center of the rational and spiritual nature of individuals, the center of moral life, and the dwelling place of Christ in us.[341]

In the Bible, the heart is never ascribed to animals. On the heart is written God's law, and the heart is where the work of grace is performed and renewed by that grace. Why? Because the heart is also the seat of sin.[342] It can even be considered the place where the soul resides. It is the heart that governs the intellectual, emotive, volitional, and physical dimensions of the inner person. It is the moral and ethical center of our lives. Integrity and authenticity find their home there. The fruit of the Spirit lives in our hearts, waiting to be cultivated and produce the character of Christ in thought, word, and deed.[343]

We can choose what will establish, inform, and condition the heart and thereby determine the outcome of our behavior. Only God can open or illuminate the heart to bring a person to faith. Only God can redeem and restore the heart. Only God can quicken and inspire the heart. Only God can see the heart for what is really there. Only God fully knows our hearts. God looks at our hearts and judges the motives of our hearts.

The Character

Horace Greeley said, "Fame is a vapor, popularity an accident, and riches take wings. Only one thing endures and that is character."[344] In his book *Uprisings*, my friend Erwin McManus profoundly observes, "The shape of your character is the shape of your future."[345]

All the preceding discussion regarding the brain, mind, conscience,

338 Esther 6:6; Job 38:36; Jer. 9:14; Deut. 4:9; Prov. 2:10; Deut. 7:17; Acts 11:23; Heb. 4:12; Eph. 6:6; Ps. 101:2; Jer. 5:23.
339 1 Sam. 16:7.
340 Jer. 3:17; Matt. 5:8.
341 Eph. 3:17.
342 Rom. 2:15; Acts 15:9; Ezek. 36:26; Gen. 6:5, 8:21.
343 Gal. 5:22–24.
344 Horace Greeley, http://philosiblog.com/2012/02/06/.
345 McManus, *Uprising*, 39.

heart, and soul comes together in what we refer to as the character—the combination of given and acquired features and traits that constitute a person's nature or fundamental disposition, and from which specific moral responses issue. Character is what people see about us and what they perceive us to be.

Merriam-Webster Dictionary defines character as "one of the attributes or features that make up or distinguish an individual; the complex of mental and ethical traits marking and often individualizing a person, group, or nation; main or essential nature especially as strongly marked and serving to distinguish moral excellence and firmness."

Author Frank Damazio states that character "will reflect either the traits of the sinful nature being influenced by the world or the traits of the divine nature being influenced by the word of God. Character is the sum total of all the negative and positive qualities in a person's life, exemplified by one's thoughts, values, motivations, attitudes, feelings, and actions. Even as the character of the world becomes more corrupt, the Lord is causing the character of the church to be matured."[346]

Our character is marked by the morality we hold. *Webster's Unabridged Dictionary of the English Language* defines morality as "the relation of conformity or nonconformity to the moral standard or rule; quality of an intention, a character, an action, a principle, or a sentiment, when tried by the standard of right. The morality of an action is founded in the freedom of that principle, by virtue of which it is in the agent's power, having all things ready and requisite to the performance of an action, either to perform or not perform it; the quality of an action which renders it good; the conformity of an act to the accepted standard of right; the doctrines or rules of moral duties, or the duties of men in their social character; the practice of the moral duties; rectitude of life; conformity to the standard of right; virtue; as we often admire the politeness of men whose morality we question."

Our Christian faith modifies and develops our character. The moral qualities we embrace are elevated, strengthened, and purified by our faith. Regeneration by the Holy Spirit gives us a solid foundation for Christian character. We partner with God to have Christ formed in us, but the source

---

346 Frank Damazio, *The Making of a Leader* (Portland: City Christian Publishing, 1996), 106–8.

of this transformation is under the sole ownership of the Holy Spirit. By "partner" I mean we must make choices and decisions that will facilitate the transformation.[347] If we are to have the character of Christ, as scripture asserts, we must submit to the gradual work of the Lord in us.[348]

We must be known as having the character of Christ if we are to have any influence in facilitating God's redemptive purposes in the world. So character matters. Once again, the fruit of the Spirit—love, joy, peace, patience, kindness, goodness, faithfulness, gentleness, and self-control—must be observable in our lives. The fruit of the Spirit dramatically impacts the character, bringing us into closer and closer congruence with the character of Christ.

There's a story about a group of women who, during a Bible study focused on the Book of Malachi, chapter three, came across verse three, which says, "He will sit as a refiner and purifier of silver." This verse puzzled the women, who wondered aloud how it applied to the character and nature of God. One of the women offered to research the process of refining silver and report back at their next Bible study. The following week, the woman called up a silversmith and made an appointment to watch him work. She didn't mention anything about the reason for her interest beyond her curiosity about the process of refining silver.

As she watched the silversmith work, he held a piece of silver over the fire and let it heat up. He explained that refining silver requires holding it in the middle of the fire, where the flames are the hottest, to burn away any impurities. The woman thought about God holding us in such a hot spot, and then she thought again about the verse, that "He sits as a refiner and purifier of silver."

She asked the silversmith if he had to sit in front of the fire the entire time the silver was being refined. The man answered yes, that not only did he have to sit there holding the silver, but he had to keep his eyes on it the entire time it was in the fire. If the silver was left in the flames even a moment too long, it would be destroyed. The woman was silent for a moment.

Then she asked the silversmith, "But how do you know when the silver is fully refined?"

---

347 Titus 2:11–14.
348 2 Cor. 3:18.

He smiled at her and answered, "Oh, that's easy. When I see my image in it."

Our character reflects the status and health of the heart. It is an outward expression of an inward transformation.

Personal Assessment

If you were to ask someone close to you to describe your character, what would they say about you?

If you were to conduct an internal audit of how you measure up to manifesting the fruit of the Spirit, what would that audit reveal?

If Christ were to look at your heart right now, what would He see?

Chapter 7: Our Journey

No one cares what you have to say until they observe how you live. If you live a life of integrity, honor, authenticity, and courage, people will ultimately want to hear what you have to say—even if they disagree with you. Why? Because they cannot get past a life well lived. They can deconstruct your faith; they can disregard your proclamations. They can disparage your beliefs. But they cannot deconstruct, disregard, or disparage a life well lived.

Being proactive about our journey will ensure that we arrive at a destination of our choosing. Understanding the landscape and what to expect on the journey helps us prevent unforeseen obstacles that can impede the journey or terminate it altogether. It's also immensely important to have a strategy for certain contingencies if we want to make progress toward our objective—a godly life of *being* the people God intended us to be and *doing* what God intended us to do.

The Landscape

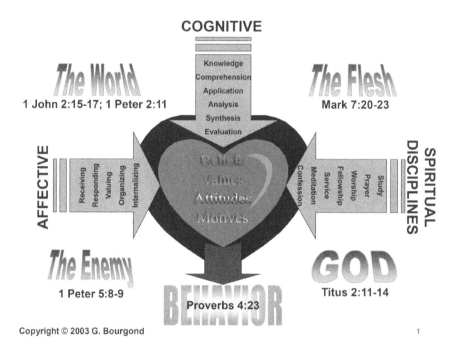

A survey of the landscape and the conditions that will affect our journey will help orient us to the lay of the land we will traverse, with its features and influences. We have already discussed the influences of the world, the flesh, the enemy, and God on our journey. The transformational center of our soul, the heart, is also bombarded with influences—cognitive, affective, and behavioral.

Cognitive Influences

Educational psychologist Benjamin Bloom developed a taxonomy of cognitive levels of progressive learning, from the simple to the complex. According to his theory, true learning begins with the acquisition of knowledge, followed by comprehension and, finally, application of that knowledge. That is where learning stops for many people. And that is where many sermons stop in proclamation. The deeper learning of analysis, synthesis, and evaluation is often left to scholars cloistered away in the offices, classrooms, and libraries of our educational institutions. It's at these deeper levels of learning that wisdom is developed.

When I was executive pastor at a church in California, John MacArthur—senior pastor of Grace Community Church, founder of Masters Seminary, and the author of numerous books—visited our church. I asked him what he thought was the biggest problem facing Christians in the foreseeable future. His answer came quickly and consisted of one word: "Discernment."

Why do so many Christians seem to lack discernment (or spiritual insight) today? Many of us are living at the information level, which is simply the ordered understanding of raw data. We do not give enough time to reflection, which leads to comprehension. The tyranny of urgency, the frenzied activity of our daily lives, and the constant bombardment of data (TV, faxes, newspapers, magazines, Internet, e-mail, radio, audiotapes, superficial conversations, etc.) rob us of an ordered analysis of our world. We operate off of sound bites instead of measured and thoughtful examination.

Many others of us are stuck at the knowledge level, satisfied with the acquisition and accumulation of information ordered in such a way as to give us an intellectual grasp of the essentials of a subject, enough to converse intelligently about it, but little more. The trouble with remaining at this level is that our mental comprehension doesn't move on to applied wisdom. The knowledge never reaches our hearts.

We need to move to the wisdom level by prioritizing our acquisition and accumulation of knowledge so it becomes godly wisdom. We do this by processing our knowledge through the filter of God's Word, the Bible. Our ultimate goal should be to apply that wisdom to life in general and our lives specifically, so that we are equipped for every good work.

In summary, information is the ordered understanding of raw data; knowledge is meaning derived through study, reflection, and comprehension; and wisdom is knowledge applied according to one's core beliefs and value system.

To illustrate, let's look at the Ten Commandments. In Exodus 20, we are exposed to basic information about them—the existence of the Ten Commandments. We develop true knowledge about them when, through study and reflection, we comprehend their meaning (e.g., the first four commandments address our relationship with God, while the remaining six address our relationship with others). Knowledge becomes wisdom when we understand the commandments' implications to us personally and we apply them to our lives, processing them through a belief system that has established our *values*.

There is a vast distance between having knowledge *about* something and having a personal knowledge *of* something. The bridge from one to the other is godly wisdom applied to our lives. When Solomon, given an opportunity to ask God for whatever he wanted, made a request motivated by his desire to justly rule his people, God gave him much more than he asked for![349]

Godly wisdom is available to every believer who asks for it in faith. "If any of you lacks wisdom, he should ask God, who gives generously to all without finding fault, and it will be given to him."[350]

We have some control over what cognitive influences inform our journey. It matters what we read, whom we listen to or hang around with, what we learn and from whom, and how we apply what we have learned. True discernment takes place at the deeper levels of learning: analysis, synthesis, and evaluation.

When dealing with the heart, we analyze the individual factors that contribute to the whole subject or topic. We look at the individual components of the heart. Analysis is followed by synthesis, where we bring in other information to inform our analysis. We have looked at other scripture bearing on our subject, the heart; we have brought in expertise from other scholars; and we have reassembled that information for a more comprehensive understanding of the journey. Now I hope to provide enough information that you will be able to discriminate, compare, and contrast what you have learned with your life and make discerning evaluations—the last level of learning.

Affective Influences

As with the cognitive domain discussed above, the affective domain also moves from simple to complex. In Bloom's scheme, these steps move from receiving (becoming aware), to responding, valuing, organizing, and then internalizing.

Previously I mentioned the fact that sometimes we admire certain values in others and resolve to emulate them, but our desire does not always result in commitment. I have identified six levels of resolve that generally correlate with Bloom's affective levels.

---

349 1 Kings 3:3–14.
350 James 1:5.

A value is not made manifest in our behavior until we commit ourselves to act on it repeatedly in the same way over a period of time. Doing so under the empowerment of the Holy Spirit will ultimately change a value into a virtue. At that point we act on it without much thought—it has become part of our spiritual DNA.

Level 1: *Aspiration*—Many of us aspire to values that are not in any way reflected in our behavior. We might esteem them, but they have no influence over us. They are an interest, but little more.

Level 2: *Preference*—Some of us have a distinct preference for one or more values over others. For instance, we might value loyalty over honesty, or mercy over justice. But in either case they are simply preferences, having little impact on our behavior.

Level 3: *Respect*—At this level of resolve, we respect a certain value to the degree that we can't understand why others don't respect it too. When we see an example of this value played out in the lives of others, it immediately gets our attention. Yet respect for a certain value is no guarantee it will influence our own behavior.

Level 4: *Affirmation*—This level of resolve may cause us to publicly affirm a value. We go "on record" that it is important to us; we are willing to declare and defend it. Still, this level of resolve might produce little consistent or repeated reflection in our behavior.

Level 5: *Commitment*—It is at the commitment stage that we are willing to act on a value we esteem. We proactively decide to intentionally live by this value. The evidence of commitment is manifest in how often it influences our behavior. We consider it so important to habitually act out that value that we are willing to be held accountable for it.

Level 6: *Virtue*—The highest level of resolve is when the habitual practice of a particular value becomes a fixed part of our character, a virtue in our lives. Again, virtues are "specific dispositions, skills, or qualities of excellence that together make up a person's character, and that influence his or her way of life."

Behavioral Influences

We have discussed the importance of spiritual disciplines in promoting spiritual maturation. These disciplines are not the end objective, but a means to a greater objective: a deep and abiding relationship with our heavenly Father through His Son, Jesus Christ. When a spiritual discipline becomes the prime objective, it ceases to be effective in bringing about any spiritual change.

On the chart you will notice a limited set of disciplines—the ones I believe will promote a healthy heart after God. These disciplines include study, prayer, worship (public, private, and personal), fellowship, service, meditation, and confession.

We have talked about the "sponge." Each of us must determine our spiritual rhythm of filling up our sponge and wringing it out in the lives of others. The question is one of rhythm between nurture and service. What fills up your sponge? How do you wring out your sponge into the lives of others? I would encourage you to join the Fellowship of the Sponge. Commit to filling your sponge through hearing, reading, studying, memorizing, and meditating on God's Word. And commit to wringing out your sponge in the lives of others by serving in your church and in your local community.

The Route

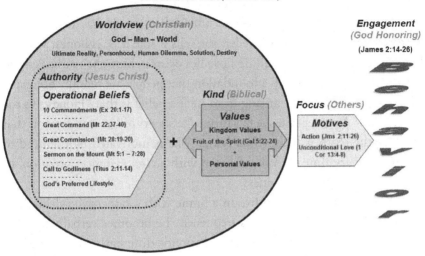

Reflected Behavior

Our *central beliefs* establish our core values; our *core values* inform our worldview; our *worldview* conditions our primary motives; our *primary motives* energize our behavior; our *behavior* reflects the condition of our heart (Proverbs 4:23).

The graphic before you depicts the route to God-honoring behavior. Our beliefs plus our values provide the bulk of our worldview, informed and conditioned by the Bible and Christ. It is from this worldview, our take on reality, that our primary motives emerge, resulting in behavior pleasing to God and benefiting others who respond.

What does this dynamic look like in real life? Consider the following scenarios, which could contain multiple variables. As I have said earlier, one belief can yield many values, and one value can be the product of many beliefs. For purposes of illustration, I will narrow each example to one possible combination.

Suppose you encounter an individual at a dinner party. During the meal he ridicules absolute truth, calling Christianity an archaic throwback to a bygone era. In fact, he belongs to an organization that publishes similar rants in a daily blog to which he is a major contributor. You realize he is no gadfly, but a devotee to the cause. His behavior at the dinner party as well as his outside actions and associations suggest an underlying belief system that could be summarized as "There are no absolutes." Given that foundation, one core value he might hold would be "Truth is relative." His worldview might include a perception "To each his own." A motive arising from such a belief system, value, and perception is a fierce commitment to "individual choice"—that is, every choice by any individual must be affirmed and accepted, and anyone who refuses to embrace this philosophy is intolerant at the least and a bigot at the most.

Or suppose you have a friend you admire because she has demonstrated repeatedly that she is a truth-teller: she tells it like it is, is honest without being hurtful, and avoids telling little lies or stretching the truth. Perhaps her belief system stands on a foundation that people are morally obligated to tell the truth. A value arising from such a belief is that "Honesty is the best policy." A perception she has formed as a part of her worldview is that "Telling the truth is better than lying." She is motivated by the need to be honest every time she is confronted with a circumstance, situation, or event that calls for truthfulness.

One final scenario: You live in a home with a father who drinks too much. When he does, which is frequently, he becomes verbally abusive, a bully. Each of your three brothers responds differently: one confronts, another pacifies, and another flees. Because you are a follower of Christ, you have chosen a different behavior. You choose intervention in the hope that it might permanently resolve the ongoing conflicts. You love your father because God loves him. You don't agree with his behavior, but you feel driven to help him. As a fully committed follower of Christ, your belief system has been calibrated with God's truth. You believe (trust in, rely on, and cling to) the idea that God loves the world, including your abusive father. Your father was created in the image of God, and God loves him even though his despicable behavior has caused great pain in the family. You do not condone your father's behavior, but you understand that it is the result of sin and corruption.

Your value is "God can change anyone—even my father." Your attitude is one of understanding how your father arrived at such a state: he used alcohol as a poor substitute for what was really bothering him, and now the alcohol is in control. Your motive to act is born out of unconditional love—a natural result of your belief system, values, and perceptual attitudes. Your behavior is not to fight, pacify, or flee, but to intervene. You know your father can change his lifestyle, but first he must deal with his alcoholism through intervention methods. Even though you have suffered like your brothers, your response is different from theirs, because you have chosen to act on truth rather than lies. Your source of truth is God.

These scenarios illustrate the interactive relationship among beliefs, values, attitudes, and motives, resulting in predictable behaviors. I firmly believe that we have everything we need to live upright and godly lives in this present age. Empowered and enlightened by the Holy Spirit, we can choose proactively to live lives distinguished by their basis in a firm, biblical foundation of truth. Our values and attitudes arising from the truth, along with a proper motive, will result in God-honoring behavior. The choice is ours.

Our Guiding Authority

The route to godliness[351] begins by establishing the Bible as your sole authority for faith and practice. Putting Christ and the Word on the throne of your life is a necessary first step on the road to transformation. Whatever you put in authority over what you believe, what you value, what defines your reality, and what powers your motives, will ultimately determine the quality of your behavior.

Remember, it is truth that sets us free.[352] John reminds us that if we wish to know the truth, we must obey God's conditions. John's phrasing, "If you hold to my teaching, *then* you will know the truth, and the truth will set you free," makes it clear that obedience precedes freedom. Compliance with Christ's teachings makes us His disciples first of all. Obedience precedes knowledge, and knowledge precedes freedom. The world will never understand such faith; it is foolishness to them. But we know different: faith is freedom to us.

We need faith so that we can be obedient and thus experience freedom. We must trust God, and so we can't get around the requirement of faith, which is simply informed trust. Any meaningful relationship is built on trust. God has our best interests at heart. He has demonstrated His unconditional love for us at the cross. He shows us mercy every day. His grace abounds. The passage from John tells us real freedom is based on

---

351 Titus 2:11–14.
352 John 8:31–32.

truth. Truth sets us free—not just any truth, but God's truth, the truth of Jesus and the Bible.

Personal Assessment

What "authority" stands over your beliefs and values?

What other influences vie for that control?

What competing philosophies or ideologies influence you?

To which authority will you give preeminence?

Our Central Belief System

In the diagram, you will note several options for operational beliefs: the Ten Commandments, the Great Command, the Great Commission, the Sermon on the Mount, the Call to Godliness, and God's Preferred Lifestyle.[353] Other biblical belief systems could be added. The point is that whichever belief system you select and proactively act upon will produce predictable behavior. Select your own, but make sure it is biblical.

Think for a moment: If the Ten Commandments were your selected belief system, what values might it establish? What worldview would it create? What motives might arise from it? What types of behavior might it produce? In Matthew 22 we are given the Great Command to love God and love others. In fact, the first four commandments are summarized as "Love God," while the last six are summarized as "Love others." Certainly your priorities would change: How you spend your time would change. What you choose to engage in would change. How you treat others, beginning with your family, would change. What you dedicate your life

---

353 Bourgond, *Rattling of Sabers*, 48ff.

to would change. What you focus on would change. What you aspire to would change. Everything would change.

How about the Ministry of Reconciliation,[354] or Christ-likeness,[355] or Living Sacrifices,[356] or Unconditional Love[357] as biblical belief systems? What values, perceptual attitudes, motives, and subsequent behavior would they produce? None of the behavior we might aspire to based on a specific belief system would ever come to fruition without our dependence on Christ and the empowerment of the Holy Spirit. This is not so much a matter of *exerting* our wills as it is of *surrendering* our wills to God.

None of the belief systems I have mentioned is better or more important than any other subset of beliefs found in the Bible. We also can't ignore the rest of the Bible in favor of our selected belief system. But choosing one system simply means that we have decided to focus our lives on it, at least for the time being, until led by God to do otherwise.

Appendix C: Operational Beliefs contains a list of operational beliefs you might want to consider. These beliefs were originally identified by Neil T. Anderson, president and founder of Freedom in Christ Ministries.[358]

Personal Assessment

What operational beliefs will you select to live your life by?

To which operational belief systems are you willing to commit, and out of which will come your values, perceptual attitudes, and motives?

What is the "truth" that will set you free?

---

354 2 Cor. 5:11–21.
355 Eph. 4:11–16.
356 Rom. 12:1–8.
357 1 Cor. 13:4–8.
358 Anderson, *Victory Over the Darkness*, 51–53.

Select five operational beliefs that you intend to live your life by. These beliefs should include supporting scripture.

Our Core Values

As I mentioned earlier, every believer receives a family set of values embedded in his or her new heart by God at the very moment of conversion. The family set is called the fruit of the Spirit and represents not only God's heart but His character, as well, lived out in the person and work of Christ. These values need to be cultivated in the believer.

In addition to these values, God places other values in the heart to be nurtured and developed in a believer. Mine include devotion to God; faithfulness to my family; commitment to responsible behavior; subservience to the authority of the Bible; and being a promise keeper, a truth seeker, a loyal servant, a man of integrity, a lifelong learner, a biblically centered leader, and a man of strength and honor. I've prioritized these values over a lifetime of following Christ.

Those of you who may be new to this way of thinking and living may want to seek God's help identifying personal values He wants to instill in you. What is it that you treasure so highly that you are irritated when other people don't? What things do you respect so deeply that you tend to be resentful when others treat them with disrespect?

Those of you in groups should work separately at first, each of you identifying the five most important values upon which you hope to establish your home. Then come together and share your results. From that combined list, identify five key values upon which you will build your life together.

Here are some examples of values and their descriptions:[359]

People—My capacity to influence is based on relationship more than expertise.
Being and doing—It is easier to do, but it is more important to be.
Learning communities—It's important to do life and ministry together.

---

359 Terry Walling, *Focus Workbook* (Anaheim: Church Resource Ministries), 16. Used by permission.

Family—My spouse and kids are my significant ministry.
Continuous improvement—I want to model a teachable spirit and do it better.
Kingdom advancement—Jesus desires more and better disciples.
Healthy local churches—The church is God's chosen vehicle today to bring light to a darkened world.
Authentic leadership—Everything rises and falls on real leaders.
Life change—I want to take the next step in a walk with Jesus Christ.
Bravehearts—We believe in hope … courage … seizing the day … taking the land.

I recommend the following process for identifying your core values. Refer to **Appendix D: Core Values** for a list of values to consider. The key is to make sure that any value you choose is biblical. That is why I am asking you to identify one or more verses to frame each value.

1. Pray and ask for God's lead in the selection of an operational belief.
2. Select an operational belief and supporting scripture.
3. Select potential values that arise from the selected belief.
4. Write a description of the value.
5. Select a scriptural reference that frames the value.
6. Identify the relational context for which you intend to apply the selected value.
7. Determine a time frame (no longer than three months) during which you will exercise that value, evaluating it at the end of the period.
8. Select one or more potential values to act upon.

Personal Assessment

From a scale of 1 (nonexistent) to 10 (fully evident), how much of each element of the fruit of the Spirit (our Kingdom values) do you have?

- *love—unselfish, loyal, benevolent, unconditional concern for the well-being of another*
- *joy—that deep, abiding, inner rejoicing that finds its strength in knowing and serving God*
- *peace—the inner tranquility and sense of well-being of someone whose trust is in God through Christ, leading to the absence of agitation or discord*

111

- *patience*—*quiet, steady, uncomplaining perseverance and endurance in the face of provocation, adversity, or strain*
- *kindness*—*gracious, pleasant, hospitable acts coupled with a readiness to help, taking notice of others, compassion, consideration, and thoughtfulness*
- *goodness*—*bountiful love and decency in action, producing consistent generosity and virtuousness*
- *faithfulness*—*dependability, loyalty, and stability; steadfastness and responsibility; being true to one's promises and fulfilling one's duties and obligations*
- *gentleness*—*control over power and strength combined with mildness and tenderness*
- *self-control*—*temperance, the rational restraint of natural impulses, and self-discipline*

What are your personal values? In the last three months, what decisions have you made or actions have you taken that prove your values are real?

What do you treasure so highly that you are irritated when other people don't? What do you respect so deeply that you tend to be resentful when others treat them with disrespect?

If you knew you had six months to live, what would become the most important thing to you? What would become unimportant to you? What core value(s) do you hope your children will adopt?

What are the principles you intend to live by? What are the filters through which you intend to make your key decisions?

Our Perceptual Attitudes

As I stated earlier, the set of perceptual attitudes we have about how life works is our view of reality. Our beliefs and subsequent values form the bulk of our worldview. When we interpret situations, circumstances, and events, we do so based on that worldview, which shapes our outlook on life. In a very real sense, it is the prescription lens through which we peer for a clear view of the world around us.

Our educational institutions try to shape our worldview by promoting one philosophy or ideology over another. Our legislators, Democrats and Republicans, liberals and conservatives, approach problems and issues from separate worldviews. The solutions they propose to societal concerns are based on their views of reality. Economic perspectives like capitalism, socialism, and communism come from different worldviews. On the spiritual front, Christianity, Mormonism, Judaism, Islamism, Buddhism, Hinduism, and other religions all hold different worldviews, even if some similarities exist among them. Even within each of the religions you will find competing worldviews.

Our worldview is shaped by many factors. Before we go further, we should also acknowledge the dynamic influence of multiple environments on our students.

Bronfenbrenner's ecological systems theory outlines five systems that impact the development of human beings, from childhood on to adulthood.[360]

The *microsystem* is the immediate environment from which an individual derives his or her sense of being, esteem, significance, values, and beliefs. The degree to which each component within this system impacts and interacts with the individual will vary. This system includes a person's immediate family, school, church, social groups, and neighborhood. Of course, the quality of the influence depends on whether the components within this sphere are healthy or unhealthy. This would be true in any of the systems that follow.

The *mesosystem* represents the interactions among various components of the microsystem. As a child grows, the degree of their influence will change depending on the power of these components and his or her attraction to them. The circumstances of life, good and bad, will adjust the influence of these components.

The *exosystem* of an individual may include extended family, friends of the family, neighbors, media, health and welfare services, legal services, the work setting, social networks, and the community.

The *macrosystem* includes the culture as a whole, where cultural values, customs, and laws exert their influence. Government, society, and global entities reside in this environment.

All these influences shape a person's worldview. For believers, a biblical

---

360 Urie Bronfenbrenner's Ecological Systems Theory, 1979.

worldview is the lens through which the world is observed, interpreted, and understood. Ultimate reality for the follower of Christ is that God created the world and breathed life into the human soul. Every human soul is created in the image of God and designed to effectively and efficiently operate through the practice of worship, law-keeping, truthfulness, honesty, discipline, self-control, and service to God and others. Our major dilemma comes when we abandon these practices and incur guilt before God and, as a result, our soul is gradually destroyed. One theologian describes this corruption as the deterioration of our conscience: our sense of shame dries up; our capacity for truthfulness, loyalty, and honesty is eaten away; and our character disintegrates.

Our biblical worldview sees only one solution to this dilemma: the person and work of Christ, who takes on our sin, satisfies the holiness of God through substitutionary atonement, gives us a new heart embedded with the character of God, imparts the Holy Spirit to help us live a godly life, and gives us new purpose and focus for our lives. Our receipt of this great gift not only provides us with everything we need to live a life of Godliness, but also reorders our priorities so that we are aligned with the Kingdom, ready to facilitate God's redemptive purposes in the world. When our days are complete in accordance with His divine plan and we have faithfully lived out our potential, a new reality awaits us: we will join Christ in another place of bliss and beauty to serve in a role commensurate with our faithfulness. Rejecting Christ and living independently of Him will garner eternal separation from Him.

Personal Assessment

What is your worldview?
  What comprises your worldview?
  How does your worldview align with the biblical worldview?

What is your understanding of the nature of ultimate reality?
  Does God figure into that understanding? If so, how?

What is your understanding of humanity?
  What makes us human?
  What makes us distinct from other living things?
  Do we bear the image of God? If so, how?

What is your understanding of the main dilemma facing humankind?
  What is the single most significant issue that prevents us from reaching our full potential?
  What holds us back from reaching perfection?

What is your understanding of the solution to our universal problem?
  What is the answer to our dilemma? How can the problem of mankind be resolved?
  What is your understanding of our ultimate destiny?
  Where will you go when you die? Is there existence after death?

Our Primary Motives

The bridge between thought and action is one's motives. Detectives seek to determine the motive behind a crime. God judges the motives of our heart. The Old Testament tells us, "And you, my son Solomon, acknowledge the God of your father, and serve him with wholehearted devotion and with a willing mind, for the Lord searches every heart and understands every motive behind the thoughts. If you seek him, he will be found by you; but if you forsake him, he will reject you forever."[361]

The New Testament tells us, "Therefore judge nothing before the appointed time; wait till the Lord comes. He will bring to light what is hidden in darkness and will expose the motives of men's hearts. At that time each will receive his praise from God."[362]

Our motives must be pure. We all operate from an array of mixed

---

361 1 Chron. 28:9.
362 1 Cor. 4:5.

motives, some pure and some impure. We should strive for pure motives, motives that will honor God and not bring dishonor upon His name. We can be motivated by generosity or greed, love or hate, kindness or cruelty, goodness or evil, gentleness or harshness, self-control or self-indulgence, empathy or apathy, morality or immorality.

Negative motives might include anger, blind ambition, conditional love, conquest, control, covetousness, destruction, domination, gluttony, greed, hatred, immorality, jealousy, lust, materialism, meanness, possessiveness, pride, racism, self-centeredness, self-protection, a sense of entitlement or superiority, sexual gratification, usury, or vengeance.

Biblical motives might include unconditional love, actualization, allegiance, a calling, care, Christ-likeness, a desire to develop or improve, equality, fairness, faithfulness, godliness, growth, holiness, honor, influence, justice, loyalty, mercy, mission-mindedness, perseverance, protection, a sense of purpose, responsibility, safety, sacrifice, security, servanthood, service, eternal significance, spirituality, or worship. There are other biblical motives, to be sure.

Personal Assessment

What motivates you?
What compels you to act? Are your motives honorable?
Are your motives godly?
Are your motives biblical?

What would others who know you well identify as your motives?
Would God be pleased with your motives?
Are you pleased with your motives?

Select a primary biblical motive and at least two secondary motives that would compel you to act given an instigating situation, event, or person.

Chapter 8: The Strategy

God is not in a hurry. He kept Abraham and Sarah waiting twenty-five years before Isaac was born, and Isaac and Rebekah waited twenty years for Esau and Jacob, Jacob had to wait fourteen years to get the bride he really wanted, and then he had to serve six more years to build up his flocks so he could be independent, a total of twenty years. Twenty-two years passed between Joseph's betrayal by his brothers and the brothers' reconciliation in Egypt. God is not in a hurry because all His works are done in love. "Love is patient, love is kind" (1 Cor. 13:4). Let's be grateful that God takes His time.

—Warren Wiersbe

On any trip into the wilderness, unforeseen events will require adjustments to the plan. A landslide will necessitate a new route. A washed-out path will require a detour. A storm will demand that shelter be found. The presence of fresh bear scat will change the location of a campsite. Maybe that promising bypass led to a dead end, and now the hiker is lost. Maybe the mountain climbed for a better view resulted in a slip and fall. Any journey can be perilous, and the experienced hiker plans in advance for such contingencies.

When I was in the navy I was responsible for certain electronic equipment. When the equipment failed to operate as designed, I had to figure out what was wrong. Using certain troubleshooting techniques and referring to schematics, I could isolate the trouble and take corrective action, usually replacing or recalibrating a part, in order to bring the system back to full readiness.

My responsibilities included periodic preventive maintenance, employing certain procedures to check out the system, calibrate it, and ensure that it was operating optimally. These measures would sometimes reveal the need to replace a part before it failed because its shelf life was coming to an end; as part of preventive maintenance, perfectly good parts are replaced to avoid future failure when you need the equipment to be operating at its best.

Corrective Contingency

Making progress on your life journey requires corrective action along the way. Sin inevitably manifests itself throughout our lives. Until God brings us home, we are saints who sin occasionally, not sinners striving to be saints. Sin finds its way into our lives when we let down our guard; succumb to life's temptations; engage in risky or destructive behavior; are negatively influenced by the world around us; take wrong cues from business practices or work associates; do not take care of ourselves physically; give in to the flesh; indulge our desires; lapse into residual patterns of independent activity; choose to live independent of God; become rebellious; fall prey to the workings of the enemy; or simply make mini-compromises with our beliefs, values, attitudes, and motives.

Generally, the first indication of sin arises when we or someone close to us observes that our behavior is inconsistent with our faith. Behavioral trends have emerged that have taken us off course and into dangerous territory. Deviation from our biblical course is more often than not gradual and almost imperceptible at first. Before we know it, we have strayed from a godly path into darkness. The Holy Spirit, who lives in us, will alert us to the fact that we need to take corrective action immediately if we want to avoid moral and spiritual implosion. As Christians, we cannot be possessed by the devil, but we are susceptible to being oppressed when repeated sin goes unanswered and strongholds of sin are created within us.[363]

When sin goes unabated, its shrill voice grows louder. Immediate corrective action is needed to recalibrate our hearts, the source of our behavior. Often we struggle with the same sin over and over again, confessing and asking God's help, only to lapse right back into the sin that so easily besets us. Why is this such a common occurrence? Aren't we promised victory and an abundant life?[364]

In *A Rattling of Sabers*, I offer a reason for this dilemma:[365]

> When an evil spirit comes out of a man, it goes through arid places seeking rest and does not find it. Then it says, "I will return to the house I left." When it arrives, it finds the house unoccupied, swept clean and put in order. Then it goes and takes with it seven other spirits more wicked than itself, and they go in and live there. And the final condition of that man is worse than the first. That is how it will be with this wicked generation … The thief comes only to steal and kill and destroy; I have come that they may have life, and have it to the full.[366]

Maybe this has been your experience—confessing the same sin over and over again. Victory over the sin is elusive at best, and your failure to defeat it is downright annoying. The Bible says the abundant life is ours this side of heaven; yet few of us seem to be enjoying the abundant life. Sin plagues us at every turn—some of us sin repeatedly. We confess our

---

363 Eph. 4:17–19.
364 1 Cor. 15:57; 1 John 5:4; John 10:10.
365 Bourgond, *Rattling of Sabers*, 210ff.
366 Matt. 12:43–45; John 10:10.

sin, asking for the Holy Spirit's empowerment not to repeat it, only to do just that again and again. Some of us simply give up—the sin is the thorn in our side we must bear, or so we think.

I believe this problem comes from having an incomplete picture of transformational change, which happens in two phases: removal and replacement. We are very familiar with the first phase but somewhat unfamiliar with the second. As the scripture above implies, if you clean out sin through confession but do not replace it with something else, it may become many times worse than it was before.

For instance, assume you have a decayed tooth that must be extracted by a dentist. Once it is removed, what will happen if a substitute tooth or bridge is not installed? Over time your remaining teeth will reposition, your bite will change, your teeth might chip, your gums may become diseased—and other diseases may follow. Removal must be followed by replacement.

The following process represents a more expanded and complete journey to wholeness and holiness. The first four steps involve *removal*; the last four entail *replacement*.

Removal

Removal begins with the awareness that something is wrong. This realization is followed by prayerful reflection to discern the cause of the problem. For change to take place, we must recognize that the sinful behavior does not measure up to God's standards for His family. Comprehension of the relationship between the beliefs, values, attitudes, and motives leading to our behavior is crucial at this point. The final step of removal is confessing our sin—a corrupt belief, value, attitude, or motive leading to corrupt behavior.

1. Realization (Awareness)
First, we must be aware of our sin if we hope to remove it. Generally, the first indication of sin is a conviction by the Holy Spirit, who resides in us and convicts the world of sin, righteousness, and judgment. He guides us into all truth—truth about ourselves. Perhaps a corrupt belief, value, attitude, or motive has led to our corrupt behavior. Knowing what underlies our corruption will help us recover from it.

2. Reflection (Prayer)

Sometimes it is not all that clear where the problem lies. It may be a pattern in our lives that was established long ago, the cause of which we've forgotten or suppressed over time, but whose effects are still being felt and played out in our behavior. We may be focusing on the symptoms rather than the actual cause, resulting in repeated sinful behavior. Prayer can clear the fog. Again, the Holy Spirit will provide counsel; He will teach us. The Bible can shed light on the cause too.

3. Recognition (Understanding)

Comprehending the relationship between beliefs, values, attitudes, and motives as they relate to our behavior is helpful at this stage. We are to guard our hearts, because it is out of the heart that good or evil springs. It gushes forth in overt behavior that either brings glory and honor to the Lord, or dishonor and shame. Examining our lives to identify the root cause or causes of our sin will ensure that the problem is dealt with properly, efficiently, and effectively by God's grace and the Holy Spirit's empowerment.

4. Removal (Confession)

Confession for the believer includes acknowledgment before God that our behavior is wrong, thankfulness and gratitude that God paid the penalty through His Son, appreciation for the fact that we are already forgiven and must simply receive that forgiveness, and finally appropriation of the strength that is in Christ to live a more godly life. True confession recognizes that Jesus is Lord—our master, mediator, and messiah. It was His sacrifice that provides atonement for our sins.

Replacement

Replacement is critical to transformational change. It begins with true repentance leading to fruitful evidence that change has truly happened; we must turn away from our sinful behavior and turn to a life of godliness. Then we must replace the lie that gave rise to the sin with the truth that will set us free. Substitution begins with a willingness to be taught, rebuked, corrected, and trained in righteousness—to experience daily renewal in Christ.[367] Renewal requires action. A belief or value is not real unless you

---

367 2 Tim. 3:16–17.

act on it; mental affirmation alone won't cut it. Finally, recalibration and realignment with our primary objective—godliness—will produce a godly life, the gift that keeps giving.

5. Repentance (Turning)
Repentance is not discussed much in churches today. We like to keep our options open and maintain control of our own destinies. We forget we were bought at a price, that we are under new management, that we must turn away from what is defeating us and toward what will give us life. Our lives should bear fruit befitting our repentance. Repentance is not an option; it is a mandate from the Lord. In God's economy there is no such thing as conditional surrender.

6. Replacement (Substitution)
Replacement with and obedience to Christ's teachings prove we are His disciples. Truth replaces the lie and brings life to the believer. The process begins with submitting to biblical authority, accepting its critique of our lives, embracing its corrective measures, and subjecting ourselves to His training with devotion, discipline, and diligence so that we will be equipped for every good work. Once the corruption has been removed, it must be replaced with a healthy and godly alternative.

7. Renewal/Restoration (Action)
The truth that replaces the lie must be acted upon at every turn if transformation is to take place. If truth is not substituted for the lie and brought to vibrant life by a vibrant relationship with our life-giver— God through Christ—it will get much worse before it ever gets better. Informed faith submits to obedience before freedom, commitment before understanding, and acceptance before realization. As James says, faith without action is dead.

8. Recalibration (Alignment)
Finally, recalibrating to our primary objective of God's preferred lifestyle will ensure advancement rather than retreat. God's grace in Christ teaches us to say no to ungodliness and worldly passions. It teaches us how to live self-controlled, upright, and godly lives in the here and now. We are not to live with our bags packed, waited to be ushered into glory. We have a godly life to live and a godly purpose to fulfill.

Again, and put simply, *removal* of sin is accomplished through heartfelt confession[368] followed by *replacement*[369] with truth and a commitment to act on that truth. It is a two-step process. Removal must be followed by replacement. Remove through confession and replace with God's truth. Then act on that truth. "If you hold to my teaching, you are really my disciples. Then you will know the truth, and the truth will set you free."

Appendix E: Confessional Prayers contains confessional prayers you can use to remove corrupt beliefs, values, attitudes, and motives and replace them with biblical counterparts. These prayers were originally adapted from Neil T. Anderson's 1992 book, *Resolving Spiritual Conflicts.* Some of you may feel uneasy about repeating written prayers, but I've recommended them because they are scripturally based and cover the intended focus and scope of each step. I would encourage you to pray them aloud; there is something to be said about the power of audible prayer. Or, if you prefer, prepare your own prayers, keeping in mind the topics and focus of the prayers contained in the appendix.

Preventive Contingency

Preventive maintenance for the Christian means setting down a prescribed plan for how we intend to live our lives in accordance with God's truth. Such a plan should include measures to ensure that we live to the glory of God, attesting to the fact that we wish to live our lives intentionally, in accordance with God's redemptive purposes. We can choose the course our lives take. We can decide in advance how we will live with integrity and authenticity.

John Maxwell, leadership expert, defines integrity as follows: "Integrity binds our person together and fosters a spirit of contentment within us. It will not allow our lips to violate our hearts. When integrity is the referee, we will be consistent; our beliefs will be mirrored by our conduct. There will be no discrepancy between what we appear to be and what our family knows we are, whether in times of prosperity or adversity. Integrity allows us to predetermine what we will be regardless of circumstances, persons involved, or the places of our testing."

Living a life of authenticity means to conform to the original, Jesus

---

368 1 John 1:8–9.
369 John 8:31–32.

Christ, and reproducing the features that reflect His character. People who do so leave little doubt as to whom they belong, because they bear the imprint of the Master.

Some Christians have an aversion to planning, believing that plans interfere with the work of the Holy Spirit and are somehow unspiritual. According to the Bible, nothing could be further from the truth. Scripture tells us that estimating cost is smart;[370] that everything should be done in a fitting and orderly way;[371] that plans succeed when committed to the Lord;[372] that whatever we do, we should do it as if we are working for the Lord;[373] that godly counsel is a part of any successful plan;[374] and that God is not a God of disorder.[375]

When preparing your personal alignment plan using as your guide the compass we described, it is good to remind yourself that a decision must be made at the outset: you have to decide where your allegiance will be focused. In this age, tolerance is a societal value; a stand for the Cross as opposed to the Crowd will be met with cries of intolerance. Just such a stand, however, is what I talked about previously—living in bold relief. The words from a music video of the song "The Crowd or the Cross" describe the juxtaposition between the two:

Listen! Two voices, which is louder to you—the crowd or the cross?
The Crowd says follow us. The Cross says follow me.
The Crowd says rely on yourself. The Cross says rely on Me.
The Crowd says earn your worth. The Cross says I am your worth.
The Crowd says bear your burdens. The Cross says nail them to Me.
The Crowd says be happy. The Cross says be holy.
The Crowd says if it feels good do it. The Cross says for love's sake, endure it.
The Crowd says honor yourself. The Cross says humble yourself.
The Crowd says Do. The Cross days Done!
Because of the cross, my interest in the crowd died long ago.
—Apostle Paul

---

370 Luke 14:28.
371 1 Cor. 14:40.
372 Prov. 16:3.
373 Col. 3:23.
374 Prov. 15:22.
375 1 Cor. 14:33.

What will it be for you and for me—the Crowd or the Cross?

The Alignment Plan

Committing to a well-thought-out personal plan aligning with the heart of God requires much prayer and thoughtful reflection. Once the plan is formulated and an implementation strategy defined, a strong commitment to executing the plan will be necessary. We are told we can do all things in Christ who strengthens us, and that He who began a good work in us will carry it on to completion until the day of Christ Jesus.[376] We are not powerless; yet it will take willful commitment, patience, courage, and perseverance, as modeled by a martyred Zimbabwe pastor who tacked the following declaration of commitment on the wall of his home.

> I'm a part of the fellowship of the unashamed. I have Holy Spirit power. The dye has been cast. I have stepped over the line. The decision has been made. I'm a disciple of His. I won't look back, let up, slow down, back away, or be still. My past is redeemed, my present makes sense, my future is secure. I'm finished and done with low living, sight walking, small planning, smooth knees, colorless dreams, tamed visions, mundane talking, cheap living, and dwarfed goals. I no longer need pre-eminence, prosperity, position, promotions, plaudits, or popularity. I don't have to be right, first, tops, recognized, praised, regarded or rewarded. I now live by faith, lean on His presence, walk by patience, lift by prayer, and labor by power.

> My face is set, my gait is fast, my goal is heaven, my road is narrow, my way rough, my companions few, my Guide reliable, my mission clear. I cannot be bought, compromised, detoured, lured away, turned back, deluded or delayed. I will not flinch in the face of sacrifice, hesitate in the presence of the adversary, negotiate at the table of the enemy, ponder at the pool of popularity, or meander in the maze of mediocrity. I won't give up, shut up, let up, until I have stayed up, stored up, prayed up, paid up, preached up for the cause of Christ.

---

376 Phil. 4:13, 1:6.

I am a disciple of Jesus. I must go till He comes, give till I drop, preach till all know, and work till He stops me. And when He comes for His own, He will have no problems recognizing me—my banner will be clear![377]

A *personal alignment plan* consists of operational beliefs you will live by, core values you will act on, a set of perceptual attitudes—your worldview—that will frame your biblical view of reality, motives that will energize your behavior, and an implementation strategy that will comprise your intentions and execution of the plan. This is called *My Compass*. Directions for developing the plan and a form with which to record it are located in **Appendix A: Focused Life Plan.**

I strongly encourage you to complete your personal alignment plan and then execute it! I would also recommend that you bring a partner along with you to hold you accountable to the specifics of your plan. Perhaps you can partner with another person who is similarly committed and has developed his or her own plan. Mutual accountability is a powerful force to keep each other on track. The plan may be amended over time and in fact is a living document.

Consider taking periodic audits of your progress, as you will experience both successes and failures on your journey. Don't give up; keep at it until the plan becomes a part of your DNA. Two steps forward and one back mean you are still making progress. Some examples of plans are included for your reference.

Appendix A: The Compass presents a framework for your compass and provides a form for your use. Your compass, as described in your alignment plan, will serve to keep you on track and provide the reference points for your journey. Pay attention to your compass, for it will help you find your way in life in alignment with God's purposes. Spend the time you need to reflect on your operational beliefs, core values, perceptual attitudes, and primary and secondary motives. Your six-month implementation plan will provide a living laboratory in which you can experiment and apply what you have learned in accordance with God's compass reference points. Get the ship away from the pier and begin a journey of adventure.

---

377 http://home.snu.edu/~hculbert/commit.htm.

PART 2:
The Map

Chapter 9: Our Trajectory

What we do in life echoes in Eternity.
—Roman General Maximus

Now that your compass is in place, the next step is to define your map for the journey. Each of us has a unique map designed by God for us to follow. When He superintended our formation in our mothers' wombs and set the days we would walk the earth, He equipped us with the wherewithal to engage our destinies and realize our full potential in Him. The features of our maps may be common to every map, but the details, locations, and topographies will be unique.

Most of us stumble through life with little direction and focus, reacting to whatever comes within our sphere of activity. We sense that there is more to life and that somehow we are missing what we have been destined to do. In the Book of Ecclesiastes we are told that God has placed a sense of the eternal in every human being, yet not so that we know what God intends.[378] This general revelation placed in our hearts drives us to find answers to the following questions: Why am I here? What is the purpose of my life? Am I making any progress? Will my life matter? Will I make any lasting mark? Will anyone notice when I'm gone?

The Bible gives us clear answers to these fundamental questions. God *does* have a purpose for our lives. We *are* here for a reason. Our lives *can* count for something of lasting value.

Most of us are trying to figure out our ultimate destinations. We have been taught that we need to determine our destinations and then make plans for how to get there. In God's economy, we are to engage the journey and leave the destination to Him. The journey will include multiple destinations.

If we focus on a point on the horizon, we develop myopia, to the detriment of our peripheral vision. Once we determine God's intended trajectory for us without focusing on a specific destination, He will bring us to places we have never been, to mountaintops we have never reached, to horizons we have never seen. The journey will be exhilarating and scary at the same time. We must trust our Creator. He has our best interests at heart.

A Destiny to Fulfill

How do we begin to live a legacy worth leaving in the lives of others? Your legacy is the aroma left in the nostrils of those God has brought within your sphere of influence. In my study of scripture, I have come to realize that God indeed has a plan for each of us that will bring meaning and significance to our lives.

Each of us has a *destiny* to fulfill ... God says so! "For I know the plans I have for you, declares the Lord, plans to prosper you and not to harm you, plans to give you hope and a future."[379] Regardless of the decisions we have made or the regret we have over poor decisions, God is not finished with us yet. Under His permissive will, we are free to choose the courses of our

---

378 Eccles. 3:10–11.
379 Jer. 29:11.

lives. Having made bad decisions along the way, as we all have done, we mistakenly think that God is through with us, that we've been benched—or, even worse, put on the sidelines, with little hope for the future.

That is a lie of the enemy. God is not finished with us. We may have made decisions we feel have disqualified us from any meaningful contribution to His Kingdom's purposes. But such a thought is far from the truth. God may have wanted us to head in a certain direction, but we chose another in the exercise of our free will. The enemy wants us to believe that the game is over: God surely won't use us now. The truth of the matter is that God will simply open up new opportunities for us. That is what scripture means when it says that God has "plans"—plural—for us.

God is not finished with us and never will be in terms of our pilgrimage on earth. He has certain destinies for us to fulfill, plans He set in motion before we ever came to be. We were on the heart of God before our creation. He has destined us to do something grand for Him. When our hearts are aligned with His, we will have the eyes to see it.

God is actively engaged in bringing about our destinies. One of the shaping tools God uses is "destiny processing," of which there are four types:[380]

Type I: Awe-Inspiring Experiences

God intervenes in a special, awe-inspiring way in the lives of leaders. This takes the form of His overpowering presence, often accompanied by some revelation from Him (e.g., a dream, a vision, or a voice). During the experience, the recipient feels God's anointing and overwhelming presence as He reveals Himself in some clear and unmistakable way. In the process, God often discloses something about the person's future purpose, such as a call to ministry. This type of experience is rare.[381]

Early in my career in the navy, I was struggling to feel God's love. Intellectually I knew it existed, but I was devoid of any emotional experience of it. One night I was sitting at the fire-control console in Combat Central, encircled by a curtain. The chatter of communications

---

380 J. Robert Clinton, *Strategic Concepts* (Altadena: Barnabas Publishers, 1995), 73–82.

381 Type I examples: Moses and the burning bush (Exodus 3); Abraham's dream (Genesis 15); Paul on the road to Damascus (Acts 9); Isaiah's call (Isaiah 6); Joseph's dreams (Genesis 37); Jeremiah's call (Jeremiah 1).

and activity was loud. All of a sudden the noise stopped and I distinctly heard the following: "Greg, I love you." I was stunned. Immediately, the chatter and noise resumed. I believe that was a Type I experience.

Type II: Indirect

Sometimes our destinies hinge on someone else's action on our behalf. This type of destiny processing involves an experience in which some aspect of the leader's destiny is linked to someone other than the leader and is done indirectly for the leader, who simply must receive its implications (e.g., prophetic word, prayer, or dedication).[382]

Type III: Providential

We can sense and affirm our destinies when, in retrospect, we see an accumulation of past experiences or providential circumstances indicating that we have been led by God and should be doing something for God because of this evidence. We usually recognize this type of destiny processing through contextual factors; we can see the hand of God through His use of circumstances that line up for His purposes. The place and timing of someone's birth or, in retrospect, the unmistakable activity of God in someone's life over time would be examples of such processing.[383]

Type IV: Blessing

When a leader enjoys the powerful presence of God in life and ministry and has repeated experiences that show that God is blessing his or her life and ministry, this accumulated evidence sustains a strong sense of destiny. This type of destiny processing comes through reflection and the realization that God's hand has been on you—that whatever you turn your hand to do, God seems to bless it.[384] Others may recognize that presence first.

---

382 Type II examples: Rachel's naming of Joseph (Genesis 30); Moses, a special child saved (Exodus 1); Hannah's contract with God (1 Samuel 1); Zechariah with the angel (Luke 1); the call of the disciples (John 1); Samson's birth and call (Judges 13).
383 Type III examples: Paul's pre-conversion experiences; Barnabas's multicultural experiences; Joseph's journey to prominence; Moses's training in the desert; Joshua's training under Moses.
384 Type IV examples: Joseph is continually blessed (Genesis 39), as are David, Elijah, Elisha, and Daniel.

Perhaps an examination of your life will reveal one or more examples of destiny processing. The point is that God is actively involved in our lives in order to bring about His plans for us. We have destinies to fulfill.

A Contribution to Make

Each of us has a *contribution* to make ... God has equipped us for His purposes! "There are different kinds of gifts, but the same Spirit. There are different kinds of service, but the same Lord. There are different kinds of working, but the same God works all of them in all men. Now to each one the manifestation of the Spirit is given for the common good."[385]

To each believer is given a manifestation of the Spirit, a spiritual gift or gifts.[386] These gifts and their use produce Christ-likeness in the followers of Christ. This occurs through the preparation of God's people for works of service so that the Body of Christ, His Church, might be built up until all people reach unity in the faith and in the knowledge of the Son of God and become mature, attaining to the whole measure of the fullness of Christ.[387]

In addition to these gifts, the Lord provides opportunities to express them. Seizing each opportunity presented to us will give us occasions to verify that indeed we have a spiritual gift. When we realize that we do, as evidenced by the spiritual results we've attained, we will be able to help others mature in Christ in ever-increasing fashion. Taking a spiritual gift inventory is not necessarily a true indication that we have a gift; it is by exercising the gift in multiple venues that we come to know whether or not it is a true spiritual gift.

God the Father determines how effectively we will exercise our spiritual gifts. When we faithfully avail ourselves of opportunities to use our gifts, we can enjoy the effect the results produced. It is God who brings about "different kinds of working." More will be said about spiritual gifts later.

---

385 1 Cor. 12:4–7.
386 1 Pet. 4:10.
387 Eph. 1:11–16.

A Purpose to Engage

Each of us has a *purpose* to engage … God has a purpose for our lives!

> For we are God's workmanship, created in Christ Jesus to do good works, which God prepared in advance for us to do … For you created my inmost being; you knit me together in my mother's womb. I praise you because I am fearfully and wonderfully made; your works are wonderful, I know that full well. My frame was not hidden from you when I was made in the secret place. When I was woven together in the depths of the earth, your eyes saw my unformed body. All the days ordained for me were written in your book before one of them came to be. How precious to me are your thoughts, O God! How vast is the sum of them! Were I to count them, they would outnumber the grains of sand. When I awake, I am still with you.[388]

Each of us has a purpose to fulfill which God determined before we were born, and knowing that purpose will bring focus to our lives. Our purpose is all about *doing* for others what God has planned for us to do. I find that many Christians have a difficult time determining God's purpose for their lives. Why? Because we often live our lives on our own terms and do not put ourselves in a place where we can hear God's still, small voice.

After an amazing victory against the prophets of Baal on Mount Carmel, Elijah's life was threatened by Jezebel, and so he fled to a cave on Mount Horeb to await his fate. God visited Elijah and asked him what he was doing there. After recounting all that he had done for God and explaining that he now feared for his life, he was told to leave the cave and go stand on a mountain. Wind, an earthquake, and fire ravaged the mountain, but God was not in any of them. Then God came as a gentle whisper.[389]

Why does God speak to us so profoundly in a "gentle whisper"? I believe it is so we have to lean forward to hear it. When is the last time you heard the gentle whisper of God's voice in your life? If you want to

---

388 Eph. 2:10; Ps. 139:13–18.
389 1 Kings 19:1–13.

know God's purpose for your life, you will have to lean forward to hear it. Tuning your heart to the heart of God will tune you in to the frequency of His gentle whisper.

A Ministry to Complete

Each of us has a *ministry* to complete … our objective is Christ-likeness!

> It was he who gave some to be apostles, some to be prophets, some to be evangelists, and some to be pastors and teachers, to prepare God's people for works of service, so that the body of Christ may be built up until we all reach unity in the faith and in the knowledge of the Son of God and become mature, attaining to the whole measure of the fullness of Christ. Then we will no longer be infants, tossed back and forth by the waves, and blown here and there by every wind of teaching and by the cunning and craftiness of men in their deceitful scheming. Instead, speaking the truth in love, we will in all things grow up into him who is the Head, that is, Christ. From him the whole body, joined and held together by every supporting ligament, grows and builds itself up in love, as each part does its work.[390]

This may come as a surprise to you: we are called to minister and to ministry. We erroneously believe that only those who go to seminary or are called to be pastors are the ones who minister and have a ministry—that they are special people singled out by God to lead His Church, while the rest of us operate on some lower level of service. Sometimes we use this false understanding to justify our lack of engagement in the church—to convince ourselves that engagement is the responsibility of those called to ministry.

The Bible suggests otherwise. We have been created for ministry.[391] We have been saved for ministry.[392] We have been called to ministry.[393] We

---

390 Eph. 4:11–16.
391 Eph. 2:10.
392 2 Tim. 1:9.
393 Eph. 4:1.

have been gifted for ministry.[394] We have been authorized for ministry.[395] We are accountable for ministry.[396] We will be rewarded for ministry.[397] We are commanded to minister.[398] The Body of Christ needs our ministry.[399]

So we have no excuse. We are all ministers of reconciliation.[400] Every one of us is a minister. So shouldn't we prepare for ministry? We each have a ministry to perform in alignment with God's purpose for our lives, the contribution we have been gifted to provide, and the destiny we are meant to fulfill.

A Legacy to Leave

Each of us has a *legacy* to leave … God wants us to invest in others! "And the things you have heard me say in the presence of many witnesses entrust to reliable men who will also be qualified to teach others … So now I charge you in the sight of all Israel and of the assembly of the Lord, and in the hearing of our God: Be careful to follow all the commands of the Lord your God, that you may possess this good land and pass it on as an inheritance to your descendants forever."[401]

Everyone leaves a legacy. Some people leave no observable legacy, which is a legacy nevertheless: a life lived in obscurity and in the shadows. Others leave a perishable legacy, such as a foundation, a name on the side of a building, or a statue erected in their honor. Many leave a bad legacy of infamy, carnage, corrupt power, or death. A few leave the only legacy worth living and leaving in the lives of others: a godly legacy, the gift that keeps giving.

If God were to call you home today, what legacy would you leave? What aroma would linger after you are gone? It is not so much how you start your journey as it is how you finish the journey. J. Robert Clinton and his colleagues have devoted their lives to ascertaining how God develops

394 1 Pet. 4:10.
395 Matt. 28:19–20; 2 Cor. 5:20.
396 Rom. 14:12; Matt. 25:14–30.
397 Col. 3:23–24; Matt. 25:23.
398 Matt. 20:28; Col. 4:17; Heb. 9:14.
399 Matt. 9:36–37.
400 2 Cor. 5:17–21.
401 2 Tim. 2:2; 1 Chron 28:8.

leaders. They have completed more than four thousand case studies to date, yielding a vast array of findings summarized as Leadership Emergence Theory. Some of the findings deal with how people finish the race.

Clinton draws a startling conclusion from his research: "There are around 800 or so leaders mentioned in the Bible. There are about 100 who have data that helps you interpret their leadership. About 50 of these have enough data for evaluation of their finish. About 1 in 3 finished well. Anecdotal evidence from today indicates that this ratio is probably generous (when contemporary leaders are considered). Probably less than 1 in 3 is finishing well today."

According to Clinton, "finishing well" means reaching the end of one's life having been faithful to God's calling. For Christ's followers, it means being more passionate about Christ and His mission as they fulfill their life purpose than they were at the beginning. It entails experiencing the depth of God's grace and love, living out one's destiny, and making one's unique and ultimate contribution to the expansion of God's Kingdom. These biblical leaders were walking with God at the end of their lives. They contributed to God's purposes at a high level. They did what God wanted them to do.[402]

In *Starting Well*, Paul Leavenworth and Richard Clinton identify three other possible finishes:[403]

Cut Off Early

These leaders were taken out of leadership because they were assassinated, killed in battle, prophetically denounced, or overthrown. Some of these circumstances are directly attributed to God. Some of these removals were positive and others were negative.[404]

Finished Poorly

These leaders were going downhill toward the end of their ministries. This downward trajectory might be reflected in their personal relationship with God or in terms of their competency in ministry.[405]

---

402 Abraham, Job, Joseph, Joshua, Caleb, Samuel, Elijah, Jeremiah, Daniel, Jesus, John, Paul, and Peter.
403 Richard Clinton and Paul Leavenworth, *Starting Well* (Altadena: Barnabas Publishers, 1998), 12–13.
404 Abimelech, Samson, Absalom, Ahab, Josiah, John the Baptist, and James.
405 Gideon, Samson, Eli, Saul, and Solomon.

Finished So-So

These leaders did fairly well but were limited in their ministries because of sin. They did not complete the plans God had for them, or there were some negative ramifications of their lives and ministries even though they personally walked with God.[406]

Several factors can prevent you from finishing well: finances (their use and abuse);[407] power (its abuse);[408] pride (self-centeredness);[409] sex (immorality and misconduct);[410] family (conflict and neglect);[411] and plateauing (complacency).[412]

Those who finish well possess three or more of the following characteristics: They maintain a personal, vibrant relationship with God right up to the end. They maintain a learning posture and can learn from various kinds of sources—life especially. They portray Christ-like character as evidenced by the fruit of the Spirit in their lives. Truth is lived out in their lives so that God's convictions and promises are evident. They leave behind one or more ultimate contributions (as a saint, stylistic practitioner, mentor, public rhetorician, pioneer, crusader, artist, founder, stabilizer, researcher, writer, or promoter). They walk with a growing sense of destiny and see some or all of it fulfilled.

Clinton's research shows that certain enhancements, when implemented, create a strong platform upon which to finish well. These enrichments include a broad perspective that will help interpret the road ahead; repeated episodes of renewal; the ongoing practice of spiritual disciplines; a well-developed, lifelong learning posture; and the use of many mentors on the journey.

Personal Assessment

How will you finish the race?

---

406 David, Jehoshaphat, and Hezekiah.
407 Gideon's ephod (Judges 8); Ananias and Sapphira (Acts 5).
408 Uzziah's usurpation (2 Chronicles 26).
409 David's numbering (1 Chronicles 21); Hezekiah's mistake (Isaiah 39).
410 David and Bathsheba (2 Samuel 11).
411 Eli and sons (1 Samuel 2–4); Solomon and wives (1 Kings 11).
412 David's latter reign (2 Samuel 15–18).

What legacy will you leave?

What will others say about you when you are gone?

What will prevent you from finishing well if you continue as you are now?

What aroma would you like to leave in the lives of others?

What are your plans for doing so?

Developing a personal life mandate, a unique map, will help you finish well.

Chapter 10: Our Calling

There are different kinds of gifts, but the same Spirit. There are different kinds of service, but the same Lord. There are different kinds of working, but the same God works all of them in all men.

—1 Corinthians 12:4–7

A common misunderstanding is that only vocational ministry is preceded by a call from God, that only ministers of the Gospel are "called." That is not true. I will let the weight of scripture support my contention that each of us is called by God not only to a life of holiness but also to a life of service.[413] Scripture is replete with verses underscoring the fact that those who have received Christ are called to ministry.[414]

What does it mean to be called? Calling is a confusing concept for many ministry leaders and followers of Jesus Christ. Does God call someone to a specific role or a specific location or a specific church or a specific ministry

---

413 Rom. 8:28–30, 11:29; 1 Cor. 7:15–24; Eph. 4:1–6; 1 Thess. 4:7; 2 Thess. 1:11, 2:14; 2 Tim. 1:9; 1 Pet. 1:15, 2:9, 2:21; 2 Pet. 1:10; Rev. 17:24.
414 Eph. 4:1.

organization, to a specific occupation or a specific company? To be sure, God can do whatever He wants: He can certainly call any of us to any role, vocation, location, church, or organization.

But more often than not, we are free to choose any of these within God's permissive will, based on whatever purpose and function He ordained for us before we ever came to be. As long as it doesn't call us to compromise our faith or violate our beliefs, we are free to choose. We are "called" to serve the purpose and function He designed for each of us specifically.

Calling and Design

First, we are called according to His design. The part we play should facilitate His redemptive plans in the world and align with His "prewiring" of us.

Second, we are called to serve a *function* rather than a role. Our function is determined by our spiritual gifts, natural abilities (intellect, aptitudes, and talents), acquired skills, personality and temperament, leadership style, values, and ministry principles—which collectively represent the general function we are to serve rather than any specific organization, location, or role we might embrace.

Third, God may open to us multiple avenues, options, or opportunities, allowing us full expression of our designed function. This would certainly include considerations of place, location, or role. When presented with such an opportunity, we simply must make sure it allows our "wiring" to operate at its best.

Fourth, under the umbrella of God's permissive will, we are free to choose the avenue, option, or opportunity that will provide the context where our purpose and function can flourish. As long as we don't compromise our faith and our practice doesn't conflict with God's commands or moral laws, we are free to choose.

Fifth, God calls us to properly steward our designed function. Again, God can do whatever He wants; He can call us directly to a specific role, location, or church, for that matter. But in my humble opinion such a calling would be an exception to the rule. In general, God calls us to serve the purpose and function for which He has designed us.

Calling and Function

Your calling has everything to do with your designed function; indeed, your function *is* your calling. You are called to serve a particular function in the outworking of God's redemptive purposes in the world. When we appear before the judgment seat of Christ, as will all true believers, we will have to account for what we have done in the faith following our conversion. "For we must all appear before the judgment seat of Christ, that each one may be recompensed for his deeds in the body, according to what he has done, whether good or bad."[415]

Unger's Bible Dictionary describes this sobering encounter:

> The manifestation of the believer's works is in question in this judgment. It is most emphatically not a judgment of the believer's sins. These have been fully atoned for in the vicarious and substitutionary death of Christ, and remembered no more.[416] It is quite necessary, however, that the service of every child of God be definitely scrutinized and evaluated.[417] As a result of this judgment of the believer's works, there will be reward or loss of reward. In any event, the truly born-again believer will be saved.[418]

Your wiring, especially your giftedness (spiritual gifts, natural abilities, acquired skills), can be expressed in many avenues and settings. By way of simple illustration, let's assume you have the spiritual gift for teaching, an aptitude for learning and communication, and you have developed skills for putting together effective lessons using educational theory and practices.

This "wiring" or *function* could be employed through a variety of *roles*, such as enrolling in graduate education, preaching, leading a small group, fulfilling any number of ministry roles, speaking at a conference, conducting a seminar, mentoring someone, or authoring books or writing articles, to mention just a few examples. It could also be employed in a

---

415 2 Cor. 5:10.
416 Heb. 10:17, referring to Jer. 31:33–34.
417 Matt. 12:36; Rom. 14:10; Gal. 6:7; Eph. 6:8; Col. 3:24–25.
418 1 Cor. 3:11–15.

variety of *settings*, such as the home, school, church, seminary, or ministry agency, or at large.

Likewise, the gift of leadership might find its full expression in roles like director of a para-church ministry organization, small-group leader in a church, trustee on a church board, senior pastor of a church, or some secular position leveraged for God's purposes.

Our calling is our wiring, the function by which we contribute to God's purposes.

Calling and Callings

God calls us to ministry in direct correlation with our God-ordained wiring: that is, our spiritual gifts, aptitudes, talents, acquired skills, temperament, passion, and spiritual maturity. He may lead us to a particular location for or expression of our calling. In the former He is the initiator; in the latter He is our partner.

In his book *Serving God*,[419] Ben Patterson draws a distinction between vocation and occupation. He says the word *vocation* refers to our calling; *occupation*, on the other hand, refers to our work. Christians can have many different occupations, but just one vocation. In other words, we are called to one vocation which can be expressed in many occupations or locations. He further makes a subtle distinction between a *calling* (vocation) and many *callings* (occupations).

According to *Nelson's Bible Dictionary*, a *vocation* is a call or invitation to a profession or way of life. But in theological discussions, the word *vocation* is not used in reference to the professional trade which one pursues; instead, it refers to the invitation God has given to all people to become His children through Christ's work. This vocation, or calling, does not come to people because they deserve it; it comes strictly as a result of God's grace.[420] However, it is up to the individual to decide whether he or she will accept and act upon the vocation.

---

419 Ben Patterson, *Serving God* (Downers Grove: Inter Varsity Press, 1994).
420 2 Tim. 1:9.

Calling and Gifts

The framework described above is applicable to spiritual gifts. In 1 Corinthians 12:4–7 we read, "There are different kinds of gifts, but the same Spirit. There are different kinds of service, but the same Lord. There are different kinds of working, but the same God works all of them in all men. Now to each one the manifestation of the Spirit is given for the common good."

In summary, to each of us has been given a manifestation of the Spirit for the common good. In 1 Peter 4:10, we read that "each one should use whatever gift he has received to serve others, faithfully administering God's grace in its various forms." There are different kinds of gifts, different kinds of service, and different kinds of influence and effectiveness. Gifts, service, and our workings comprise what I call the gift package.

There are different kinds of gifts. The list of possible gifts can be found essentially within three scriptural passages: 1 Corinthians 12:8–10; Ephesians 4:7–13; and Romans 12:3–8. Each believer is given one or more gifts at the moment of conversion to help the body of Christ become more like Christ in thoughts, words, and deeds.

There are different kinds of service through which the gifts can be expressed. These could include avenues of expression, such as roles or occupations; or settings or contexts, such as churches, location, or ministry organizations.

There are different kinds of working. When people are faithful in the expression of their gifts, using the avenues the Lord provides for such expression, they will enjoy a measure of godly effectiveness as they seek to serve the Lord faithfully.

We may have one or more gifts that don't change, but how we express those gifts and our effectiveness in expressing them varies.

Calling and Free Will

In his book *Decision Making and the Will of God*,[421] Garry Friesen proposes that we have the freedom to choose alternatives without fear of missing

---

421 Garry Friesen and J. Robin Maxon, *Decision Making and the Will of God* (Colorado Springs: Multnomah Books, 2004), 116.

what we may perceive is only one possibility in God's will. Unless God intervenes or the Word of God gives clear direction, we are free to choose from many possible alternatives in fulfilling His will. Friesen calls this the way of wisdom and sets forth four principles for following God's will:

1. In those areas specifically addressed by the Bible, the revealed commands and principles of God (His moral will) are to be obeyed.
2. In those areas where the Bible gives no command or principle (non-moral decisions), the believer is free and responsible to choose his own course of action. Any decision made within the moral will of God is acceptable to God.
3. In nonmoral decisions, the objective of the Christian is to make wise decisions on the basis of spiritual expediency.
4. In all decisions, the believer should humbly submit, in advance, to the outworking of God's sovereign will as it touches each decision.

In summary, first we are *called* (or set apart) for the ministry of the Gospel—our vocation. Second, we express our *calling* in one or more *callings*—occupations. Third, we may be led to a particular situation—a setting. Our calling is initiated by God, our callings are our response to His gifting, and we may be led to a specific setting. In the last scenario, we are free to choose without fear of penalty, for all things work together for good to those who love God and are called according to His purpose.

What's most important to remember at this stage is that each of us is called to serve a function that may be embodied in several different roles and exercised in several different settings. Being called to a role or a setting is an exception to the normal or common experience. It is the function of our ministry that will be assessed and weighed at the judgment seat of Christ.

Personal Assessment

What are your spiritual gifts?

What spiritual results have been produced in the exercise of your spiritual gifts?

How have others benefited from the exercise of your spiritual gifts?

What natural abilities do you possess (aptitudes, talents, personality, temperament)?
How have these natural abilities been demonstrated within your sphere of influence?

What skills have you acquired that might be used to further God's redemptive purposes?
What schooling or training have you received that could be used by God to further His Kingdom?

What work experience have you had that could be leveraged for God's purposes?
What vocational expertise have you gained that could be used for eternal ends?

What is your calling—the function God has called you to serve? Are you currently being led to rethink your contribution to the Kingdom's purposes? If so, how?

Chapter 11: Our Shaping

Does who you are determine what you do, or does what you do determine who you are? Your understanding of who you are in Christ will greatly determine how you live your life.

—*Neil T. Anderson*

Our Pattern

God develops leaders over a lifetime—and we have an important part in the process. Cooperation with God will lead to growth in character, competence, and alignment with God's design for us. In such collaboration, the integration of spiritual, ministerial, and strategic formation will help a leader finish well. Ignorance of these processes, outright resistance to them, or passive apathy toward them will result in stagnation and stunted growth. Leavenworth and Clinton identify three basic truths that form the basis for our growth, maturity, effectiveness, and influence as we progress in our development as Christian leaders: [422]

---

422 Richard Clinton and Paul Leavenworth, *Living and Leading Well* (Seattle: CreateSpace, 2013), xviii.

- God initiates development throughout our lives so that we will become more Christ-like.
- We can respond positively or negatively to God's sovereign initiation in our lives.
- If we respond positively, we grow in Christ-like character, maturity, effectiveness, and influence; but if we respond negatively, we will stagnate until we respond positively to God's initiation.

My mentor, J. Robert Clinton, identified six developmental phases God employs to develop followers and leaders. People progress through the phases at different rates, and in some situations the phases will overlap. Willful obstinacy or neglect will interfere with our development. As a result, we may not experience all six phases. God intends for us to realize our full potential. My dream is to crash through the gates of heaven exhausted and spent, having left everything on the field of ministry, with no regrets about having held anything back. My wife contends that there will be more than one exhausted angel relieved that his or her watch is over.

On the average, each developmental phase lasts approximately ten years and is punctuated by subphases lasting anywhere from one to six years. Foundational and inner growth take place in the early stages of development. Ministry- and life-maturing phases take place in the middle stage of development. In the latter stage, convergence and afterglow may be experienced. Few leaders reach convergence, and fewer yet attain afterglow. Provided God's development of them is not impeded by sin or some other issue, leaders in their late fifties or early sixties may reach convergence.

Sovereign Foundations (Phase I)

In this phase, which usually continues until conversion, very early foundations are laid—some good and maybe some hurtful, all used to foreshadow what is coming. In this early phase, God is concerned primarily with shaping the emerging leader's personality and character. He accomplishes this mainly through the family of origin, other social influences, and the historical context within which the emerging leader lives.

Leavenworth and Clinton acknowledge the less-than-favorable contexts we may experience: "He knows of our self-centeredness and what it will take to bring us to him. He allows us to be exposed to the devastating consequences of sin in our lives, relationships, societies, and world affairs so that we will recognize our need for him … Human heartache and tragedy can become the context for growth and blessing."[423]

Even in the midst of such circumstances, the early development of basic leadership skills may be present during this phase, as well as possible hints of the emerging leader's personal destiny. J. Robert Clinton makes the following observation: "Personality characteristics, both good and bad experiences, and the time context will be used by God. Character traits are embedded … and will be adapted and used by God."[424]

Inner-Life Growth (Phase II)

This phase normally begins at conversion and involves grounding believers in the basics and helping them learn to sustain their walk with Christ and become self-feeding servants of God. As a result of their growing relationship with God and the gradual formation of Christ-likeness in them, self-centeredness gives way to Christ-centeredness.

It is during this phase that the emerging leader establishes a more mature commitment to God, evidenced by the continued development of a Christ-like character. It is also during this phase that the emerging leader begins to reflect on his or her own potential for ministry, and the initial testing of leadership potential by God and others begins.

Circumstances, events, situations, and people create a laboratory of sorts to refine leaders. The shaping of a person, precipitated by these variables, is accomplished through means like *integrity checks, obedience checks, word checks*,[425] and *isolation*, whose use by God will continue into other phases.

- **integrity checks:** special tests that God initiates to reveal the true intentions of our hearts, and which, when passed, serve as a springboard for the expansion of our capacity to be trusted by God.

- **obedience checks:** special tests that reveal our willingness to obey God regardless of circumstances and apparent

---

423 Rom. 8:28–30.
424 Clinton, *Making of a Leader*, 28.
425 Leavenworth and Clinton, *Living and Leading Well*, xxi.

consequences, and which, when passed, lead to the realization of God's promises.

- **word checks:** special tests that reveal our ability to receive and understand a word from God and allow Him to work out the fulfillment of this word.

- **isolation:** a maturity-building process in which we are separated from normal activities for a time through a sickness, a crisis, a conviction, or an awareness that recalibration is essential to experiencing God in a new and deeper way.

These processes may be initiated by an "inconvenient moment" when we are not feeling particularly spiritual, are rushing to something else demanding our attention, or are interrupted by the need of another when seemingly more pressing matters are before us. God often does His greatest work through us at the inconvenient moments in our lives. Why? Such moments require our utter dependence on Him. Pay attention to the inconvenient moments: Resist the urge to speed past them. Stop and submit to the conviction of the Spirit. Do what God is compelling you to do, even though you are not prepared for it.

Ministry Maturing (Phase III)

In this phase, a leader experiences a variety of ministry assignments—formal (an established position on staff), nonformal (an intern or apprentice), and informal (a volunteer)—and God is primarily working *in* rather than *through* the leader, with each experience adding to his or her awareness of giftedness and calling. (Calling generally emerges in one's forties.) During this phase, the leader is given growing responsibility for ministry and leadership assignments. Training is more incidental and often not intentional. In conjunction with this, the leader becomes increasingly aware of his or her giftedness and seeks to develop both relational and task-oriented ministry skills that augment that set of gifts.

In this phase, believers are thrust into new settings with which they have little experience. These settings help hone their gifts—spiritual gifts, natural abilities, and acquired skills—as they identify and apply them. They begin to see what they are good at and what they are not, what they are called to do and what should be left to others. This process of exploration can take place in any context, including a vocational setting, a ministry, the marketplace, and other service venues.

A leader's gift mix begins to take shape at this point. His or her reach of influence begins to expand, becoming more extensive, intense, and comprehensive. There will also be many challenges in terms of tasks, relationships, conflicts, and authority and submission to authority. Remember, character is forged on the anvil of difficulty. During this phase, God is quietly convincing the person to see that we minister out of who we are, our beingness.

Also during this phase, the leader begins to feel God's calling. He or she may even enter formal training such as graduate school or seminary; seek out nonformal venues, such as conferences, seminars, or workshops, for further development; or shadow an accomplished leader to learn firsthand how to live and serve.

In addition to the process items in the Inner-Life Growth phase, God introduces other chisels to shape a person, such as the following:[426]

- **ministry task:** an assignment from God that primarily tests a person's faithfulness and obedience, but that often also allows application of ministry gifts to a task requiring closure, accountability, and evaluation.

- **ministry skill:** refers to the definite acquisition of one or more identifiable skills which facilitate a ministry assignment.

- **ministry conflict:** those instances in ministry when a leader learns lessons (positive and negative) regarding the nature of conflict, possible ways to resolve or avoid conflict, ways to creatively use conflict, or how God shapes people through conflict.

- **authority insights:** refers to those instances in ministry when a leader learns important lessons through positive or negative experiences about submission to authority, authority structures, the authenticity or power bases underlying authority, authority conflict, or how to exercise authority.

---

426 J. Robert Clinton, *Leadership Emergence Theory* (Altadena: Barnabas Publisher, 1989), 137, 157, 205, 172, 208, 165, 222, 220.

- **leadership backlash:** the reaction of followers, other leaders within a group, and/or Christians outside the group, to the ramifications of some course of action taken by a leader. The situation is used to test the leader's perseverance, clarity of vision, and faith.

- **giftedness discovery:** any significant discovery or development of gifts, and the event, person, or reflection process that was instrumental in bringing about the discovery or development.

- **faith challenge:** an instance in ministry when a leader is challenged to take a leap of faith is met with divine affirmation and ministerial achievement that increase his or her willingness to trust in God in future ministry.

- **destiny revelation:** a grouping of incidents or process items with an unusual sense of God's presence working in them— significant acts, people, providential circumstances, or timing that confirm a person's destiny and perhaps begin to clarify its nature.

God uses other process items to shape us, but these are the more dominant and frequently seen items during this phase of development.

Life Maturing (Phase IV)

In this phase, life crises and new limitations begin to drive believers deeper into their faith. God begins to work through them; proficiency in ministry gives way to a call for deeper intimacy, and often a revisiting of past struggles. During this phase, leaders come to terms with the fact that ministry is inextricably linked to identity, that doing and being can never be separated in the context of Christian leadership. This realization helps them develop a mature, biblical philosophy of ministry that finds a firm foundation in obedience to God. They can then use their spiritual authority to help followers navigate both positive and negative situations.

A personal sense of calling becomes clearer. Calling has more to do with "wiring" (life purpose, committed passion, and giftedness), the function we are called to serve, rather than the role we fill or the location in which we serve. A biblically based ministry philosophy takes shape during this phase and includes core values, principles, proven strategies, and axiomatic truths that have been learned along the way.

The operational ministry philosophy is the conduit through which leaders minister. It forms the foundation on which they stand and the platform from which they serve. Such a philosophy develops over time and is enriched by a leader's giftedness, learning, experiences, and imitation. (Imitation operationalizes Hebrews 13:7–8: "Remember your leaders, who spoke the word of God to you. Consider the outcome of their way of life and imitate their faith. Jesus Christ is the same yesterday and today and forever.")

In this phase, a person uses his or her giftedness with authority and power and knows the best contexts in which to exercise it. Mature fruitfulness—with attendant spiritual results—is evident. Clinton says, "The principle that 'ministry flows out of being' has new significance as the leader's character mellows and matures ... The leader's experiential understanding of God is being developed. Communion with God becomes foundational; it is more important than success in ministry."[427]

God uses several types of processing during this phase:

- **ideal influence-mix discovery:** any significant discovery or use of the combination of influences that results from the harmonizing of major and minor convergence factors.

- **ideal role discovery:** any significant discovery or use of a role that enhances a leader's giftedness and maximizes the effectiveness of the influence mix.

- **gifted power:** a specific instance of using a spiritual gift through which the Holy Spirit is channeling power.

- **sovereign guidance:** God's guiding intervention in the life and ministry of a leader through the unique alignment of circumstances which He uses to develop the emerging leader.

- **negative preparation:** the special processing through which God uses the negative (events, people, conflict, persecution, or

---

427 J. Robert Clinton, *The Making of a Leader* (Colorado Springs: NavPress, 2012), 39.

experiences) to free a person from a situation so he or she can enter the next phase of development.

- **ministry affirmation:** a special kind of destiny experience in which God gives approval to a leader in terms of some ministry assignment in particular or some ministry experience in general, which results in a renewed sense of purpose.

Convergence (Phase V)

Ministry experiences and a deeper walk with Christ begin pointing a believer to a unique and fulfilling way of ministering. Here the leader moves toward his or her ideal role in ministry, a role that fits the leader's calling, passion, giftedness, and style. This is the most highly productive and effective period of ministry, and visionary leaders use this position of effectiveness as a platform from which to multiply themselves in emerging leaders.

I define convergence as a situation in which 80 percent of who you are overlaps 80 percent of what you do. Convergence involves the coming together of who God shaped you to be and your sense that "I was born for this." This phase involves "the mature coming together of inner-life preparation, ministry maturing, and life maturing to fulfill your destiny or ultimate purpose. Convergence involves the coming together of five major and five minor factors. The major factors include dependence upon God, giftedness, ministry philosophy, role, and influence. The minor factors include our experience, focus, methodology, destiny, and legacy."[428]

Reaching convergence means that you are operating from your sweet spot. Everything seems to be clicking. You feel the power of God working through you; it humbles you and scares you at times. Your script often gives way to the Spirit's leading. You quickly recognize God's presence in a situation and adjust to what He is doing at the moment. You can sense God's movement in a context and can quickly align what you are saying or doing accordingly. You feel tuned to the heart of God.

According to Clinton, leaders experiencing convergence use the best they have to offer and are freed from ministries for which they are not gifted or suited. Clinton also states that many leaders do not experience convergence because they are hindered by their own lack of personal

428 Clinton and Leavenworth, *Living and Leading Well*, xxv.

development. At other times, he says, an organization may hinder a leader by keeping him or her in a limiting position. In some cases, leaders are promoted to roles that take them out of convergence. In convergence, a leader's potential is maximized, and so leaders selecting a new role or context should take into consideration whether it would allow them to have maximum effectiveness.[429]

Process items used by God during this phase might include the following:

- **double confirmation:** when God makes clear His will by giving direct guidance to a leader and then reinforcing it through someone totally independent and unaware of the leader's guidance.

- **divine affirmation:** a special kind of destiny experience in which God gives approval to a leader so that the leader has a renewed sense of ultimate purpose and a refreshed desire to continue serving God.

- **destiny fulfillment:** a grouping of process items—significant acts, people, providential circumstances, or timing—which represent the completion of destiny processing that has gone on previously.

- **destiny revelation:** a grouping of incidents or process items with an unusual sense of God's presence working in them— significant acts, people, providential circumstances, or timing that confirm a future destiny and perhaps begin to clarify its nature.

- **power:** demonstrations of God's intervention that convince followers that God is indeed supporting a leader in his or her ministry.

- **spiritual authority discovery:** any significant discovery, insight, or experience that advances the development of a leader's spiritual authority.

---

429 Clinton, *The Making of a Leader*, 39.

- **mentoring:** the process by which someone with a serving, giving, encouraging attitude (the mentor) sees undeveloped leadership potential in someone else (the protégé) and promotes or otherwise significantly influences the realization of that potential.

- **word:** refers to an instance in which a leader receives a word from God that affects his or her guidance, commitment, decision making, personal value system, spiritual formation, spiritual authority, or ministry philosophy.

Afterglow (Phase VI)

In this phase, which few leaders attain, limited ministry happens. This phase is characterized by the satisfaction and influence available to the leader who has substantially completed his or her life calling or destiny. The leader's stature—what he or she has accomplished in life, and the integrity and authenticity he or she enjoys—is often used as an encouragement to others.

In this last period of life, the leader takes time to enjoy the fruits of a life that is finishing well, all the while using the influence gained from a reputable life of ministry to enable others to go even further in their service and leadership. Leaders at this point in life are often looked to by other leaders as sources of blessing, encouragement, and validation. Mentoring others becomes a dominant feature of their ministry. What they have learned, how they have lived their lives, the observable fruits of their lives, and their life-giving legacies have powerful influence directly, indirectly, and organizationally.

Clinton observes that in this phase, "the fruit of a lifetime of ministry and growth culminates in an era of recognition and indirect influence at broad levels … leaders have built up a lifetime of contacts and continue to exert influence in these relationships … they are sought out because of their consistent track record in following God."[430]

---

430 Ibid., 40.

Developmental Tasks

J. Robert Clinton has identified developmental tasks for each stage. In the *early stage*, when sovereign foundations and inner-life growth phases occur, the following development tasks are suggested:

- Mold embryonic leadership personality.
- Mold inner character.
- Initiate discovery of leadership potential.
- Facilitate committal to a lifetime of leadership.

During the *middle stage*, when ministry maturing and life maturing occur, the following development tasks are recommended:

- Facilitate development of leadership potential.
- Develop ministry skills, including the initial discovery and use of spiritual gifts.
- Develop ministry values that uniquely fit the leader.
- Recognize any "mini-convergence"—that is, factors that work together to increase effectiveness and a sense of accomplishment.

During the latter stage, when convergence and afterglow occur, the following development tasks are stressed:

- Develop maturity in spiritual formation (character), ministry formation (competence), and strategic formation (congruence).
- Develop spiritual authority as the foundational powerbase.
- Maximize leadership effectiveness toward convergence.
- Provide guidance toward convergence roles.

Personal Assessment

As you look at your life, where would you place yourself along the continuum of the development phases?

What is currently keeping you from advancing to the next phase? What do you intend to do to eliminate any hindrances?

What role or context will give you an opportunity to advance along the continuum and take advantage of what you have to offer?

What process items have you experienced so far? How have you responded to God's processing thus far?

What plan will you put into action that will support God's development in your life? What decisions must you make that will bring you into alignment with God's purposes?

Our Authority[431]

Early on I referred to "spiritual authority"; now I think further discussion of the subject is warranted. When we examine secular and Christian leadership across the spectrum, one common concept emerges: influence. *Webster's Ninth New Collegiate Dictionary* defines *influence* as follows:

- an emanation of spiritual or moral force
- the act or power of producing an effect without apparent exertion of force or direct exercise of command
- corrupt interference with authority for personal gain
- the power or capacity of causing an effect in indirect or intangible ways
- one that exerts influence

Power, on the other hand, is best understood by first describing what it is not. Power is not the production of intended effects, the ability to apply force, the intended and successful control of others, or the extent to which A can get B to do something B would not normally do. Power is

---

431 Much of what follows is taken from J. Robert Clinton's research in leadership emergence theory. The information is used by his permission.

the resource that enables a person to induce compliance from others or to influence them—his or her influence potential.

When we think about power and the exercise of power, we must consider several concepts: power bases, power resources, authority, power styles or forms, power types, and spheres of influence.

Generally speaking, the power base from which a leader exercises his or her influence draws its utility from underlying resources. The degree to which a leader possesses such power and the influence he or she wields by exercising it is called "authority." A leader's style of exercising power can range from the use of force, manipulation, or persuasion to the use of authority. The scope of one's authority may include direct influence, organizational influence, and indirect influence.

Several types of power may be used to influence others, from coercive power to spiritual power; spiritual power and authority is the preferred type for ministry leaders. As a leader grows, his or her spheres of influence—direct, indirect, and organizational—also grow.

Power Bases

J. Robert Clinton suggests that a leader leads from a power base, which he defines as "the source of credibility, power differential, or resources which enables a leader (power holder) to have authority to exercise influence on followers." He essentially identifies three possible power bases:

Positional Power is induced compliance from others because of one's position in the organization and the degree of power delegated by the organization to that position. The extent to which a manager develops a rapport with and the confidence and trust of senior management will determine management's willingness to empower that manager's position.

Positional power, especially in ministry, has a short shelf life. If positional power doesn't move to personal power in a relatively short period of time, the leader's influence and authority will wane. People may follow a leader who derives his or her authority solely from a job description, but over time they will do so begrudgingly. And if that situation continues, especially if the leader continually reminds followers of his or her authority, followers might become resentful.

Personal Power derives from a leader's personality and behavior and the power delegated to him or her by those being led. This kind of power depends on the confidence and trust a leader generates in the people he or she is attempting to influence. It usually takes longer to build this kind of power.

While positional power is delegated from the top down, personal power is given from the bottom up. People follow good leaders, and good leadership happens, when personal power is developed based on the leader's charisma, expertise, or character.

Spiritual Power exercised by a leader is backed by the spiritual authority of God. As defined by Clinton, "spiritual authority is that characteristic of a God-anointed leader developed upon an experiential power base which enables a leader to influence followers through persuasion, force of modeling, and moral expertise towards God's purposes."

An individual may begin with positional power, but over time, if the leader handles the position properly, he or she will earn positional power from the confidence and trust of those being led. Positional power is authority delegated down. Personal power is authority delegated up. Spiritual power, however, is a by-product of a deep, abiding reliance upon God, who is the source of such authority and who bestows it on whomever He chooses based on an intimate relationship with that leader.

A leader's power base comes from one or more power resources, defined by Clinton as "those individual and collective assets such as organization, money, reputation, personal appeal, manipulative skills, interpersonal skills, kinds of knowledge, information, the indwelling Holy Spirit, and giftedness."

A leader's ability to influence followers to go places they would not go on their own may come, in part, from an ability to manipulate or persuade through personal appeal. Then again, it may be due to interpersonal skills, expertise in a certain area, or the weight of the leader's reputation. Obviously, the base of spiritual power must have one indispensable resource, the indwelling Holy Spirit.

Whether a leader has positional, personal, or spiritual power, the degree to which he or she possesses such power and the amount of influence wielded in the exercise of that power is called "authority." According to Bobby Clinton, *authority* is a leader's right to exercise influence over followers within a certain realm. For a spiritual leader, the field of influence has to do with God's purposes and His directions for accomplishing specific aims that He reveals.

Authority with regard to positional power comes with the position and is enforced by the organization from which it was assigned. Authority with regard to personal power is earned over time, given to a leader by those being led. Authority with regard to spiritual power is not earned, but temporarily assigned by God Himself based on a vibrant relationship with the leader over time. The degree of authority a leader possesses is directly proportional to the credibility the leader has with those he or she wishes to lead.

Power Styles

Power styles (or power forms) are the approaches a leader may use to influence others. In exercising a certain power style, a leader hopes to bring about compliance from followers. There are essentially four power styles:

- *force:* This style refers to the use of physical and psychic influence to gain compliance. The leader influences followers by exercising physical strength over them, or uses psychological measures to make them submit to his or her will.

- *manipulation:* This style refers to influencing a follower by covert measures. In other words, the follower isn't aware of the leader's intentions and therefore does not necessarily have the freedom to exercise moral responsibility in the situation.

- *persuasion:* This style refers to the use of arguments, appeals, or exhortations to gain compliance from followers. The difference between manipulation and persuasion is that the latter gives the follower freedom to exercise moral responsibility.

- *authority:* This style refers to various means a leader can use to influence followers, including coercion, connection, inducement through rewards, positional legitimacy, competency through expertise, critical access to information, and spiritual authority.

The style used to exercise influence often depends on a leader's temperament, leadership style, learned practices, modeling of other respected leaders, and spiritual maturity. More specifically, a leader's central belief system, core values, worldview (perceptual attitudes), and primary motives will often influence his or her style.

For example, if a leader has a driver-type temperament, he or she may gravitate to force or manipulation. If a leader has an expressive or amiable temperament, he or she may use persuasion to influence others. Or a leader may admire another leader and therefore adapt or adopt his or her style accordingly.

Our central belief system (Christian, secular) establishes our core values. Those core values, the principles we live by, inform the set of perceptual attitudes or worldview we use to interpret and understand our observations of life around us. Our attitudes condition the primary motives behind our observable behaviors. All these internal factors help determine our use of one leadership style over another.

Finally, the status and vibrancy of our relationship with Christ, our active pursuit of meaningful fellowship with the Father, and our reliance upon empowerment from the Holy Spirit will determine in great measure the degree of spiritual authority we hold and the spiritual influence we have over a specific group of God's people in accordance with His purposes.

Power Types

Let's look at eight types of power. The first four are generally associated with those holding positional power and authority, while the last four pertain to those holding personal power and authority.

- *Coercive power* is the perceived ability to provide sanctions, punishment, or consequences for not performing. The leader obtains compliance by threat of force or punishment. This type of power is not always a bad thing. For instance, when there is danger involved or someone's safety is at stake, orders must be followed. The military in war operates from this type of power base. In the church, a pastor or ministry director may use coercive power when a child's welfare is threatened or legal sanctions must be adhered to for his or her protection. This type of power is eroded when used continually but without delivering the punishment promised or threatened—when a person is repeatedly warned but no action is taken. The threat of consequences diminishes because there is no follow-through with penalties for violating policy or procedures.

- *Connection power* is the perceived association of the leader with influential persons or organizations. In other words, the perceived influence of this individual is directly proportional to the relationship he or she holds with those in higher positions in the structure, those who run the organization or possess power to sanction activity with impunity. This type of power is eroded when people begin to see that the higher connection does not make any disciplinary interventions or provide any favors or sanctions. If word gets out that the leader does not garner respect from those above him or her, that leader's authority quickly wanes, resulting in reduced influence.

- *Inducement (reward) power* is the perceived ability to provide things that people would like to have. The leader obtains compliance by promising a reward or some other gain. Leaders who use this type of power must be able to deliver the goods. I have personally witnessed the demise of many leaders who promised their followers more than they could deliver. If you make a promise, keep it—or don't make it at all. This type of power is also eroded when everyone gets the same reward regardless of performance, or when reward is not earned, but meted out based on seniority or whose "turn" it is.

- *Legitimate power* is the perception that it is appropriate for the leader to make decisions because of his or her title, role, or position in the organization. The leader obtains compliance by using influence commensurate with followers' expectations for someone in his or her position. This type of power base often fails when those being led can choose whether to cooperate. This type of power is eroded when a leader fails to make decisions that people think he or she should make, given his or her position. When leaders fail to exercise the authority given them, these failures erode respect and compliance by followers.

- *Competency power* is the perception that the leader possesses expertise or information necessary to the success of the organization. This particular category can be subdivided into two forms: information power and expert power.

- *Information power* is the perceived access to or possession of useful information. Leaders who effectively use this type of power base are in the know. They know how to get needed information or possess an institutional understanding of how to get things done: they know the right people, the right procedure, the applicable policy, and the informal rules of the road. In general, they have a working knowledge of the system. This type of power is eroded when the leader gives away information to people whose goals are not organizational goals, or they use information to impress followers and garner their admiration and respect. It also erodes when a leader claims to know more than he or she really does and uses such erroneous information to get others to comply.

- *Expert power* is the perception that the leader has relevant education, experience, and expertise. It is also called "competent authority"—the leader obtains or can expect (but not demand) compliance by virtue of acknowledged expertise in some limited field. These subject-matter experts wield significant authority because they possess knowledge and demonstrated expertise in areas needed or desired by those being led. This type of power is eroded when the leader gives away expertise to people whose goals are not organizational goals or holds back his or her expertise to serve selfish interests. It also erodes when the leader shows favoritism by sharing his or her expertise only with those who are in good standing with or are favored by the leader.

- *Personal (referent) power* derives from the perceived attractiveness of interacting with a leader. It is also called "personal authority"—that is, the leader obtains or expects compliance (but cannot demand it) by virtue of his or her attractive personal characteristics: charisma, leadership qualities, motivational abilities, or personal communication skill. This type of power base is eroded when the leader "strokes" those who are not performing. If difficult employees are coddled or deferred to for the purpose of getting them to perform, and therefore a sense of fairness is not evident, this type of power base can be severely limited.

Power Preference

Spiritual power is the influence that followers confer upon a leader because they perceive him or her as a spiritual person. Spiritual authority is the characteristic of a God-anointed leader developed through experience; it enables him or her to influence followers through persuasion, modeling, and moral expertise. It includes a combination of persuasion and legitimate, competent (expert/information), and personal (referent) power.

Have you ever been in the presence of someone who emanates spiritual authority? He or she wears it like a mantle; you sense it and feel its influence. Two people quickly come to mind: Billy Graham and Mother Teresa. In my own experience, Bobby Clinton exudes spiritual power. People who have it don't have to tell you. If they do, they don't have it. You can "feel" spiritual authority in someone who possesses it.

According to Bobby Clinton, spiritual power and its authority come from a life and ministry that demonstrate the presence of God. Credibility is demonstrated in a life when a leader *is* what he or she teaches. Credibility comes from a ministry that manifests results that are from God. A leader with spiritual authority knows God and His ways and demonstrates this in life. Spiritual authority is a major power base of godly leadership. Followers perceive leaders' spirituality in terms of character, the demonstration of power, and the perceived knowledge of God and His purposes.

Spiritual power and authority come to the leader in three major ways:

- through an experiential knowledge of God and deep experiences with God
- through a life that models godliness characterized by evidence of spiritual fruit

- through gifted power, a clear testimony to divine intervention in one's ministry

In other words, spiritual power and its authority are not earned by the leader. They are by-products of the leader's experiential knowledge of God (versus a knowledge about God); his or her deep experience with God; the manifestation of the fruit of the Spirit in his or her life; and God's imprimatur, or seal of approval, on the leader, as evidenced by His personal presence in and through who the leader is and what he or she does.

Here's another way to look at it: spiritual power and authority are leased to the leader under certain conditions. The lease can be revoked at any time. One dominant reason for revoking the lease is because the leader used it to manipulate others for the purposes of his or her private agenda. The abuse of spiritual authority is particularly loathsome because followers are hurt deeply as a result.

Having studied spiritual power and authority and the leaders who have manifested them, Clinton makes the following observations:

- *essential source:* One who exercises spiritual power and authority in ministry must recognize the essential source of all authority—God!

- *delegated authority:* God's delegated authority is His authority and does not belong to the person exercising it. That person is just a channel.

- *responsibility:* The person through whom that delegated authority is channeled is responsible to God for how that authority is exercised.

- *recognition:* A leader is one who recognizes God's authority manifested in real-life situations.

- *submission:* Subjection to authority means that a person is subject to God Himself and not to the channel through which the authority comes.

- *rebellion:* Rebellion against authority means that a person is not subjecting him or herself to God, though it may appear that the person is rejecting some impure manifestation of God's authority through the human channel.

- *sensitivity:* People who are under God's authority look for and recognize spiritual authority and willingly place themselves under it.

- *ultimate purpose:* Spiritual authority is never exercised for one's own benefit, but for those under it.

- *power base:* A person in spiritual authority does not have to insist on obedience or manipulate or coerce. Followers are responsible for recognizing and following God's spiritual authority in leaders.

- *defense:* God is responsible for defending spiritual authority.

Clinton has also identified six characteristics and limits of spiritual power and authority. Spiritual authority has its ultimate source in Christ. It is His authority and presence in us that legitimates our authority. Accountability to this final authority is essential.

Spiritual authority rests upon an experiential power base. A leader's personal experiences with God, and the accumulated wisdom and development that come through them, are the reason why followers allow that leader to influence their lives. The genuineness of spiritual authority is confirmed in the believer by the presence and ministry of the Holy Spirit who authenticates that experiential power base through the leader.

Spiritual authority influences by persuasion. That influence is granted by virtue of legitimate authority and buttressed by other authority forms such as competent (expert) authority and personal (referent) authority.

Spiritual authority must be used for the ultimate good of the followers, as prescribed by the basic Pauline leadership principle in 2 Corinthians 10:8. Momentary judgments made by leaders must meet this criterion.

A leader's spiritual authority is best judged over time by gauging the spiritual development of his or her followers. Using coercion and manipulation will usually reproduce similar behavior in followers. A leader with spiritual authority will produce mature followers who will make responsible, moral choices because they have learned to do so.

A leader using spiritual authority recognizes submission to God, who is the ultimate authority. Authority is representative; God is therefore the responsible agent for defending spiritual authority. A person leading by spiritual authority does not have to insist on obedience. Obedience is the moral responsibility of the follower. Disobedience—that is, rebellion against spiritual authority—means that a follower is not subject to God Himself. He or she will answer to God for that. The leader can rest upon God's vindication if it is necessary.

Considerations of influence, power, and spiritual authority are unavoidable if we seek to serve our Lord as leaders. Our objective should be to possess spiritual authority derived by spending time with its Giver, our Lord. Remember, spiritual authority is not earned; it is given as a result of the following:

- an experiential knowledge of God and deep experiences with God
- a life that models godliness characterized by evidence of spiritual fruit
- gifted power, a clear testimony to divine intervention in one's ministry

Personal Assessment

What power base are you operating from—positional, personal, or spiritual? What power base would those you lead say you possess?

What power style is most closely aligned with your own? How do you exercise influence over those you lead? What power style do you exercise in your home?

What power types have you employed? Under what circumstances were they employed? Which power type would you prefer to employ? Why?

Do you personally know someone who exudes spiritual power?
What is it about his or her life that leads you to conclude that he or she has spiritual power?

Do you know someone who possesses spiritual authority?
Under whose spiritual authority have you placed your life?

How do you plan to provide an environment in which spiritual authority will emerge and be a primary base of influence for you?

Chapter 12: Our Story

Thank you for placing this dream in my heart. Thank you for this passion. Thank you for the desire to use my gift to bring glory to You. Father, there are people in this world who will try their best to trample on my dream, hide my light, and stop my progress. But, I know what you have planned for my life, no man can stop. Father, give me laser focus. Give me the wisdom to go to you for strength through prayer, reading your word, and worship. Father, give me the strength to complete my assignment and bless me to one day hear these three words from your mouth, "Job well done." In Jesus name. Amen.

—*@pastornaccm*

Regardless of our age, each of us has a unique story to tell. From the moment we were born to this present day, our lives have been filled with circumstances, events, and people that have shaped our stories. Some of the situations we've faced have been good, and some have been bad; some have been encouraging and some have been discouraging; some have been supportive and some have been hurtful; some have been of our doing and some have been done to us.

The story is told of a nearsighted art connoisseur who would spend hours at the local museum examining works of art. He especially appreciated vivid and colorful paintings in which contrasts were obvious; after all, he could only see them close up. One day as he was appreciating a multicolored painting, a bystander came and stood alongside him. The stranger remarked that such paintings reminded him of life: full of contrasts between dark and light. We can travel through life bemoaning the dark times and celebrating the light times, but what makes us appreciate life more deeply is the realization that it is full of dark colors and bright colors, and that together they form an amazingly rich picture.

Admittedly, I could do without some of the darkness I have experienced in my life, but I understand that both the dark times and the light times have made me who I am today. I am convinced that in all things God works for the good of those who love Him and have been called according to His purpose.[432] To this day, however, I wonder how certain circumstances, events, or people could possibly work together for good.

But I am not the artist who painted the picture. I have to trust in Him. He uses the paint He has available from our life's experiences and adds some of His own, creating different hues. He applies those hues as only a master painter can. The result is a thing of beauty—when He is done with it. A quality painting takes time to produce, even though the sketch may have been drawn a long time ago. Even before sketching, an artist has in mind what he or she wants to convey when he or she takes pencil to paper. Sometime later, the painting is seen for what it is: a work of art by a master painter who took what was available at the time, mixed in his pigments, and brushed onto canvas a breathtaking painting of a life.

Only in retrospect, when the pain of a bad experience dissipates and ceases to have unhealthy control of our emotions, do we begin to appreciate what we have become as a result: stronger, more persevering, more empathetic, more reflective, possessing a deeper and more mature faith, and more convinced than ever that we will not be defined by events

---

432 Rom. 8:28.

that have brought great misery. Certainly we do not want to repeat the negative experience, but we come to realize that the contrast between light and dark can be used to bring about something of value not only to ourselves, but to others.

Our Narrative

Writing out in short form the story of your life will help put your life experiences into perspective. There are situations that shaped you that you may have forgotten or that are buried deep in your subconscious, and they may still affect you today even though you don't remember the specifics.

Some life events have undue influence over us, but when brought to the light of day cease to have the control they once did. When time removes us from the circumstances, we have an opportunity to be more objective.

I have taken many people through the process of recording their stories in written narrative form. I generally start by warning them that they will experience a range of emotions in journaling their story, especially as they recount painful experiences. In every case, once they write their story, they are glad they did. Many are released from the power of negative events, are reminded of the positive things that happened, and see the journaling experience as somewhat therapeutic.

Journaling your story is the first step in developing a personal graphic of your historical timeline. Once the significant or critical circumstances, events, and people have been placed on your timeline, the groupings of which are demarcated by transition moments from one period of your life to the next, you can add God's processing and derive the lessons learned—all of which will help you develop perspective for the road ahead.

I am indebted to Terry Walling of Leader Breakthru[433] for granting permission to use guidelines for journaling and developing a personal timeline. I have used these materials countless times as I've taken people through the process. The experience has proven richly rewarding for those who have completed it.

I cannot improve on Terry's introductory words: "Today, more than ever, believers like you are searching for ways to recognize the hand of God

---

433 Terry Walling, *Perspective Workbook: Personal Timeline* (Anaheim: Church Resource Ministries), 1–31.

at work in their lives. To see again that the God of the universe is personally involved in our lives, brings hope and a greater desire to persevere through the turbulent days in which they live. A personal time-line is a big-picture overview of your life. It is a chronological map of a believer's development, highlighting those critical incidents and circumstances that God has used to shape character and purpose. Developing (your story and) personal time-line will help you gain a:

- Greater understanding of your personal contribution and roles.
- Greater capacity to assess future ministry opportunities.
- Greater capacity to understand and process difficult times.
- Greater capacity to help others understand their development."[434]

Terry also reminds us that "the heart cry of every genuine believer is to stand at the end and hear Christ say, 'well done thou good and faithful servant.' It is the reason behind seeking to live a focused life. A simple definition of finishing well: To be more passionate and committed to Christ at the end of one's life than in the beginning. Perspective begins your journey toward living a focused life that pleases God, and finishes well."[435]

To begin the process of writing *your* story, brainstorm about the circumstances, events, and people that have shaped your life. Don't bother to record all the incidents in your life, but just the ones that had a shaping influence on you. Some incidents will be positive, while others will be negative. Either way, if they had a significant impact on you, add them to your list.

Keep in mind the following descriptions:

- The *events* of your life that have had an impact on who you are today, such as graduation, a new job, a school incident, a move to a new city, a promotion, a conflict, a challenge, an achievement, the birth of a child, a calling, the loss of a loved one, marriage, divorce, etc.
- The *people* who influenced and shaped your life, such as friends, families, relatives, pastors, classmates, your spouse, teachers,

434 Ibid., 3.
435 Ibid., 4.

heroes, mentors, church members, work associates, antagonists, protagonists, etc.

- The significant *circumstances* that have affected your life direction, including any incidents or statements made about you before your birth, or circumstances like childhood experiences, conflicts with others, societal changes, spiritual conversion or ministry, your education or intellectual pursuits, service, etc.

Sometimes it is hard to distinguish between events and circumstances. Events are usually episodic or singular happenings, while circumstances are a series of related activities. An *event* might be a promotion, a marriage proposal, an accident, an accomplishment, a new job, being laid off or fired, some special certification, or passing a test. A *circumstance* might be ongoing struggles, family dynamics, spiritual maturation, being coached, suffering chastisement, being discipled, or developing a skill or competence. A simple example: an *event* would be selecting a mentor; a *circumstance* would be being mentored.

I encourage you to take out three sheets of paper. On the first page write Significant Circumstances. On the second page write Significant Events. And on the third page write Significant People. Brainstorm about the critical or significant incidents of your life and write them down under the appropriate heading. Once you've made those random lists, put them in sequential or chronological order. Above all, take your time.

Once the lists are complete, you are ready to start putting them in story form, a chronological narrative not to exceed five pages. Once again, not every incident in your life will be recorded, only those that are significant and have shaped who you are today. Be open and honest, including both positive and negative situations. As you write your narrative, other incidents will come to mind, things you haven't thought about for years. Revise your story accordingly.

Your narrative summary and the lists you prepared will be the resource you need to start putting your personal timeline together. The entire process will make you more sensitive to God's shaping activity, help you realize your potential more quickly, make you more capable of making good decisions, and give you a clearer focus on factors that will help you finish well.

Our Timeline

Walling states that certain assumptions undergird timelines: "When Christ calls a believer He intends to develop them to their full potential. Each believer is individually responsible for his or her own development, as opposed to a spouse, pastor or church leader. God continually develops a believer. Effective Christians are shaped through times of spiritual renewal and formation. Every believer operates from a set of convictions and values. Focused living comes from learning to identify these values and convictions from the past and use these to provide guidance into the future."[436]

You can develop a personal timeline using an Excel spreadsheet, mind-mapping software, or old-fashioned tools—poster board and Post-it notes.

1. Using your lists and narrative, jot down *positive* shaping incidents (people, events, or circumstances), one each on a Post-it or cell on a spreadsheet. Use one color (e.g., green) for each incident. On a computer you can choose a specific color for the font or a colored shade for the cell on a spreadsheet. Place the Post-it notes randomly on the board or put them in cells.

2. Using your lists and narrative, jot down *negative* shaping incidents (people, events, or circumstances), one each on a Post-it or cell on a spreadsheet, again using one color (e.g., yellow) for each incident. Place the Post-it notes randomly on the board or put the incidents in cells.

3. Some episodes in our lives are both positive and negative or are neither, but have shaped us nevertheless. If an incident has *positive and negative* features, use a third distinctive color (e.g., purple). Place the Post-it notes randomly on the board or put the incidents in cells.

4. Arrange the Post-it notes or cells in *chronological order*, with the earliest memory on the top left and moving down, leaving space at the bottom, and then moving back up to the top and repeating the process until all the incidents are represented on the chart.

5. Now that the timeline is organized chronologically, divide your life, as represented by the incidents, into *three to five phases or chapters,*

---

436 Ibid., 14.

each of which represents a distinct era in your life. You might arrange them using the nomenclature of the generalized development phases we discussed earlier (i.e., sovereign foundations, inner-life growth, ministry maturing, life maturing, etc.). Or you may choose to partition your chart by major incidents that moved you from one life stage to another. In this case, determine a title for each era. Try to have three to five.

6. As you review each era, determine what *lessons* you learned and record them at the bottom of your chart. Consider the following questions to uncover lessons learned.

- *What was God trying to teach me during this chapter of my life?*
- *What are some important lessons that God has taught me concerning my character?*
- *What character traits have I learned to value the most?*
- *What important lessons has God taught me about my uniqueness as a child of God?*
- *What important lessons has God taught me concerning my effectiveness in serving Him?*
- *What are my core convictions about people and relationships?*
- *What are my core convictions about the church and ministry?*
- *What important lessons and insights has God taught me from my painful moments?*
- *If I could describe my passion for ministry in one sentence, what would it be?*

From lessons learned we derive insights from which we will develop our ministry philosophy—the framework from which we will operate and the foundation of understanding we will employ as we fulfill our calling.

Our Processing

All followers of Christ experience God's processing in their lives. His processing can be a chisel that shapes us into the image of Christ. His processing can be a scalpel that removes spiritual disease preventing our growth. His processing can be a tuning fork that tunes our hearts to His.

His processing can be a wrench that tightens down our beliefs and values. His processing can be a caliper that measures our growth.

Walling provides further clarification: "Process items are key instruments God uses to shape an individual. The concept of processing is central to the study of lifelong development. Process items take many forms. They are used by God to indicate issues for greater growth, expand potential vision and passion, confirm role and ministry responsibility, and direct the believer to God's appointed contribution. Not everything in an individual's life is a process item—it is the significant, identifiable items, where it does appear that God has used it to form a believer's life or ministry."[437]

Process items are the ways and means God uses to develop a person's character, competence, and congruence with how He has wired us, all of which is to be leveraged for His redemptive purposes in the world. Bobby Clinton and his team of researchers have identified more than fifty process items. Different process items accomplish different ends, all to help a person reach his or her designed potential. **Appendix F: Process Items** includes a complete list of Clinton's process items.

For our immediate purposes, I'll describe ten common process items to be considered for placement on your personal timeline. They are divided into two groups. The first five items deal with God's ongoing processing throughout a believer's life, and they are recurring. The second five deal with conflict or negative processing; they tend to be situational and often lead to reevaluation and new development.[438]

- **integrity check (IC):** a test God uses to evaluate the heart and consistency of inner convictions with outward actions (temptation, conflict, persecution, values check, follow-through).

- **word check (WC):** tests the capacity to hear from God through His Word and apply insights to life situations (personal and ministry guidance, submission, lordship, direction).

- **divine contact (DC):** the presence of a key person at a crucial moment to help ensure ongoing growth and development

---

437 Ibid., 21.
438 Ibid., 22.

(ministry guidance and challenge, an open door, new paradigms).

- **faith challenge (FC):** tests someone's willingness to take steps of faith and grow in his or her capacity to trust God (ministry crossroads, decision, new direction, lack of growth, plateau).

- **destiny revelation (DR):** tests the capacity to hear from God concerning future direction and willingness to realign life (listening to God, giftedness, life-ministry direction).

- **negative preparation (NP):** special experience or conflict that focuses and frees individuals for the next stage of development (failure, restlessness, temptation to believe "the grass is greener" in a new situation).

- **life crisis (LC):** a special, intense situation that tests and teaches dependence (health or financial problem, difficult personality, life-stage issue, family change).

- **ministry conflict (MC):** a conflict that occurs as a believer serves—used by God to shape values and core convictions (struggle with people or leadership, authority issue, organizational change).

- **obedience check (OC):** a circumstance where God calls for obedience, even in confusion and apparent contradiction (perseverance, clarity-of-life situation, new opportunity, test of submission).

- **isolation (I):** the separating of an individual from normal involvements to enable him or her to hear from God in a deeper way (sickness, new education, self-renewal, spiritual retreat or reflection, solitude).

Back to your personal timeline: Not every life event can or should be categorized. But sometimes it is helpful to use a processing template to see how God is at work. Look at your timeline in light of the *ten process items*. Do you see any of the ten occurring in your life? Do any reoccur? Go back through the Post-it notes on your timeline and identify as many of the ten process items you can, writing its abbreviation (e.g., IC) on the corresponding Post-it note or cell. One incident may include more than one process item.

Depicting your life in such a linear fashion may not appeal to you. Some people prefer a visual timeline using graphics and pictures to depict their journeys. Others might prefer storyboarding. Still others might prefer mind mapping.[439] Whatever your preference, I urge you to take up the challenge and create a timeline in the way that is most meaningful to you. Your timeline will be a document that you will come back to often to reflect and gain perspective, to update, and to make revisions as new insights come to light.

Our Social Base

Social base refers to the personal living environment out of which a leader operates; it provides emotional, economic, and strategic support and basic physical needs. Picture it as a platform on which a believer or leader stands that provides balance and support for him or her to effectively and efficiently expedite his or her unique calling. Supporting the platform are four pillars. If any of these pillars cracks or becomes weak and unable to support the platform of ministry, the whole thing could collapse in a heap.

I have known many leaders who sought to fulfill their calling while neglecting one or more of those pillars: their emotional, economic, strategic, or physical support needs. I have declared publically that my wife gives me the platform I get to dance on. I am acutely aware of the fact that whatever success I have enjoyed to date is in great measure due to the emotional and strategic support she has given me. I am deeply grateful to God for the gift of my wife.

Emotional support involves such things as having companionship, someone to listen to you, someone to emphasize with and understand you, someone who can recreate and relax with you, and someone who can

---

439 A mind map is a diagram used to visually outline information, concepts, or processes. A mind map is often created around a single word or phrase, placed in the center. Associated ideas, words, and concepts are added. Major categories of data radiate from a central node, and lesser categories are sub-branches of larger branches.

affirm you. Your spouse or close friends or mentor can provide this kind of support.

Economic support is required by every leader. We all need a financial base that covers living expenses, medical and educational costs, and other basic physical needs like food, clothing, shelter, transportation, and recreation. If any of these necessities is missing, the leader becomes distracted, devoting his or her limited energy to finding economic support.

Strategic support involves a deep level of communication about our ministry, career, ideas, philosophy, problems, or personal development, as well as our dreams, visions, and hopes about life and ministry. Sharing our perspective with someone close helps give meaning to life and affirms that what we are doing is important. Our major life choices are influenced in this arena. Again, a spouse, close friend, or mentor can provide this kind of support.

Social support is concerned with the basic necessities of life. How we eat, where we sleep, how we wash our clothes, and how we satisfy our physical drives are all issues related to basic living. Social support can also include the network of relationships through which we communicate and seek advice and counsel. This network may also introduce us to people who can help us reach our potential or find avenues by which we can thrive and leverage our wiring for greater effectiveness.

Personal Assessment

How would you assess the stability and strength of your ministry platform in terms of the four pillars of your social base?

Who within your sphere of relationships provides emotional support to you? Do you have someone you can go to for this support?

How are your financial needs being met? Do you need help developing a plan to provide the financial support you need to do ministry?

Who within your sphere of relationships provides you with strategic support? Do you have someone you can go to for this support?

Who within your sphere of relationships provides you with social support? Are your basic needs being met? Are you cultivating a network of supportive relationships?

Our Boundaries

Bobby Clinton defines a boundary event as a major passage or shaping activity that provides a unique opportunity to deepen your relationship to God, bring closure to a recent experience, expand your perspectives, and make decisions that will launch you into a new, challenging phase of development. Boundary events often usher you from one phase of development to the next, although that is not always the case.

In an article describing boundary events and their significance,[440] Clinton summarizes his findings this way:

> Every leader goes through critical times of transition in his or her ministry. The key to these times is to put them into the perspective of a lifetime of development. Looked at directly, with the narrow focus of the now, the events of the present, they can be overwhelming and discouraging. We can feel like giving up, backing out of leadership altogether. But placed in the context of a lifetime of development they can be seen to serve at least four major purposes. (1) They deepen one's relationship to God. (2) They bring closure to recent experiences—that is, we learn lessons concerning the situation that has catapulted us into the boundary time. We make amends in terms of our inner life—recognize the need

---

440 J. Robert Clinton, *The Leadership Theory Reader: Boundary Processing* (Altadena: Barnabas Publishers, 2005), 1–43.

for forgiveness and reconciliation, where we can. We put that time behind us with a sense of having gained as much positive from it as we can. (3) They expand our perspectives to see new things. We may be released to consider or to be led into something new and different that we otherwise would never have opted for. We may be taken to a new level of realization of our potential that God has put in us. (4) We will make decisions that will launch us into a new aspect of ministry, or a new ministry altogether, or a new phase of development.

These boundary times are times of confusion, turmoil, sometimes pain, and almost always reflection with uncertain resolution. They last from as short a time as 2 or 3 months to as long a time as six years. There is a pattern to them. There is the (1) entry stage and its characteristic backward reflection—a seeking to understand what has happened to bring about the boundary. There is the (2) evaluation stage and its characteristic upward reflection—the drawing of God to see the meta-goals behind the whole process—the deepening of relationship with the sovereign God. And there is the (3) termination stage with its characteristic forward look. The light in the tunnel is ahead, not now behind as it was in stage (1). Decisions are made with a confidence, even though made with details not always clear, that God is moving one forward with excitement to a new time of expansion, of purpose, and of release.

Major boundaries might include your conversion, the event of God's calling in your life, a crisis that propelled you into a new ministry phase, the initiation and completion of a growth cycle, a new vision or paradigm that ushered in a different ministry focus, lordship committal (when you surrendered to Christ and realized you were under new management), or divine guidance that forced you to rethink what you were doing.

Every boundary has an *entry phase* when you try to make sense of what precipitated the situation, looking to the past and trying to understand what happened to bring you to this point. Often you don't arrive at absolute clarity about the factors that contributed to the situation; ultimately you come to terms with the circumstances even though many questions remain unanswered.

You then enter an *evaluation phase* when you hunker down and look at the present. Given what's happened, you start from there and try to reassess what it means for you in the here and now. Often in this phase you'll conduct a personal audit of your gifts and look at options you wouldn't have considered in the past. You attempt to reposition yourself for some new, future event, although you may have no idea what that is.

Once you have completed the evaluation, you enter the *exit phase*, looking to the future and seizing the moment to embrace your new reality. You reengage with the world around you with renewed vigor and set out to enjoy the next big phase of your life. You are now ready for the new, having let go of the past. You have transitioned to a new and exciting era of the life and ministry.

During this process, you conduct retrospective reflection, inward assessment, future thinking, and decision making. Process items God uses may involve conflict, a life crisis, a leadership commitment, a paradigm shift, ministry structure, ministry insights, isolation, training progress, negative preparation, divine contact, destiny revelation, and divine guidance—and there are other issues, I am sure.

There are many types of boundary events, and they range in duration from one or two months to six or seven years. *The Surprise Boundary* can be short and is instigated by some unexpected ministry challenge, opportunity, or invitation that requires immediate acceptance. *The Growth Boundary* refers to a growing restlessness, usually involving a need to grow or expand (as well as an increasing sense of being stifled in a role that is not using much of your potential). This boundary usually takes place over a one- to three-year time period. *The Creeping Vine Boundary* refers to a relatively long process during which God gives guidance little by little over a period of time, frequently through negative preparation. It slowly dawns on you, after an accumulation of numerous indicators, that you need to make a change in your ministry. Frequently, this boundary is seen to be relatively longer—three to six years. *The Expansion Boundary* refers to a situation in which you are challenged to a new level of ministry. The challenge may come as the result of a paradigm shift or some destiny experience in which you face an expansion in your kind of ministry, ministry role, faith, or influence.

Boundary processing is helpful for many reasons. It deepens your relationship with God, instills hope for tomorrow, brings closure to grief over recent experiences, releases you from former visions, invites "new sight" through paradigm shifts, realigns components of your identity, and assists in strategic decision making for new development and direction. Sometimes boundary types overlap in a particular case.

After having faithfully served an institution of higher learning for close to fourteen years, my position was eliminated to reduce expenses. I was initially shattered. I had given much of my productive adult life to the school. I went through a period of second-guessing my circumstances. I tried to make sense of what had happened to me, but little made sense. My feelings of being cast aside and my loyalty and service having been so callously discarded put me on an emotional roller coaster. I had never been fired before. I struggled for several months, looking to the past to try to connect the dots. I didn't arrive at many satisfying answers.

I knew it was time to assess the present; do a personal audit of my gifts, expertise, and experience; rethink my circumstances; make temporary arrangements to provide finances for my family; and try to find a new avenue to express my wiring. I dabbled in several things, cobbling together consulting arrangements that brought in additional income to supplement my severance package. My obligations didn't go away, just my means to fulfill them. Gradually doors began to open, but my funds were running out. To my humiliation, I applied for unemployment benefits once the severance package was depleted. I was too young to retire and too old to be attractive to other organizations, which were also cutting back.

Finally, an opportunity presented itself and I embraced ministry on the front lines once again. I had no idea how satisfying that new ministry would be on so many levels. I realized that what I had to offer could be utilized in significant ways. I hadn't planned to go back to church ministry, but God had other plans for me. These last three years have been the most satisfying and productive of my life. I went through a yearlong boundary event that was not of my choosing. God used almost all the process items I mentioned as prevalent in boundary events.

A typical believer will experience as few as three and as many as six major boundaries in a lifetime. The point is to understand that each boundary or transition has three phases: an entry phase that looks to the past or backward, an evaluation phase that looks to the present or upward, and an exit phase that looks to the future or forward. The other point to understand is that God often provides or uses circumstances to help a believer transition from one phase to another in His developmental plans for him or her. Terry Walling has written extensively on these types of transitions. I would encourage the reader to pick up a copy of his book *Stuck!*[441]

Personal Assessment

What boundary events have you experienced in your life thus far? How have you processed them?

Having experienced a boundary event, what conclusions have you reached about its purpose and subsequent results?

Given a significant boundary in your life, how would you characterize the entry, evaluation, and exit phases of the boundary? What did you learn in each phase?

Which process items were used by God in the boundary event? How were they used? Which process items were used during each of the three phases of the boundary event?

Having come out on the other side of a boundary event, how would you assess the experience?

---

441 Terry Walling, *Stuck! Navigating the Transitions of Life and Leadership* (St. Charles: ChurchSmart Resources, 2008).

Our Giftedness

When I speak of a person's giftedness, I include spiritual gifts, natural abilities, and acquired skills. We all have natural abilities and acquired skills. Spiritual gifts are added when we receive Jesus Christ as Savior and Lord—an appreciation of the person and work of our Creator; a recognition of our sin and rebellion separating us from God; an acknowledgment that Jesus atoned for our willfulness and transgressions; a receipt of God's provision of salvation through His Son; and a surrender of our independence to the lordship of Jesus Christ, with an understanding that we are now under new management.

Spiritual Gifts

Spiritual gifts are God-given, unique capacities for service that are imparted to each believer for the purpose of releasing Holy Spirit–empowered ministry. Common spiritual gifts are listed in Romans 12:3–8, 1 Corinthians 12:8–10, and Ephesians 4:7–13. From scripture we learn the following key information about spiritual gifts:

- Every Christian has at least one spiritual gift.[442]
- No Christian has all the gifts.[443]
- We cannot choose our gifts; God does that.[444]
- There is no gift that every Christian possesses.[445]
- Believers will account to the Lord for how they use their gifts.[446]
- Spiritual gifts indicate God's call and purpose for a Christian's life.[447]
- Gifts used without love do not accomplish God's intended purposes.[448]
- Spiritual gifts are for the common good to build up the Body of Christ.[449]

---

442 1 Pet. 4:10.
443 1 Cor. 12:28–30.
444 1 Cor. 12:7–11.
445 1 Cor. 12:29–30.
446 1 Pet. 4:10.
447 Rom. 12:2–8.
448 1 Cor. 13:1–3.
449 1 Cor. 12:27.

- There are different kinds of gifts but the same Spirit; different kinds of service or venues of expression but the same Lord; and different kinds of working, spheres of influence, or effectiveness, but the same God.[450]

Identifying your spiritual gifts may begin with taking a survey or completing a questionnaire. The results revealed by these instruments are not proof perfect that you indeed have the gift or gifts indicated. The only way to ensure that one gift or another is truly your spiritual gift is exercising it in a variety of contexts and assessing the spiritual results.

More specifically, a true spiritual gift is used in accordance with biblical teaching.[451] There is affirmation and positive feedback within the Body of Christ for the expression of the gift.[452] There is agreement within the Body of Christ that the Holy Spirit is at work.[453] The Holy Spirit provides peace in our spirits as we offer our gift(s) to the Body of Christ.[454] There is evidence of godly fruit in the life of the Body.[455] We offer the gifts for the common good, as others have need of it.[456] Unless gifts are offered in love, they have no worth.[457] Finally, we should strive to live lives worthy of our callings.[458]

There is little agreement among Christians about exactly how many different spiritual gifts there are. When we look at the key Bible passages on spiritual gifts, we see the gifts manifested as prophecy, service, teaching, encouragement, giving, leadership, and mercy;[459] as a message of wisdom, a message of knowledge, faith, healing, miraculous powers, the ability to distinguish between spirits, speaking in tongues, and interpreting tongues;[460] and by an apostle, prophet, evangelist, pastor, and teacher.[461]

Some believe that certain spiritual gifts, such as the ability to speak

---

450 1 Cor. 12:4–7.
451 2 Tim. 3:16; Rom. 12; 1 Cor. 12–14; Eph. 4; 1 Pet. 4.
452 1 Cor. 12:7; Eph. 4:16.
453 1 John 4:1; 1 Thess. 5:21.
454 John 15:26; Rom. 8:16.
455 John 15:8; Matt. 7:16–20.
456 Acts 2:44–45; 1 Cor. 12:7.
457 1 Cor. 13:1–3.
458 Eph. 4:1.
459 Rom. 12.
460 1 Cor. 12.
461 Eph. 4.

in tongues, interpret tongues, and perform miracles, were given to people only by the direct laying on of hands by the original apostles, and that these gifts ceased to exist after the first century. Some add the possibility of other gifts, including celibacy, hospitality, martyrdom, mission work, voluntary poverty, intercession, prayer, and writing.[462]

However, it is not particularly important whether any specific ability is a spiritual gift, a blessing from God, a God-given talent, an inherited trait, a natural human ability, or something learned. The thing that is important is that we discover what gifts are more pronounced in us and how to use them to serve God. God is just as pleased when we use a learned ability to serve Him as when we use a spiritual gift to serve Him. The key is to discover our abilities and then learn to use them to love, worship, and serve God.

Clinton makes the following observations regarding giftedness, discovery, and validation. He represents his findings as stages that progressively make gifts and abilities more evident, effective, and influential:

- Stage 1: A person begins to get some ministry experience, which leads to …
- Stage 2: the discovery of a spiritual gift or natural ability, which leads to …
- Stage 3: the increased use of that gift or natural ability, which leads to …
- Stage 4: effectiveness in using that gift or ability, which leads to …
- Stage 5: more ministry experience or new ministry roles, which …
- Stage 6: stimulate the further discovery of gifts to meet a new situation, which …
- Stage 7: over time reveals the identification of the gift mix,[463] which leads to …
- Stage 8: the development of a gift cluster,[464] which leads to …
- Stage 9: convergence or maturity in giftedness.[465]

462 1 Cor. 7:1–9; 1 Pet. 4:9–10; 1 Cor. 13:1–3; Eph. 3:6–8; 1 Cor. 13:1–3; Eph. 6:18; Luke 1:1–3.
463 Gift Mix: describes the set of spiritual gifts repeatedly used in ministry.
464 Gift Cluster: refers to a gift mix that has a dominant gift supported harmoniously by other gifts and abilities.
465 Clinton, *The Making of a Leader,* 251.

The difference between a talent and a spiritual gift is fuzzy for most people. These comparisons may help:

Innate Talent	*Spiritual Gift*
natural	supernatural
inherited from others	received from the Holy Spirit
received at physical birth	received at spiritual birth
possessed by everyone	possessed by saved people
needs to be developed	needs to be exercised
used for personal gain	used to serve God's purposes
produces a natural result	produces a spiritual result
reveals us	reveals Christ
builds up ourselves	builds up the Church
can be used for others	must be used for others
self-centered	God-centered
horizontal focus	vertical focus
exercised in our power	exercised in His power
can be used for nonspiritual purposes	must be used for spiritual purposes
facilitates man's contribution to mankind	facilitates God's redemptive purposes

Natural Abilities

Natural abilities refer to those capacities, skills, talents, or aptitudes that are innate and allow someone to accomplish a variety of activities. These natural abilities may also include strengths, leadership style, and personality or temperament.

Strengths

Strengths are our innate, God-given abilities, aptitudes, or talents. They are naturally recurring patterns of thought, feeling, and behavior that can be productively applied consistently in a given activity. For instance, you may have a natural aptitude for some form of artistry (drawing, painting, poetry, sculpture, writing, dancing, or drama), athleticism or physical prowess, communication, clerical work, creativity, innovation, intellectual acumen, emotional awareness, language acquisition, intuitive leadership, logic, mathematics, mechanical know-how, medicine, music (instrument, voice), organization, spatial perception, science, verbal comprehension, or visual acuity.

Gallup's StrengthsFinder helps people identify signature themes—clusters of related talents that, when appropriately understood and leveraged effectively, become strengths. My top five themes are "learner," "activator," "achiever," "input," and "belief." *Learner* describes people who have a great desire to learn and continuously want to improve. In particular, the process of learning, rather than the outcome, excites them. *Activator* describes people who can make things happen by turning thoughts into action. They are often impatient. *Achiever* describes people who have a great deal of stamina and work hard. They take great satisfaction from being busy and productive. *Input* describes people who have a craving to know more. Often they like to collect and archive all kinds of information. *Belief* describes people who have certain core values that are unchanging. Out of these values emerges a defined purpose for their lives.

If you search the Internet you will find sites that offer the StrengthsFinder instrument, which you can take to determine your top five strengths. I have found the results have strong validity and reliability—the instrument measures what it says it measures and does so consistently. I have taken the survey several times, and it always reveals the same strengths. Over several trials, one or more new strengths may pop into the top five, merely indicating that they were already very close to the top.

Leadership Style

Leadership style refers to the individual behaviors a leader uses to influence others. It includes characteristics like how the leader motivates or relates to followers, is perceived as a leader by followers, solves group problems, attempts to bring about obedience among followers, and resolves differences. Each of us leads sometime and somewhere. We are not exclusively followers and never leaders; nor are we leaders and never followers. You lead every time you take the initiative to solve a problem, resolve a conflict, provide for a family, or make a decision that will impact others. You may be a reluctant leader, but you are a leader nevertheless.

There are many theories about leadership styles. For instance, situational leadership postulates that there are basically four styles: director (telling, guiding, directing, and establishing); coach (selling, explaining, clarifying, and persuading); partner (participating, encouraging, collaborating, and committing); and mentor (delegating, observing, monitoring, and advising). The style most appropriate for any given setting depends on the readiness of those being led in terms of their competence (ability) and confidence (security).

> In a given situation, when a follower is *unable or too insecure* to do what is needed, the leader should assume the role of *director* and provide specific direction about what should be done, when it should be done, or how it should be done. In this case, direction, guidance, and the establishment of standards are needed. As a director, the leader tells the follower what action is appropriate and how it should be accomplished.
>
> When the follower is *unable but willing to try*, the leader adjusts his or her leadership style to that of *coach*—giving explanations, clarifying specifics, and using persuasion. This is the same function a coach provides in sports. A coach doesn't do what is required of the player; instead, he or she sets strategy, encourages the player, and motivates performance in accordance with the player's skill set.
>
> When a follower demonstrates that he or she is *able but still insecure*, the leader becomes a *partner* who models the appropriate behavior or procedure, provides encouragement as the follower attempts to replicate that behavior, and collaborates with the follower as he or she is doing it. In essence, the leader has moved from a sage on a stage to a guide by the side.
>
> When the follower is *willing, able, and secure*, the leader changes his or her engagement style to that of *mentor*— observing, counseling, and sponsoring the follower as he or she becomes adept. A mentor is fully a guide by the side, offering

wisdom, insight, advice, suggestions, recommendations, and, on occasion, cautions and warnings.

Erwin McManus has identified primary, secondary, and team leadership styles. Primary styles include vision, passion, and mission. Secondary styles include corporate, catalytic, and causal. Team styles include strategic, tactical, and logistical. Each style has its unique features. Bobby Clinton has identified four primary leadership styles, including commander, motivator, participator, and delegator—similar to the situational leadership categories described earlier. Details regarding the McManus and Clinton models can be found in **Appendix I: Leadership Style**.

Personality temperament is a set of characteristics or habitual inclinations or a predisposed emotional response that represents a personal pattern for interaction and reaction. Each of us is born with a predisposed temperament that helps make us unique. You may be a driver, expressive, amiable, or analytical. You could be a doer, influencer, relater, or thinker. You could be a lion, otter, golden retriever, or beaver. Tim LaHaye, internationally known author, teacher, and expert on Bible prophecy, identified four temperaments, including choleric, sanguine, phlegmatic, and melancholy.[466]

I have read extensively on this subject and seen patterns suggesting four primary temperaments, each manifested as a particular leadership style, leadership strength, personal motivation, leadership practice, demeanor under tension, set of needs God must provide, set of needs others must provide, ideal leadership situation, and primary area for improvement.

I have also noted biblical characters that model each temperament. In **Appendix G: Personality Temperament** you will find the composite temperament matrix I just described, as well as a simple instrument for determining your personality temperament using the Myers-Briggs categories of extroversion/introversion, sensing/intuitive, thinking/feeling, and judging/perceiving. Both resources will help you identify your dominant temperament. We generally have a combination of characteristics from more than one temperament, but on the whole, we fit one the description of temperament more than the others.

---

466 Tim LaHaye, *Spirit-Controlled Temperament* (Wheaton: Tyndale House Publishers, 1994).

Our *strengths* are our predisposition to act a certain way given a set of circumstances or events. Our *personality temperament* is our expression of being. Our *leadership style* is our method of influence.

Clinton makes the following assessment concerning leadership styles:

> The dominant leadership style of a leader is that consistent behavior pattern that underlies specific overt behavior acts of influence pervading the majority of leadership functions in which that leader exerts influence; that is, highly directive, directive, nondirective, or highly nondirective. One's leadership style is conditioned by four major factors. Based on personality and cultural conditioning, the leader is oriented around task (highly directive behaviors) or relational (less directive behaviors). Follower maturity affects how a leader influences. The more mature the followers the more options available to the leader. Less maturity breeds more directive styles. The more intimate the relationship between the leader and group the more a whole range of behaviors can be used. Followers will respond to different behaviors from leaders they love and trust knowing that he/she will use the most appropriate style for the situation.[467]

Acquired Skills

Acquired skills refer to those capacities, skills, talents, or aptitudes that someone has learned in order to accomplish something. Ministry competencies such as conflict resolution, problem solving, personal management, mentoring, team building, communication, interpersonal skills, systems understanding, organization, project management, and effecting change are acquired skills.

Basic ministry competencies might include ministry planning, relational communication, resolving conflicts effectively, solving problems creatively, mobilizing a team, maximizing leadership influence, managing time efficiently, motivating and empowering others, displaying your giftedness set, and determining your leadership style.[468]

---

467 J. Robert Clinton, *Leaders, Leadership and the Bible* (Altadena: Barnabas Publishers, 1993).

468 Gregory W. Bourgond, *Reader: Ministry Competencies,* 2.

Other acquired skills might include assessment and evaluation, Bible study, bookkeeping, budgeting, building, coaching, marketing and communication, computer skills, cooking, counseling, environmental analysis, development, effecting change, empowerment, financial planning, gardening, interpersonal skills, graphics, leading and managing, mentoring, networking, organizing, parenting, personal management, personal soul care, photography, planning, prayer, problem solving, resolving conflict, recruitment, sales, research, resourcing, scrapbooking, speaking, teaching, strategic planning, systems understanding, team building, electronic technology, time management, training, typing, visioning, witnessing, or woodworking.

These competencies and skills can be picked up through organizational training opportunities, conferences and workshops, seminars and classes, higher education, leadership and management publications, mentoring and modeling, and repeated practice in a variety of contexts.

One way to depict your giftedness is to create a Giftedness Venn Diagram. Terry Walling describes the value of doing so:

> A Venn Diagram is a special way of illustrating the relationship of a person's spiritual gifts, natural abilities and acquired skills. Symbols are given to each of these three elements, with size representing the dominance of each element, and the overlap depicting how the elements relate to one another. Venn was a mathematician that developed set-theory … the ability to look at groups of items (numbers) at the same time and discover how they relate to each other. Developing a Venn diagram of your spiritual gifts, natural abilities and acquired skills provides the bridge to help you identify a major role and clarify your effective methodologies.[469]

Appendix H: Giftedness Venn Diagram contains guidelines for how to construct your Giftedness Venn Diagram.

---

469 Terry Walling, *Advancing*, 23.

Personal Assessment

What are your spiritual gifts?
  How have they been validated?
  What spiritual results have they produced?
  How have your gifts been exercised?

What natural abilities do you possess?
  What are your strengths, talents, and aptitudes?
  What is your personality temperament?
  What is your dominant leadership style?

What competencies and skills have you acquired?
  What abilities have you developed?
  What learned skills do you have?

Chapter 13: Our Focus

If you invest all of who you are in one venue (a profession, initiative, project, an avenue of endeavor) you are headed for abject misery. Instead, determine who you really are (who God created you to be) and invest different aspects of who you are in multiple venues, the composite of which represents all of who you are. That way you will not be subject to the perturbations of any one venue. That is what I call the modern day Renaissance person.

—Leonard Sweet

My wife and I were sitting outside our cottage in Cong, Ireland, taking in the sun and fresh air, when we noticed a covey of butterflies flitting about a flowered bush and some bees searching out nectar. The scene conjured up in my mind the notion that we are either butterflies or bees: butterflies flit around with little intentionality, while bees are very intentional about their activity. The question I would ask at this point is, Are you a butterfly or a bee? Are you intentional about the way you live your life, or are you simply flitting from one thing to another, with little purpose? Are you living a focused life, or are you lacking focus for your life?

A focused life is defined as follows:

Beginning with an all-out commitment to Him, a focused life is dedicated exclusively to carrying out God's unique purposes by identifying the focal issues—that is, the biblical purpose, life purpose, committed passion, major role, unique methodology, and ultimate contribution—that allow and increase prioritization of life's activities around the focal issues, resulting in a satisfying life of being and doing.

Terry Walling makes the following observation: "Today, more than ever, believers like you are searching for ways to recognize the hand of God at work in their lives, and to know that their lives will count for the building of God's Kingdom. But the difficulty comes in knowing how to bring focus to one's life and knowing that the course direction one has chosen is truly designed by the Lord."[470] Developing and implementing a *personal life mandate* can help.

Walling suggests that a good personal life mandate—our unique map—reflects our unique personal destiny; blends together our biblical purpose, life values, and personal vision; helps us understand our roles in the Body of Christ; provides encouragement and perseverance in difficult times; and helps with decision making about future life and ministry opportunities.

Terry also believes, as I do, that

> at the core of a personal calling is the concept of destiny. Personal calling (or mission) presupposes a unique, personal destiny for each of us. God has brought each of us into existence, at this point in time, to bring glory to His name and to fulfill our part in the expansion of His Kingdom. *Destiny* is the living out of God's purposes in one's own generation. Paul said of David, "For when David had served God's purposes in his own generation, he fell asleep."[471]

> The Lord told Jeremiah, "Before I formed you in the womb I knew you. Before you were born I set you apart; I

---

470 Walling, *Focus Workbook*, 3.
471 Acts 13:36.

appointed you as a prophet to the nations."[472] Jeremiah had a
unique destiny to fulfill. Jesus obviously lived with a sense of
purpose and destiny. Jesus said, "My food is to do the will of
Him who sent me and to finish His work."[473] On the cross He
cried out, "It is finished."[474] Jesus' life had purpose. Jesus came
to die. His death on the cross completed what He had come
to do. His resolve was to live out His own personal destiny.
This focus caused Him to make daily choices in line with His
personal mission.

Paul, too, lived with a sense of destiny and purpose. Paul
reflects on his call "to be a minister of Christ Jesus to the
Gentiles ... so that the Gentiles might become an offering
acceptable to God."[475]

Paul reminds each of us that we are God's craftsmanship,
"created in Christ Jesus to do good works, which God prepared
in advance for us to do."[476]

Each of us is called by God to live out our godly purposes,
to love and worship Him, to share His love with one another
and a hurting world, to glorify the God and Father of our Lord
Jesus Christ.[477] But we also have been gifted to play a specific
role as members of Christ's body.

Throughout history, God has called His servants to use
their gifts and abilities to influence the hearts and lives of
their generation. Destiny processing is a believer's ability to
focus his or her ministry according to God's unique call on
his or her life.

Our Biblical Purpose

As followers of Christ, we share a common purpose. Clarifying your
biblical purpose helps you in several ways: It explains why you exist. It

472 Jer. 1:5.
473 John 4:34.
474 John 19:30.
475 Rom. 15:16.
476 Eph. 2:10.
477 Rom. 15:6.

captures the essence of why you are on this planet and what it means to live in relationship with God. It defines your life not by what you think, but by what God thinks. It anchors your life in the character of your Creator. It clarifies the nonnegotiable. It tells what never changes about who you are, regardless of the circumstances.[478]

There are certain biblical purposes we must all embrace as followers of Christ: evangelism, passion for God, passion for others, worship, spiritual growth, and service.[479] Each of us is mandated to fulfill these biblical purposes. And I would add one more biblical purpose to the list: the pursuit of godliness.

> For the grace of God that brings salvation has appeared to all men. It teaches us to say "No" to ungodliness and worldly passions, and to live self-controlled, upright and godly lives in this present age, while we wait for the blessed hope—the glorious appearing of our great God and Savior, Jesus Christ, who gave himself for us to redeem us from all wickedness and to purify for himself a people that are his very own, eager to do what is good.[480]

Your biblical purpose answers the *why* of your life. It is a statement of being. It answers the question of why you do what you do. It should focus on self. It can be applied to many people. It is general in nature. It should represent your commitment to The Great Commandment and The Great Commission.[481] As an example, I offer my biblical purpose:

> My biblical purpose is to live with abandon, fulfilling the mandate God has given me. My mandate is to live in such a way as to exemplify and model Christ-likeness in all I think, say, and do. The hills I will die on include fidelity to my personal relationship with Christ and my loyalty and faithfulness to Him; faith in the saving grace of the Gospel in all its implications, even if it takes me to uncomfortable places; family, as I strive to

---

478 Josh. 24:15; Phil. 3:10.
479 Matt. 28:18–20, 22:37–40; Ps. 34:1–3; Col. 2:6–7; Isa. 58:6–12.
480 Titus 2:11–14.
481 Matt. 22:37–40, 28:19–20.

be and do what serves their best interests; and a focus on God's purposes for my life in alignment with what He has called me to be and do. I seek to tune my heart to the heart of God and live accordingly. The Bible is my sole foundation, and I submit to its authority for faith and practice. My objective is to model the character of Christ and leave a pleasing aroma in the nostrils of all who come within my sphere of influence.

Personal Assessment

How would you define your biblical purpose?

What factors encompass the "why" of your life?

What provides a biblical foundation for your beingness?

How would you draft a biblical purpose that takes into account evangelism, passion for God, passion for others, worship, spiritual growth, and service?

Our Life Purpose

Our life purpose is a burden-like calling, a task or driving force or need for achievement that motivates a leader to fulfill something or see something done. Frequently leaders will have one to three dominant life purposes, some combination of one or more, or at least an umbrella one which is clarified by more detailed subpurposes. Your life purpose is the dominant focal issue in your life. The following principles apply to it:

- A leader cannot have a focused life apart from some life purpose which lies at the core of his or her being. However, life purpose is not enough to generate a focused life.

- Life purpose is the primary integrating factor around which a focused life revolves. The seeds of a believer's life purpose are contained in his or her unusual experiences with God. These experiences are called sense-of-destiny experiences. All believers generally and leaders specifically have a sense of destiny.

- God uses various means to intervene in a person's life in order to create a sense of destiny and bring clarity to his or her life purposes. Destiny processing provides the seedbed for discovering life purposes. As we discussed in an earlier chapter, there are four types of destiny processing: awe-inspiring experiences, indirect destiny experiences, providential circumstances, and the blessing of God over time.

Your life purpose answers the *what* of your life. It is a statement of *doing*. It answers the question of what you are called to do for others. It should focus on others but apply only to you. It is specific in nature. It should include a hint of the strategies you will employ to make your life purpose a reality. It should include action verbs (e.g., to influence, to facilitate, to align, to encourage, to exhort, to teach, to counsel, to mentor). It does not have to include every dimension or role in your life. What we are all called to do is a given and should not be wrapped up in your life purpose statement. By way of example, I submit to you my life purpose:

> My life purpose is to influence leaders directly and indirectly to live "all-out" for Christ; to facilitate a process to determine how God has "wired" them; to help them align their lives according to God's predetermined plans; to encourage them to become proactive partners in God's purposes and redemptive activity; and to exhort them to live a legacy worth leaving in the lives of others.

Randy Reese, founder and president of VantagePoint3, an organization dedicated to developing leaders, offers helpful questions to help clarify one's life purpose:

> *How would you articulate the "burn" in your soul or your sense of destiny?*

> *To which biblical character's calling and sense of destiny can you most relate?*[482]
>
> *What biblical books or specific verses reflect your life purpose?*
>
> *What biblical text is encouraging you presently toward your life purpose?*

To these questions I would add the following:

> *What must you do that, if you couldn't do it, you would feel a great loss?*
>
> *What has God equipped you to contribute to His redemptive purposes?*
>
> *Where and how do you feel you can make your greatest contributions?*
>
> *What unique strategies will help you fulfill your sense of purpose for the benefit of others?*
>
> *What is your life purpose?*

Our Committed Passion

I am indebted to Bobby Clinton for introducing me to focused living. Much of what I convey in this chapter comes from the strategic concepts he developed and taught for years. Biblical purpose, life purpose, role characteristics, unique methodologies, and ultimate contribution are his original concepts. I have adopted and adapted these concepts and added one of my own: committed passion.

In my view, committed passion is focused, intentional, energized action defined by your inner drive to fulfill your revealed destiny and be all God has equipped and wired you to be. Life purpose without the follow-through of committed passion is merely a dream with little chance of becoming a reality. It's the magnetism of passion that causes the needle

---

482 Some possible examples are Isaiah (Isaiah 6); Samuel (1 Samuel 1); Jeremiah (Jeremiah 1); Barnabas and Paul (Acts 4); Joseph (Genesis 39).

in your internal compass to point to directed effort and focus. It's the dedication and devotion to realizing one's full created potential.

Our passion is a God-given desire that compels us to make a difference in a particular endeavor or in ministry. Your passion will lead you to some compelling action. Passion addresses *who* you would like to help most and *what causes* you feel strongly about. As an example of life purpose, I will share my own:

> My committed passion is to help men and women realize their God-given potential in Christ and to develop to the fullest their God-given gifts, abilities, and capacities for godly leadership from the inside out and within legitimate limitations, such as temperament, aptitude, and maturity.

Personal Assessment

Regarding people you'd like to help, the following questions have been excerpted from the book *Network* by Bruce Bugbee, Don Cousins, and Bill Hybels.

If you could snap your fingers and know that you couldn't fail, what would you do?

At the end of your life, what would you like to have done for others?

If your name were mentioned to a group of your friends, what would they say you were really interested in or passionate about?

What conversation would keep you talking late into the night?

What would you like to do for others?

What categories of people would you like to help the most? (Some examples might be abuse victims, addicts, agnostics, atheists, business leaders, children, church leaders, college students, people with disabilities, divorced people, doctors, those involved in education, the elderly, empty nesters, fatherless children, foreigners, foster children, government workers, the homeless, hospitalized people, the hungry, immigrants, infants, the infirmed, laborers, lay leaders, leaders, workers in the marketplace, married couples, men, mentally challenged people, people in midcareer, members of the military, missionaries, nurses, orphans, parents, pastors, the police, politicians, the poor, prisoners, refugees, retirees, seekers, service providers, single mothers, single parents, singles, social workers, teachers, teen moms, the unchurched, the unemployed, the unsaved, veterans, widowed people, women, young career people, or youth.)

Regarding causes you feel strongly about:

What issues or causes do you feel compelled to embrace?

What causes stir your soul and urge you to respond?

What issues pique your interest and passion?

What concerns capture your attention every time they are raised? (Some examples might be abortion, abuse, addictions, AIDS, childcare, church, community outreach, community service, discipleship, economics, education, employment, the environment, evangelism, the family, global concerns, health care, homosexuality, human slavery, human trafficking, hunger, immigration, injustice, intolerance, development, literacy, marriage, missions, politics, poverty, prisons, racism, secularism, the sex trade, social needs, technology, violence, or women's rights.)

What are the top five to seven positive experiences you've had in your life, what did you do about them, and why were they meaningful to you?

What is your committed passion?

Our Role Characteristics

Role characteristics include the official or unofficial position, status, platform, leadership function, or job description by which you are recognized and which uniquely fits who you are and lets you effectively accomplish your life purpose(s) and committed passion. This is a place where 80 percent of who you are overlaps 80 percent of what you do!

Many of us have jobs that provide income and security for our families. These jobs may or may not be conducive to our life purposes and committed passions, but they are gifts from God to provide our needs and fulfill our responsibilities and obligations.

Perhaps you can adjust your job to accommodate God's calling in your life; perhaps you can't. You may not have the freedom to quit your job to find one more suitable to your calling. If that is the case, you may need to identify outside venues where your life purpose and committed passion can be expressed. These options may be in some volunteer role or ministry.

According to Clinton, five components combine to make up an effective major role: a suitable sphere of influence for ministry; a job description that covers the major thrusts needed; ministry activity compatible with giftedness; the freedom to proactively choose actions that enhance life focus and refuse actions that do not; and a respected status that enables effective entrance to a ministry opportunity, bespeaks spiritual authority, and gives a good hearing.

As I noted previously, you may not be able to carry out your life purpose(s) and exploit your unique methodologies unless you have the freedom to adjust your present role. A major role will usually have to be adapted, if possible; organizations rarely define such a role to fit an individual. The major role may be a combination of formally recognized functions related to your position or qualifications, and informal ones done implicitly within the functions of your job description or in addition to your job description.

A suitable major role is one that enhances giftedness and allows you to use unique methodologies that will lead to ultimate contributions—a legacy. Remember, the giftedness set includes natural abilities, acquired skills, and spiritual gifts. Natural abilities are those capacities, skills, talents, or aptitudes which are innate and allow you to accomplish things. Acquired skills are those capacities, skills, talents, or aptitudes you learned in order to accomplish something. A spiritual gift is a God-given, unique capacity imparted to you for the purpose of releasing a Holy Spirit–empowered ministry, producing supernatural results.

Early on, you'll find it necessary to try out various assignments in order to really discover your gifts and the roles they best match. As you experience a number of mini-convergences over time, and as you get a better understanding of your giftedness, you will know the ideal role for you. Your major role is the best fit between your gifts and the job you must do. It allows you to use unique methodologies effectively and enjoy the satisfaction of fulfilling your life purpose(s).

The environment in which you perform your role should not require you to compromise your beliefs and values. If the role you assume requires you to sacrifice any aspect of your compass, moves you away from the exercise of your giftedness, or does not provide you time to meet your spiritual needs or your family's needs, avoid it. Although it might provide you with the economic means to support your family, it should not require you to sacrifice your faith and practice on the altar of expediency. Having clarity regarding your personal life mandate will undoubtedly change the kinds of questions you ask in job interviews. Remember, the time to negotiate is before you accept a position, not after. As an example, my role characteristics follow:

> The major role that will provide the platform for my life's purpose is one in which I'm allowed to focus my energies on investing in the lives of budding leaders (who are in the process of becoming but have not yet arrived) and malleable leaders (who

have the potential for greater purposes but do not have clarity or understanding about how to realize their full potential in Christ). This role will allow me to cultivate relationships with these leaders through networking, teaching, writing, and one-on-one mentoring or in small groups and workshop settings, and expose them to leadership-development concepts, values, principles, and practices. My spiritual gifts exercised in these settings find their primary application in the word cluster gifts, including teaching, exhortation, and leadership. Less dominant, but observable, are the spiritual gifts of words of wisdom, discernment of spirits, and governance.

Personal Assessment

What must the ministry or vocational environment look like so that your life purpose, committed passion, and giftedness (spiritual gifts, natural abilities, and acquired skills) can thrive?

What are the nonnegotiables, the deal breakers, or the irreducible minimums that must be present if you are to be a faithful steward of God's embedded trust in you?

What must be present in order for you to make your greatest contribution to God's redemptive purposes?

What ministry or vocational settings have allowed your gifts to be unleashed and exercised?

If you could rewrite your present job or ministry description, what would it look like?

Our Unique Methods

A unique methodology is the box of tools that you use to carry out your life purpose, committed passion, and vocational or ministerial roles. Many of these tools have come to you naturally, while others have been acquired along the way. Spiritual giftedness, natural abilities, and acquired skills are the primary tools you will use. Included in this toolbox are the core values you act upon and consider in key decisions, as well as operational principles you have gleaned over time that have proven to be axiomatic and spiritually functional. They are the lessons you have learned that now inform how you think and act.

To this toolbox are added insights you can pass on to others: the essentials of doing something or using something or being something, some important contribution you make to a person's vocation or ministry which enhances your life purpose or moves you toward the ultimate contribution.

Your unique methodologies are insights and abilities that fit who you are, help you carry out your life purpose(s) and committed passion, and become effective vehicles for you to carry out your calling, responsibilities, obligations, and service to and for the Lord. They may include an approach, a method, a design, a technique, a philosophy, a framework, a format, a concept, a procedure, a process, a strategy, an ability, or developed materials that move people toward results in line with your life purpose(s) or ultimate contributions.

Unique methodologies describe the major means by which life purpose and ultimate contributions are realized. They relate to the how you operate, achieve, or make progress in delivering your contributions. They are the filters through which you express your ordained uniqueness.

More specifically, your unique methodologies include spiritual gifts, natural abilities and aptitudes, personality temperament, leadership style, core values, and operational principles. Filling your toolbox with appropriate tools will reflect your uniqueness. Answering the personal assessment questions at the end of this section will stock your toolbox with the necessary equipment to carry out your calling, life purpose, committed passion, and distinctive role. It will also facilitate an ultimate contribution that will leave a pleasing aroma with those God has brought within your sphere of influence, beginning with your family, extending to your church, serving your community, and fulfilling your vocational and ministerial responsibilities.

Once again I submit an example from my own life. My unique methodologies find their roots in six major ministry insights that I have seen played out repeatedly in my ministry experience:

- Effective, godly leadership flows from being, is a matter of the heart, and is primarily character-centered and secondarily skill-centered. Skills are the tools of effective leadership; character is the power of effective leadership.

- Lasting behavioral change that brings glory to God begins with the heart in general and our core belief system in particular. Satan's battlefield has always been the heart. What we store in our hearts will evidence itself in our behavior. Our central beliefs establish our core values, our core values inform our worldview, our worldview conditions our motives, and our motives energize our behavior.

- Authentic spirituality is a prerequisite for godly leadership and is produced when we tune our lives to God's standards of excellence. Its vitality comes from living our lives for an "audience of One."

- Effective, godly leadership is developed over a lifetime, is exercised through our God-given passion and gifts, finds its source and authority in God, is built on biblical principles and values, and is practiced in culturally sensitive ways.

- The only legacy worth leaving is the godly legacy we live out daily and leave in the lives of others. Our legacy is the sweet-smelling aroma that lingers in the lives of others long after we're gone from this earth.

- We must make decisions and evaluate options by seeing situations, circumstances, and events through four frameworks: structural or systems (systems theory); human resources (personal needs); symbolic (mission, vision, and values); and political (stakeholder and constituency concerns).

These major ministry insights influence how I cultivate my network of relationships, my style of teaching, the foci of my writing, and the emphases of my mentoring activities. I intend to act faithfully by behaving in accordance with my core values, by leveraging my natural strengths, by finding appropriate expressions for my personality temperament, and by exercising my leadership style in appropriate and life-giving ways.

> Core Values: devoted to God, keeper of promises, seeker of truth, loyal servant, man of integrity, faithful to family, lifelong learner, spiritually informed leadership, submission to biblical authority, responsible behavior, and strength and honor

> Natural Strengths: learner, activator, achiever, input, belief, relator, responsibility, command, focus, self-assurance, and strategic

> Personality Temperament: introverted (I), intuitive (N), thinking (T), judging (J); driver/analytical, choleric/melancholy, lion/beaver

> Leadership Style: primary—passion; secondary—corporate/causal; team—tactical

Personal Assessment

What are your spiritual gifts?

What are your strengths?

What are your aptitudes?

What are your acquired skills?

What is your dominant personality temperament?

What is your dominant leadership style?

What are your core values?

What are your operational principles?

Our Ultimate Contribution

An ultimate contribution is a Christian's lasting legacy for which he or she is remembered and that furthers the cause of Christianity by one or more of the following means:

- setting standards for life and ministry
- impacting lives by enfolding them in God's Kingdom or developing them once they are in God's Kingdom
- serving as a stimulus for change that betters the world
- leaving behind an organization, institution, or movement that will further channel God's work
- discovering, communicating, or promoting ideas that further God's work

An ultimate contribution is a legacy you leave behind after your life is over. It is possible to leave several ultimate contributions, which help set the boundaries for what you want to accomplish in terms of the big picture. They will relate to the means and the ends. When all is said and done and God calls you home, the mark you leave, the legacy you impart, the contribution that lingers, is your ultimate contribution.

It is never too late to begin living a legacy worth leaving in the lives of others. Clinton has identified thirteen legacies that you might leave in the lives of others now, and which, ideally, will endure even after they are gone:[483]

- **saint:** a person who has lived a model life—not a perfect life, but one others want to emulate

- **stylistic practitioner:** a person whose ministry style sets the pace for others and which other ministries seek to emulate

- **family:** a person who promotes a God-fearing family, leaving behind children who walk with God, carrying on that godly heritage

- **mentor:** a person who has a productive ministry with individuals, small groups, etc.; end product is changed lives

- **public rhetorician:** a person who has a productive public ministry with large groups; end product is changed lives

- **pioneer:** a person who starts new works for God; end products are new churches, new movements, and new works for God

- **change person:** a person who rights wrongs and injustices in society and in church and mission organizations; end products are changed institutions, societies, etc., that reflect justice and fairness

- **artist:** a person who has creative breakthroughs in life and ministry and introduces creative ways of doing things; end products are whatever is created as well as a model for how to do things differently

- **founder:** a special category of pioneer who starts a new Christian organization; end product is an organization that

---

483 Clinton, *The Making of a Leader*, 206.

meets a need or captures the essence of some movement or the like

- **stabilizer:** a person who can help a fledgling organization develop or an older organization become more efficient and effective in order to solidify the organization and keep it alive and consistent; end product is a revitalized, efficient organization

- **researcher:** a person who finds out why things happen the way they do in Christian endeavors; end products are new ideas as a result of study and a further understanding of how to facilitate Christian work

- **writer:** a person who can capture ideas in writing in order to help and inform others in Christian work; end product is the writing that is produced

- **promoter:** a person who can motivate others and inspire them to use ideas, join movements, and so on; end product is people committing themselves to new ventures

There are certainly other contributions that can promote God's redemptive purposes. My ultimate contribution is as follows:

Although I am in the process of becoming, having not yet arrived, I believe at this time that my ultimate contributions could coalesce around the roles of mentor, saint, researcher, writer, and stabilizer. I am beginning to see significant results as a mentor (leading a productive ministry with individuals and small groups); saint (living a model life focused on leaving a godly legacy in the lives of others within my sphere of influence); researcher (advancing new ideas about spiritual formation and leadership development); writer (capturing and recording in written form ideas and concepts that are relevant to spiritual and leadership development); and stabilizer (stabilizing and maximizing organizational objectives that coincide with my life's purpose and passion). My "end game" is to live a legacy worth leaving in the lives of my family and the leaders I have had the privilege of influencing for the glory of God.

Personal Assessment

What vocational or ministry dynamics continued to bear fruit after you left the scene?

What is the signature of your activities?

How will you be remembered?

What would cause you disappointment or pain if you were ninety-four and reflecting upon your life?

What legacy do you want to leave in the lives of those God has called you to lead?

What legacy or legacies do you want to leave in the lives of your loved ones?

How does your current vocational or ministry activity reflect the legacy you would like to leave?

Our Personal Mandate

A *personal life mandate* is the map you intend to follow to navigate through life. The components of a mandate include your biblical purpose, life purpose, committed passion, role characteristics, unique methodologies, and ultimate contribution. I have laid out the framework for your mandate in **Appendix A: The Map**. A form for you to complete is also in the appendix. Once you have answered the questions listed under each component of the mandate, you are ready to draft your personal life mandate. This declaration is a living document that will serve as a benchmark and touchstone for a focused life. It is something you will go back to time and again to evaluate your progress.

The examples of my own declarations, provided near the end of each description, are the result of continual revisions and updates over many years. Your mandate initially may not be as specific or detailed as mine. That is okay. The point is to be thinking strategically about how you will live your life. The Chinese are right: the journey of a thousand miles begins with the first step. Pray about what God wants from you. Share your mandate with others. Find a partner who understands the journey and give him or her permission to hold you accountable. Redeem the time!

PART 3:
The Guide

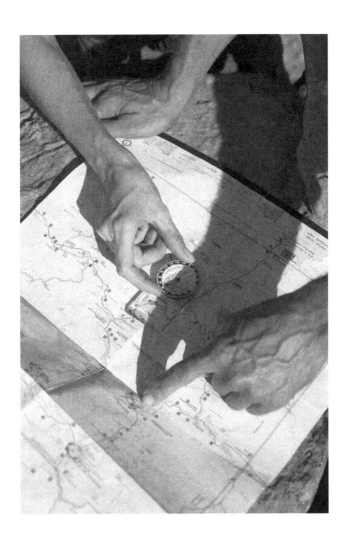

Chapter 14: Finishing Well

Every conscience needs instruction. Its delicate mechanism has been thrown off balance by the Fall. Just as a bullet will reach the bull's eye only if the two sights are in correct alignment, so, correct moral judgments are delivered only when conscience is correctly aligned with the Scriptures.

—J. Oswald Sanders

No one I know wants to finish his or her journey poorly. No one I know gets up in the morning looking for ways to tarnish his or her reputation. Yet that is how many of us end our journeys. What legacy will you leave in the lives of others? What legacy are you living now that's worth leaving in the lives of others? What kind of legacy do you want to leave to your friends, your loved ones? If your life continues as it is right now, without any changes, what kind of *legacy* will you leave?

Each of us has something of value to pass on to someone of value. Each of us has been given something of value by God to give to someone He values. Are you investing the treasure God has given you in the lives of your loved ones, in the lives of your friends, in the lives God has allowed you to influence on His behalf?

Psychoanalytic theorist Erik Erickson introduced the concept of generativity more than fifty years ago. But it was not until the 1980s that it caught the imagination of psychological theorists, researchers, and clinicians. Erikson argued that in adulthood, mature men and women work to ensure the well-being of their children in particular and the next generation in general.

Generativity is the concern for and commitment to the well-being of future generations. It may be expressed through teaching, mentoring, volunteer work, charitable activities, religious involvement, and political activities. It may be expressed as conserving and nurturing that which is deemed to be good in life and as transforming that which is believed to be in need of improvement, with the common aim of fostering the development and well-being of future generations. It is the desire to invest your substance in forms of life and work that will outlive you. At the same time, it involves relatively selfless nurturing and caring for the next generation, even to the point of giving yourself up for your children, your community, or your people. A number of scholars have linked generativity to a desire for symbolic immortality.

Some adults are more generative than others. Highly generative parents prioritize education and values in their approach to their children's socialization, and they take advantage of opportunities to impart lessons and pass on wisdom to the next generation. In Erikson's research, generativity was positively associated with church attendance and involvement in church activities.

Erikson conceived of *identity* as, among other things, a personalized and self-defining configuration of drives, talents, values, and expectations that positions the young adult in historical time and within society. Beginning in late adolescence, he theorized, a person constructs and internalizes this configuration to give his or her life a sense of unity, purpose, and meaning: I may die, but my children will live on. My own story may end, but other stories will follow mine, due in part to my own generative efforts.[484]

---

484 Dan P. Adams and Regina L. Logan, *What Is Generativity?* (2004). The generative society: Caring for future generations, (pp. 15–31). Washington, DC: American Psychological Association, xiii, 292.

Generativity is often about progress, improvement, transforming the bad into good. So, according to social science, we do have something of value to pass on to others. In fact, we are driven to do so.

Legacy Features

I define *legacy* as the aroma left in the nostrils of those we leave behind, those whom God brought within our sphere of influence, long after we are gone. What fragrance will linger when God calls you home? Maybe you think that you have nothing of value to offer others or that no one cares about what you have to offer. That is a lie from the pit of hell, and it certainly doesn't correspond to God's plans for our lives.

There are only four legacies one can live and leave: no legacy whatsoever, a perishable legacy, a bad legacy, or a godly legacy. Living and leaving a godly legacy will help us finish well. Some people drift through life, gliding from one experience to the next, causing no major fuss and living undistinguished lives. Their legacy is leaving no legacy at all. Others leave a perishable legacy, the memory of which fades with time. Their monuments may still be standing, but few people know why. Still others leave a bad legacy, having given in to their dark side, often supported by people who condone their behavior. What distinguishes these people is their badness. Then we have people who leave a godly legacy in the lives of others, the gift that keeps giving, growing more meaningful as time passes.

Earlier we described several types of finishes: being *cut off early* because the wake being left is capsizing the lives of too many people; *finishing poorly*, having possibly started well but ultimately succumbing to barriers along the way; *finishing so-so* because of repeated sin and strongholds of the enemy impairing progress; and *finishing well*, regardless of how the journey started. I am sure you see the correlation between legacies and finishes.

Leaving a godly legacy and finishing well are interrelated. A refresher: Someone who is finishing well is walking with God at the end of his or her life, has contributed to God's purposes at a high level, and has fulfilled what God intended for him or her. Biblical examples of finishing well would include Abraham, Job, Joseph, Joshua, Caleb, Samuel, Elijah, Jeremiah, Daniel, John, Paul, and Peter. When you read about the lives of these people, you will notice that some of these leaders experienced moments or seasons of weakness and failure but still finished well. I don't know about you, but for me that's encouraging.

In summary, finishing well means reaching the end of life having been faithful to the calling God has placed upon that life; it's about Christ's followers being more passionate about Christ and His mission as they fulfill their life purpose than they were at the beginning. It also entails experiencing the depth of God's grace and love. It is living out one's destiny and making one's unique and ultimate contribution in expanding God's Kingdom.

Legacy Characteristics

When Clinton and his colleagues researched scripture, they came to a startling conclusion: There are around eight hundred leaders mentioned in the Bible. We have enough information on one hundred of them to enable us to analyze their leadership, and enough information on fifty of them to enable us to evaluate their finish. Of those fifty, about one in three finished well. Anecdotal evidence from today indicates that for Christian leaders today, this ratio is probably generous. Probably fewer than one in threes finishes well today.

When the lives of those who finished well were carefully analyzed, some equally interesting conclusions emerged. Those who finished well exhibited common characteristics. Many leaders had several of the characteristics, and a few possessed them all. The Bible encourages us to remember our leaders who spoke the Word of God to us. We should consider the outcome of their way of life and imitate their faith. Jesus Christ is the same yesterday and today and forever.[485] Notice that their legacies were less about what they said than about how they modeled what they believed. Notice also that a singular quality found in such people and modeled by Christ is consistency.

Bobby Clinton makes the following observations about the characteristics of those who finish well. I would humbly suggest that anyone seeking to finish well would be wise to heed the lessons embedded in these characteristics.

---

485 Heb. 13:7–8.

Comparative study of effective leaders who finished well has six identified characteristics. While there may be other characteristics that I have not seen, certainly these are important ones. Not all six always appear but at least several of them do in leaders who finish well. Frequently, effective leaders who finish well will have four or five of them seen in their lives. And some like Daniel in the O.T. and Paul in the N.T. demonstrate all of them.

They maintain a personal vibrant relationship with God right up to the end. They maintain a learning posture and can learn from various kinds of sources; life especially. They manifest Christ-likeness in character as evidenced by the fruit of the Spirit in their lives. Truth is lived out in their lives so that convictions and promises of God are seen to be real. They leave behind one or more ultimate contributions. They walk with a growing awareness of a sense of destiny and see some or all of it fulfilled.

The classic example in the O.T. of a good finish is Daniel who manifests all six characteristics.

The classic example in the N.T. other than Christ is Paul. There are gradations of finishing well. Some finish well but not quite having all six or lesser intensity on one or the other major characteristics. This list of characteristics is probably not complete. But these are certainly evident in many leaders who have finished well.[486]

Legacy Barriers

Barriers along a path impede progress. Barriers to finishing well impede us from advancing. Clinton identifies six such barriers, but it only takes one to destroy our witness and bring discredit upon ourselves and the Lord we say we serve. In many such cases, the person who fails in one area will

---

486 J. Robert Clinton, *Finishing Well—Six Characteristics* (Altadena: Barnabas Publishers, 2007), 1-3.

also fail in others. Scripture tells us that sensible people will see trouble coming and avoid it, but an unthinking person will walk right into it and regret it later.[487]

What follows are Clinton's descriptions of the six barriers, to which I will add another called "woundedness." Although he speaks in terms of leaders, these barriers apply to every follower of Christ. You will notice, as well, that these barriers are a common malady of humans, whether or not they follow Christ.

Finances—Use and Abuse

Leaders, particularly those who have powerful positions and make important decisions concerning finances, tend to use practices that can encourage the incorrect handling of finances and eventually their abuse. Greed is often a deeply rooted character trait, and eventually it will cause impropriety with regard to finances. Numerous leaders have fallen due to some issue related to money.

Power—Use and Abuse

Leaders who are effective vocationally or in ministry must use various power bases in order to accomplish their responsibilities. When power is so available and used almost daily, there is a tendency to abuse it. Leaders who rise to the top of a hierarchical system tend to assume privileges with their perceived status. Frequently, these "privileges" include the abuse of power, and the leaders usually have no counterbalancing accountability.

Pride—Self-Centeredness

Pride, which is commonly inappropriate and self-centered, can lead to the downfall of a leader. Leaders must maintain a dynamic tension between a healthy respect for themselves and the recognition that they have nothing that was not given to them by God, who is the one who really enables us.

Sex—Illicit Relationships

Illicit sexual relationships can be seen as a major downfall both in the Bible and throughout Western culture. Joseph's classic integrity check with respect to sexual sin is the ideal model that should be in every

---

487 Prov. 22:3.

leader's mind. Pornography, with its easy availability, has become a major contributor to immoral behavior.

Family—Critical Issues

Problems between spouses, between parents and children, or between siblings can destroy a leader's work and ministry. What is needed are biblical values lived out in family relationships. Of growing importance in our day is the need for social base support systems (i.e., economic, emotional, strategic, and social) for singles and married couples in ministry. Every family has conflicts; they do not disqualify us from service unless we neglect our responsibility to deal with them strategically.

Plateauing—Living on Fumes

Leaders who are competent tend to plateau. Their very strength becomes a weakness: they can continue to operate at a certain level without reality- or Spirit-empowered renewal. Most leaders will plateau several times in their developmental lives. Some of the five enhancement factors for a good finish will counteract this tendency (lifetime perspective, life-long learning posture, repeated times of renewal, many mentors, spiritual disciplines). Again, there is a dynamic tension that must be maintained between leveling off for good reasons, (consolidating your growth and/or reaching the level of potential for which God has made you) and plateauing because of sinfulness or loss of vision.

Woundedness—Victim Mentality

Some leaders wear their misfortunes and wounds on their sleeves, repeatedly sharing how they have been victimized. They wear their hurt like a badge of honor; not only can they not get over it, they cannot get past it. The pain they endured now defines who they are. But if they continue to allow pain to define them, their effectiveness will be severally impaired. Those they hope to lead will avoid them or disregard what they offer.

Clinton cautions us at this point. "Forewarned is forearmed. There are many other reasons why leaders don't finish well—usually all related to sin in some form. But at least the six categories are major ones (plus one) that have trapped many leaders and taken them out of the race. Leaders who want to finish well, Take heed!"

Legacy Enhancements

What can we learn from the preceding remarks? Clinton offers five strategies that will help us finish well.[488] You'll find it helpful to consider these strategies as you think through your Focused Life Plan—and implementing them would be a game changer.

Perspective

We need to have a lifetime perspective on life, work, and ministry. Effective leaders view their present actions in terms of a lifetime perspective. We gain that perspective by studying the lives of leaders, as commanded in Hebrews 13:7–8. I (Bobby) have been doing intensive study of leaders' lives over the past many years. Leadership emergence theory is the result of that research. Its many concepts can help us understand more fully just how God does shape a leader over a lifetime.

Renewal

Special moments of intimacy with God, challenges from God, new vision from God, and affirmation from God, both personal and ministerial, will occur repeatedly in the life of a growing leader. These destiny experiences will be needed and appreciated and will make a difference in how well a leader perseveres in life, work, and ministry. All leaders should expectantly look for these repeated times of renewal. Some can be initiated by the leader (usually extended times of spiritual discipline), but some are initiated by God. We can seek them, of course, and be ready for them.

Most leaders who have been effective over a lifetime have needed and welcomed renewal experiences from time to time. And some times of renewal are more crucial than others. Apparently in Western society, the mid-thirties, early forties, and mid-fifties are crucial times in which renewal is frequently needed in a leader's life. Frequently during these critical periods, discipline slackens, there is a tendency to plateau and rely on past experience and skills, and there is a sense of confusion about achievement and new direction.

Unusual renewal experiences with God can overcome these tendencies and redirect a leader. Openness to them, a willingness to receive them, and

---

488 J. Robert Clinton, *The Leadership Emergence Theory Reader: Finishing Well— The Challenge of a Lifetime* (Altadena: Barnabas Publishers, 2005), 11–15.

knowledge of their importance for a whole life can be vital enhancements for finishing well. Sometimes these renewal experiences are divinely originated by God, and we must be sensitive to His invitation. At other times we must initiate the renewal efforts ourselves.

Disciplines

Leaders need disciplines of all kinds, especially spiritual disciplines. A strong surge toward spirituality now exists in Catholic and Protestant circles. This movement, combined with an increasingly felt need for discipline due to the large number of moral failures, has leaders hungering for intimacy with God. The spiritual disciplines are a means of achieving this intimacy. Authors like Eugene Peterson, Dallas Willard, and Richard Foster are making headway with Protestants concerning spiritual disciplines. Leaders who don't use these leadership tools are prone to failure through sin, as well as plateauing.

Clinton concurs with Paul's admonitions to discipline as a means of ensuring perseverance in the ministry. When Paul was around fifty years old, he wrote to the Corinthian church what appears to be both an exhortation to the Corinthians and an explanation of a major leadership value in his own life. We need to keep in mind that Paul had been in ministry for about twenty-one years at this point, and he was still advocating strong discipline. I will paraphrase his message here: I am serious about finishing well in my Christian ministry. I discipline myself for fear that after challenging others into the Christian life, I myself might become a casualty.[489]

Lack of physical discipline is often an indicator of laxity in the spiritual life as well. Toward the end of his life, when he was probably between sixty-five and seventy, Paul was still advocating discipline. This time he wrote to Timothy, who was probably between thirty and thirty-five years old: "Instead exercise your mind in godly things. For physical exercise is advantageous somewhat but exercising in godliness has long term implications both for today and for that which will come."[490]

From time to time, leaders should assess their state of discipline. In addition to standard Word disciplines involving the devotional life and

---

489 1 Cor. 9:24–27.
490 1 Tim. 7b–8.

biblical study, I recommend other disciplines such as solitude, silence, fasting, frugality, chastity, and secrecy. Foster and Willard identify a number of disciplines that, when practiced habitually, can shape character and increase the probability of a good finish.

Learning Posture

The single most important antidote to plateauing is a well-developed learning posture. Such a posture is also one of the major ways through which God gives vision. Effective leaders maintain a learning posture all their lives. It sounds simple enough, but many leaders don't see the need for it. Two biblical leaders who certainly were lifelong learners and exemplified this principle were Daniel and Paul. When Daniel was quite old, he was still studying his Bible and still learning new things from it. And he was alert to what God wanted to do through what he was learning. Consequently, Daniel was able to intercede for his people and receive one of the great messianic revelations.[491] Paul's closing remarks to Timothy show he was still learning: "And when you come, don't forget the books, Timothy!"[492]

There are many nonformal training opportunities, such as workshops, seminars, and conferences, covering a variety of learning skills. Take advantage of them. A good learning posture is insurance against plateauing and provides a helpful prod along the way as you persevere in leadership. A disinterest in learning is an almost sure precursor to a so-so or poor finish.

Mentoring

A comparative study of many leaders' lives indicates the frequency with which other people significantly challenged them into leadership and offered timely advice and help to keep them there. Leaders who are effective and finish well will have ten to fifteen significant people who helped them at one time or another.

Mentoring is a growing movement in both Christian and secular circles. Generally, it involves a relational empowerment process: someone who knows something (the mentor) passes on something (wisdom, advice, information, emotional support, protection, links to resources) to a person

---

491 Dan. 9.
492 2 Tim. 4:13 (paraphrased).

who needs it (the mentee or protégé) at a sensitive time so that it impacts that person's development. The basic dynamics of mentoring include attraction, relationship, response, accountability, and empowerment.

All leaders need mentors during their lifetime of leadership. Mentors are available. Just look for people who can help with specific areas rather than an ideal mentor who can do it all. God will provide a mentor in a specific area of need if you trust Him and are willing to submit to and accept responsibility for His choice.

Simply stated, a final way to facilitate a good finish is to find a mentor who will hold you accountable in your spiritual life and ministry and who can warn and advise you, enabling you to avoid pitfalls and grow throughout your lifetime of ministry.

In summary, if you want to finish well, learn from godly leaders who have gone before you, eliminate barriers that will interfere with finishing well, and implement the enhancements above.

I encourage you to complete the **Five Habits Checklist** in **Appendix J**. The results will help you assess the degree to which you have adopted the habits that will help you finish well.

Personal Assessment

What legacy characteristics would be trues of your personal journey?

What legacy barriers are you currently struggling through?

What legacy enhancements need to be addressed in your life?

Chapter 15: Mentoring

The unexamined life is not worth living.

—Socrates

Few people finish well. Those who do had other individuals who gave them timely help along the way and significantly enhanced their development. Clinton's research indicates that people who finish well have had ten to fifteen significant mentors in their lives. I have met with many people who long to be mentored but do not know how to find a mentor, much less risk rejection when they ask someone to mentor them.

While speaking at a conference one day, I approached the subject of mentoring by declaring that many people who are young in the faith desire older, more mature Christians as mentors, but they are hesitant to ask for help because they are afraid of rejection, or because they believe the people they have selected are too busy and won't have time for them. On the other hand, older Christians who have something of value to offer younger Christians often feel that no one really wants to hear what they have to say. Sometimes a mentoring opportunity is passed by because we feel we are not worthy to mentor or be mentored.

In either scenario, the enemy wins. He is encouraged that such a divide exists, and he would like for it to remain. Why? Because the last thing he wants is for any Christian to become a fully devoted follower of Christ. He knows effective mentoring will result in spiritual growth, confidence, and a deeper commitment to Christ. God's mandate, however, is that we are to pass on what we have learned to others.[493] Mentoring provides the mortar that holds the foundation of our faith together.

The Bible stresses the importance of mentoring when it exhorts us to love one another, bear with one another, accept one another, forgive one another, submit to one another, pray for one another, serve one another, instruct one another, greet one another, teach one another, offer hospitality to one another, be at peace with one another, be devoted to one another, encourage one another, build up one another, be kind to one another, be patient with one another, spur one another on, live in harmony with one another, confess to one another, admonish one another, have compassion for one another, and stop judging one another. You can see why the enemy does not want mentoring to take place.

Mentoring In General

Why consider mentoring? Randy Reese offers the following reasons: People are longing for their stories to be heard and their lives to be shaped. Mentoring is one of the most effective ways to change lives. It provides an avenue for passing on what we have learned. It is one of the most effective ways to shape a person's character. It can be a significant means of facilitating discipleship. It connects us to a deeper sense of the community of the Church. It is essential to finishing well as a Christian leader. And it reflects a primary way Jesus impacted lives and practiced ministry.

Mentorship Description

Mentoring is a relational process in which a mentor, someone who knows or has experienced something, transfers that something (resources for

---

493 2 Tim. 2:2.

wisdom, information, experience, confidence, insight, relationships, status, etc.) to a mentee at an appropriate time and in an appropriate manner, facilitating development or empowerment. More succinctly, mentoring is a relational experience through which one person empowers another by sharing God-given resources.

In *The Iliad*, Odysseus—better known as Ulysses by the Romans much later—contracts his "wise and trusted counselor" as a tutor for his son, Telemachus, before leaving on a twenty-year journey precipitated by the kidnapping of Helen by Paris, the son of the king of Troy. The name of that trusted counselor was Mentor. Mentor's name—with a lowercase *m*—has passed into our language as a shorthand term for a wise and trusted counselor and teacher.

Words like *mentor*, *mentee*, and *mentoring* can conjure up various meanings for each of us. For some, the words evoke memories of positive, life-changing relationships; for others, the words are reminders of their yearning for something they know they need to develop as a person, a professional, a Christian, or even as a leader, but which they have yet to find.

A *mentor* is a person with a serving, giving, encouraging attitude who sees potential in a younger person and is able to promote or otherwise significantly influence the realization of that potential. A mentee or protégé is a person who receives empowerment in the mentoring relationship.

Mentor Categories and Types

Intensive mentors help forge the foundations of our faith and practice through means like a one-on-one discipleship. *Occasional* mentors come in and out of our lives to address specific needs that arise on our journeys. *Passive* mentors are people we probably have never met; they may not even be alive. But every time we read something they have written, listen to something they have said via recording, or watch a video of one of their presentations or sermons, God feeds our souls. On occasion, a divine contact will enter our lives, generally unannounced, and pass on a word of encouragement, the importance of which we may or may not realize at the moment.

Intensive mentors include disciplers, spiritual guides, and coaches. *Disciplers* provide enablement in the basics of following Christ. *Spiritual guides* provide accountability, direction, and insight regarding questions, commitments, and decisions affecting spirituality and maturity. *Coaches* provide the motivation, skills, and application needed to meet a task or challenge.

Occasional mentors include counselors, teachers, and sponsors. *Counselors* provide timely advice and correct perspectives on viewing self, others, circumstances, vocation, or ministry. *Teachers* provide knowledge and understanding of a particular subject. *Sponsors* provide career guidance and protection as a leader moves within an organization. They also might provide access to their network of relationships.

Passive mentors include contemporary, historical, and divine contacts. *Contemporary* mentors provide living, personal models for life, ministry, or profession; they serve as examples and inspire emulation. *Historical* mentors are deceased people whose lives still teach dynamic principles and exemplify values for life, ministry, and/or profession. They encourage ongoing development and press us to finish well. *Divine contacts* may offer timely guidance from God at critical junctures in our lives.

The type of mentor needed will depend on the expectations the mentee has or the objectives a mentee hopes to reach—the goal he or she hopes to attain. It's not unreasonable to expect ten to fifteen mentors during a lifetime, when all the categories and types of mentors are considered. We all have passive mentors. There is a divine reason why certain individuals we have never even met feed our souls when we read or hear what they have said or have to say to us today.

Mentoring Constellation

Bobby Clinton stresses that "Christian workers need relationships that will mentor us, peers who will co-mentor us, and people that we are mentoring. This will help ensure a balanced and healthy perspective on life and ministry."[494] Who is mentoring you? Whom are you mentoring? Who is a peer mentor with you?

Lifelong development is greatly enhanced by a balance of mentoring relationships. Terry Walling makes the following observations regarding the mentoring constellation:

---

494 Clinton, *Please Mentor Me*, 27.

There are three basic kinds of mentoring: upward mentoring, co-mentoring (internal and external), and downward mentoring.

- *Upward Mentoring*—upward mentoring pushes people forward to expand their potential. Upward mentors see the bigger picture and how the current situation fits into that picture. Their experience and knowledge base is more advanced than the mentoree. They give valuable advice and challenge the mentoree to persevere and grow.

- *Co-mentoring*—Co-mentoring is lateral mentoring that comes from peers who are either inside or outside a person's daily frame of reference. Internal co-mentors are peers in the same ministry environment and about the same level of spiritual maturity. They provide mutual growth and accountability, contextual insights within the organizations, and friendship during difficulty.

- *External Co-mentors*—Includes peers like internal co-mentors, except they are outside the ministry situation. They are also at about the same level of development and maturity. They provide objective perspective. They challenge a person to think through the way they act and apply insights.

- *Downward Mentoring*—Believers need to identify, select, and help develop emerging disciples. Downward mentoring means empowering younger or less experienced individuals. Downward mentors provide accountability, challenge, insight, and critical skills. Downward mentoring also counter-balances the tendency for disciples to plateau and become inconsistent in living out their values.[495]

Every Christian, regardless of whether he or she is relatively young in the faith, is growing in maturity, or has reached maturity, should consider who is in his or her mentoring constellation. Being mentored, mentoring others, and forming peer–mentor relationships with people who are essentially at the same place in their walk should be a high priority.

---

495 Terry B. Walling, *Mentoring Workbook,* Leader Breakthru (2013), 18.

The resources shared in a mentoring relationship could include wisdom and discernment, life and ministry experience, timely advice, new methods, skills, principles, important values and lessons, organizational influence, sponsorship, networking, and, on occasion, financial resources.

Mentoring Guidelines

First of all, mentoring is relational,[496] autobiographical,[497] a partnership with the Holy Spirit,[498] purposive,[499] requires listening[500] and discernment,[501] and is intentional.[502] Second, following certain mentoring guidelines will make for more effective mentoring. Whether you are the mentor or the mentee, these guidelines will help establish the best environment for God to work through the mentor and in the life of the mentee.

- Establish the mentoring.
- Jointly agree on the purpose of the relationship.
- Determine the regularity of interaction.
- Agree on a system for accountability.
- Set up communication mechanisms.
- Clarify the level of confidentiality.
- Set the life cycle of the relationship.
- Evaluate the relationship from time to time.
- Modify expectations to fit the real-life mentoring situation.
- Bring closure to the mentoring relationship.

Good mentors possess the following characteristics: the ability to readily see potential in a person; a tolerance of mistakes, brashness, abrasiveness, etc., in order to see that potential develop; flexibility in responding to people and circumstances; patience and a recognition that time and experience are needed for development; perspective—the vision

---

496 John 1:14.
497 Luke 19:1–10.
498 Isa. 48:17–18.
499 Deut. 31:7–8.
500 Mark 5:24–34.
501 1 Thess. 5:21.
502 Phil. 4:9.

and ability to see down the road and suggest the next steps that a mentee needs; and gifts and abilities that build up and encourage others.[503]

A good mentor is one who is honest with you, a model for you, deeply committed to you, open and transparent, a teacher, successful in your eyes, open to learning from you as well as teaching you, and willing to stay primarily on your agenda, not his or her own. He or she believes in your potential and can help you plan and turn your dream into reality.[504] Put more simply, a good mentor possesses the following qualities: availability, confidentiality, honesty, accountability, boundaries, and a capacity for honest assessment.

A good mentee, on the other hand, is easy to believe in, easy to like and spend time with, and easy to keep helping. A good mentee is like family, is teachable, respects his or her mentor, is self-motivated, and feels comfortable with (and to) the mentor.[505] Put more simply, a good mentee is honest, vulnerable, accountable, committed, and teachable. When I mentor someone I look for these qualities.

Mentoring Accountability

Effective mentoring hinges on five relational dynamics. First, like attracts like. People naturally move toward those who seem helpful. Mentees may be attracted by a mentor's approachability, personality, spirituality, competence, skills, expertise, or experience. Second, the best environment for sharing empowerment resources happens when mentors and mentees trust each other. Third, a mentee's willingness to respond to the mentor's information, advice, assignments, evaluation criteria, instruction, criticism, correction, and training is vital to learning empowerment. Fourth, empowerment that bolsters a mentee's confidence and competence makes him or her more receptive to growth, leading to spiritual and personal maturation. Finally, accountability is crucial to honest, transparent, and candid exchanges.

Truth be known, we are as accountable as we want to be. Unless there is a concrete agreement from the start about what constitutes accountability, how

503 Paul D. Stanley and J. Robert Clinton, *Connecting* (Colorado Springs: NavPress, 1992), 215.
504 Bobb Biehl, *Mentoring* (Nashville: Broadman & Holman Publishers, 1997), 100–104.
505 Ibid, 122–25.

it will be implemented, to what degree it will be upheld, and the consequences of an accountability breakdown, mentoring will falter if not fail altogether. The management adage "Inspect what you expect" applies here.

Patrick Morley, author of *The Man in the Mirror*, provides additional insights regarding accountability.[506] Although his comments are directed to men, they apply to women as well:

> One of the greatest reasons that men get into trouble is that they don't have to answer to anyone for their lives. Ask around. You will learn that very few men have built accountability into their life. Every day men fail morally, spiritually, relationally, and financially; not because they don't want to succeed, but because of blind spots and weak spots which they think they can handle on their own. They can't. Some have spectacular failures in a moment of passion they burst into flames, crash, and burn. More often, they make hundreds of tiny, undetected decisions that slowly, like water tapping on a rock, wear down their character. Not blatantly or precipitously, but subtly, we get caught in a web of cutting corners, compromise, and self-deceit. And no one asks us, "How? Why? What? And Who?" Men fall because they don't have to answer to anyone for their behavior and beliefs. Most of our conversations in life revolve around the cliché level news, sports, and weather. But this is the tip of the iceberg, the "visible" you. The "real" you wrestles with gut-wrenching issues in the key areas of your life every day, and like me, you need someone to help you navigate around the submerged dangers of an unexamined life.

Morley describes Christian accountability as "nothing less than to each day become more Christ-like in all our ways and be ever more intimate with Him." He goes on to say that you can't stay on track with your God, family, friends, morality, money, and vocation unless you have an accountable relationship with other like-minded people. The truth for the biblical Christian is that there is power in vulnerability, strength in numbers, and safety in visibility.

---

506 Adapted from *The Man in the Mirror and The Seven Seasons of a Man's Life*. Also found at http://www.maninthemirror.org/printthis/alm/alm9.htm.

Are you doing everything you can to guard yourself against the epidemic of falling and failure to which so many people have succumbed? Make a commitment today to regularly account to qualified people for each of the key areas of your life. It may be the missing piece that helps you synchronize your behavior with your beliefs and keeps you from spinning out of control.

Appendix K: Accountability Guidelines provides accountability guidelines which, when followed, will help ensure that the journey you are on will be one of integrity and authenticity.

Being Mentored

Many mentoring relationships happen with little discussion of the dynamics, responsibilities, and requirements involved or the type and scope of mentoring needed. More commonly, both mentor and the mentee are uncertain about the relationship and need help defining it. They need to clarify their roles and agree on the kind of mentoring the mentee seeks.

Needs Assessment

I routinely make the following requests of those who seek me out for mentoring: I ask them to read a recommended book on mentoring.[507] I ask them to think through the area or areas in which they need mentoring. I ask what type of mentor they need, their expectations of the mentoring relationship, clarification about what they would deem a successful mentoring experience, and why they asked me to mentor them. Once they've read the book I recommended, I have them write down their answers and send me their responses via e-mail. Then I pray about them to determine if I am the right person to mentor them and if I can indeed help them with their concerns.

In 1999, I was in Dallas attending an invitation-only gathering to determine what it would take to develop lay leaders in the coming decade. Many luminaries were present, which made me wonder why I was invited. Bobby Clinton was there. I had never met him, but I had read everything

---

507 I normally recommend *Connecting: The Mentoring Relationships You Need to Succeed in Life* by Paul Stanley and J. Robert Clinton. I keep several copies on hand for this express purpose.

I could get my hands on that he'd produced. Having gained a deep appreciation for his leadership emergence theory and findings, I secretly coveted a mentoring relationship with him. As we shared our stories at the beginning of the meeting, it became apparent that Bobby had mentored many of the leaders gathered there.

During lunch one day, I got to him before he was surrounded by others wanting his time. Not wanting to scare him away, I asked general questions about how he determined whom he would mentor. He said he didn't seek anyone out; people came to him of their own volition. If he thought he could help them, he would ask them to fulfill certain tasks, and once those were completed he would decide whether or not to mentor them. Then he added that he turned down most requests. That was a discouragement to me, and I concluded that my secret desire would go unmet.

But at the end of the meetings, to my great surprise and delight, he came up to me and asked me to complete a certain task. When I got home I did just that; it was no easy assignment. When I sent him the results, he followed up by giving me additional assignments over the next several weeks. As I completed each one, my impatience grew. Finally, I wrote him a short e-mail: "Are you going to mentor me or not?" He sent a one-word reply: "Yes." Bobby has been my mentor from that day to the present. God has used him at several critical junctures in my life. Bobby's advice, guidance, care, and accountability have proven to be priceless.

The point I am trying to stress is that an assessment must be conducted to ascertain the needs and expectations in a proposed mentoring relationship. Many people just want to be mentored, having given little thought to the specifics. Such mentoring encounters often end in unmet expectations or disappointment with the experience. Unless there is clarity at the beginning, there will be no clarity at the end.

Personal Assessment

If you are seeking to be mentored, consider answering the following questions:

What are my current goals for personal growth?

What help do I need to accomplish my life goals?

Based on my needs, what type of mentor should I seek?

What are my expectations for a mentoring relationship?

What end result do I hope to obtain?

What would constitute a successful and worthwhile experience?

What kind of accountability will I need?

Am I willing to take responsibility for my growth?

Am I willing to submit to a mentor?

The following information will help you determine your mentoring needs. In what specific area are you seeking mentoring?

Spiritual Disciplines	Spiritual Leadership	Relationships	Self-Management	Life Management	Foundations
Bible Study	Children with Special Needs	Marriage	Spiritual Growth	Time Management	Seeker/Inquirer
Prayer	Unbelieving Children	Unbelieving Spouse	Self-Discipline	Priorities	Basic Discipleship
Quiet Time	Parenting Teenagers	Divorce	Trusting God	Home and Career	Spiritual Disciplines
Witnessing	Blended Families	Singleness	Anger Management	Career Fulfillment	Prayer Life
	Family Skills	Relatives	Addictions	Finances	Worship
		Friendships		Organizational Skills	Evangelism
		Unbelievers			Service
		Workplace			Biblical Leadership

Mentor Selection

A mentee usually seeks out a mentor to help in a particular area of need. Successful mentoring depends on a healthy relationship between the mentor and mentee. Willingness to submit to a mentor is critical; effective mentoring cannot take place if the mentee resists the advice and counsel given, cannot accept criticism, or passively thwarts the process. Respect for the mentor, appreciation for his or her investment of time, and energy and recognition of his or her advanced spiritual standing are important. Being teachable is a prime criterion.

To find a mentor, you must be aware of the opportunities that pass before you. Walling calls this awareness "mentoring eyes"—recognizing divine appointments and growth opportunities that God puts in the mentee's path.

Identify potential mentors based on your current needs. Who within your sphere of relationships might be a suitable mentor? Ask others you trust to point out possible mentors. Ask your pastor who might help you. Talk to others who have been mentored to get the names of additional candidates.

Walling makes the following recommendations: If you don't know whom to ask first, start with the top three candidates related to your top needs. Mentees are often surprised by how willing mentors are to help. Approach the mentor with your mentoring goals and the ways you feel he or she might be able to help. Allow the mentor to give input and help clarify your issues and define your goals. Ask for a first meeting to discuss the issues. After such a meeting, you and the mentor will have a much better idea about whether the relationship is something you want to pursue.

Mentoring Contract

Establishing a mentoring contract, whether you are being mentored or mentoring someone, will help you avoid any misunderstandings. In fact misunderstandings will certainly occur if such a contract is not defined ahead of time.

1. Jointly agree on the purpose of the relationship. Determine the objective for the mentoring relationship. Determine the type of mentor needed. Identify the area or areas that need to be addressed.

2. Set the criteria for evaluation. What will a successful outcome look like? How will you know the objective has been accomplished? Have the mentee describe what he or she hopes to accomplish.

3. Determine the regularity of interaction. It should be at least twice a month but could be more, depending on the needs of the mentee and the availability of the mentor.

4. Determine accountability parameters. Consideration should be given to honesty, vulnerability, accountability, and whatever else is required by the mentor and agreed upon by the mentee. What accountability parameters will be applied? Refer to the **Accountability Guidelines** in **Appendix K**.

5. Set up communication mechanisms. Will you communicate face-to-face; by e-mail, phone, video connection, or a combination; or whatever is most convenient? At least one face-to-face meeting is required per month in addition to second or additional meetings by other means.

6. Clarify the level of confidentiality. What is shared on a personal level must remain confidential unless it is of a legal nature (e.g., abuse of any kind, a crime, etc.).

7. Set the life cycle of the relationship. Three months is recommended as a preliminary time frame, at the end of which each of you should evaluate the relationship. If you agree to continue, set an end date

not to exceed six additional months. Nine months should be enough time to complete the mentoring process. Potential mentors often are unwilling to commit to a mentoring relationship if it is open-ended.

8. Evaluate the relationship from time to time—I would recommend every two to three months. If, during the course of a periodic evaluation, the mentor or mentee no longer wants to continue the relationship, it should be terminated.

9. Modify expectations to fit the real-life mentoring situation. If an issue or concern arises that needs more focused attention, both parties should decide whether the parameters of mentoring need to be changed.

10. Bring the mentoring relationship to a close. Celebrate the completion of the journey. Have the mentee write about the experience and what was accomplished.

Passive Mentoring

Many people do not realize that they are more than likely already enjoying passive mentoring. God, in His infinite care for us, sends us passive mentors regularly. They may come in the form of *historical personages* long since passed away, whose biographical information, written work, or recorded messages feed our souls. They may be *contemporary living people* we may not know personally who model in their own lives important values, attitudes, principles, or guidelines that help us during particular life stages or circumstances. They may also be sent as *divine contacts* that intersect our life at particularly important moments, providing timely insight and help from God.

Rather than relying solely on coincidental exposure to passive mentors, we can also proactively seek them out based on a thorough assessment of our needs. We can do this by seeking resources, written or recorded, that apply to our needs. People we respect or trust with our spiritual well-being can provide counsel or share resources that are or have been especially meaningful to them. Footnotes and bibliographies in the books we read can also provide passive mentoring.

The book tables and resource centers at conferences, workshops, and seminars can be valuable resources. Listening to messages from notable speakers on the Internet or visiting the websites of churches or ministry organizations can provide valuable passive mentoring. Paying attention to the sermons you hear in your own church, with a mind to hearing God's voice in the message, is another valuable source. Scanning Christian magazines can provide a plethora of different passive mentoring resources. Perusing book and video offerings can be helpful as well.

Listen to interviews of noted Christian speakers and thinkers. Request book and video lists from publishers, or secure syllabi from undergraduate, graduate, and postgraduate professors or institutions. Solicit additional resources from ministry organizations and ministry leaders.

One treasure trove is finding out what respected Christian leaders are reading and listening to. When you read classic devotional material, see if other devotional resources are cited. Find out what your mentor recommends for additional reading.

All these sources can provide timely help for whatever stage of life you are in, circumstances you are facing, problems you are dealing with, subjects you are interested in, and topics that address your needs.

The aforementioned information is also applicable to mentors.

Personal Assessment

Who are your passive historical mentors?

Who are your passive contemporary mentors?

Who and what do you read for spiritual nourishment?

What video or audio messages do you listen to for spiritual nourishment?

Chapter 16: Being a Mentor

The greatest use of life is to spend it for something that will outlast it.
—William James

Mentoring others is not just a priority; it is a mandate. We are to pass on to others what we have learned.[508] Mentoring is obviously not a new phenomenon. The Bible mentions many mentoring relationships. In the Old Testament, Jethro mentored Moses, providing valuable advice when Moses was overwhelmed by his responsibilities. Moses, in turned, mentored Joshua over many years and so trusted him that Joshua, certified by God, became his successor. Moses fulfilled several mentoring roles for Joshua, including spiritual guide, counselor, contemporary model, and sponsor.

David and Jonathan enjoyed a peer-mentoring relationship in which they shared advice and encouragement, with David being the primary beneficiary. King David mentored his son Solomon by providing counsel and advice, modeling how a king rules and sponsoring Solomon as the

508 2 Tim. 2:2.

next king of Israel. Elijah mentored Elisha, his replacement, and recruited him as a protégé. Elijah was a contemporary model and counselor for Elisha.

In the New Testament, Jesus formed a close bond with Peter, James, and John. In a wider circle He mentored all twelve apostles. In a yet wider circle, He mentored seventy followers, and He became a passive mentor to the crowds who gathered to hear Him. He served as a discipler, spiritual guide, coach, teacher, counselor, contemporary model, and sponsor, placing His mentees in significant roles to expand his Church on earth.

Barnabas mentored Paul, previously known as Saul, the persecutor of early Christians, acting as Paul's contemporary model, teacher, and sponsor. Barnabas later relinquished his lead role and became a follower of his mentee. Paul, in turn, mentored young Timothy by being his disciple, spiritual guide, and coach. Paul was also a counselor, teacher, and contemporary model, and he sponsored Timothy to other churches.

Paul also mentored Titus as a spiritual guide, counselor, teacher, contemporary model, and sponsor. He continued his mentoring with Onesimus, the servant or slave on whose behalf he wrote the epistle to Onesimus's owner, Philemon. He discipled Onesimus and became his teacher, contemporary model, and sponsor when he interceded on his behalf to Philemon.

Mentoring has gone on for centuries. Modern-day mentors recognize that helping others has a reciprocal effect, causing growth in the mentor's life. Walling identifies four common objections that often prevent potential mentors from mentoring others. He offers a rebuttal to each obstacle:

"I can't mentor someone else; I am not there yet myself!" Like attracts like. People are drawn to those they feel might be helpful to them. They are not looking for experts; they are looking for others on a similar journey.

"There are so many people who would be better than me!" There is always someone more qualified than you. The point is not whether you are fully qualified, but whether what you have learned along the way might help someone else be more effective.

"I am not equipped to be a mentor!" Mentoring is a relationship. By reviewing the concepts in this workbook, you now have the framework you need to be a mentor. Make yourself available and you will be amazed at how God will use you.

"What if the mentoring I offer is not what he or she really needed?" Mentoring relationships can always be renegotiated. All relationships should be reevaluated. You may be the one who uses your network to connect a mentee with needed resources.

Finding Your Niche

Knowing what you have to offer a mentee and what type or types of mentor you can be will help you find your niche. You have something of value to pass on to someone God values, some specific resources or area of knowledge or expertise: wisdom and discernment, life experience, ministry experience, wise counsel, timely advice, proven or new methods, life or leadership skills, key paradigms or insights, important values and life lessons, occupational or vocational expertise, organizational systems, cultural assessment, sponsorship, networking, resource identification, management competencies, problem-solving or conflict-resolution competencies, personal soul care, practice in spiritual disciplines, life-maturation processes, intercessory prayer, organizational sponsorship, financial resources, spiritual development, discipleship, leadership development, parental guidance, marriage counseling, stage-of-life transitions, financial planning, or job-placement advice, among many other talents, competencies, or skills.

Personal Assessment

Brainstorm about the experiences, expertise, and resources you may be able to pass on to others. Conduct a personal audit. Determine specifics by responding to the following questions.

What do you have to offer?

What life areas can you address?

What subjects or topics are you knowledgeable about?

What experience do you have?

What competencies and skills do you possess?

What lessons have you learned that can benefit others?

In what areas do you have expertise?

What God-given gift do you have to impart?

What values can you model for others?

What evaluation and assessment skills can you offer?

What networks can you introduce to others?

What knowledge or wisdom can you impart?

What new methods, practices, or strategies can you share?

Defining Your Style

Based on your temperament, roles you have enjoyed in the past, experiences you have cherished, relational dynamics you have appreciated, previous mentoring you have done, or styles you are comfortable with, what type or types of mentoring are you interested in providing?

Review the three categories of mentoring and the nine mentor types. First, select the category of mentoring you prefer:

- Intensive and Foundational _____
  This category of mentor usually follows a prescribed process of some kind, using pertinent prepared materials for a designated period of time to accomplish the objective of building strong foundations.

- Occasional and Needs-Based _____
  This category of mentor responds to a declared need for a period of time adequate to meeting that need, with the objective of helping the mentee develop an ability to resolve that need.

- Passive and Indirect _____
  This category of mentor provides some service indirectly to others through audio or video media, presentations to large groups, or written resources or materials that will be made widely available.

Second, select the type of mentoring you would like to do in the future:

- discipler _____

- spiritual guide _____

- coach _____

- counselor _____

- teacher _____

- sponsor _____

- contemporary model _____

- indirect resource _____

- situational contact _____

Third, given your time limitations and sphere of influence, determine how many people you can mentor and what intensity of mentoring you can provide based on the following criteria:

- Formal Mentoring   ————
  Formal mentoring requires direct engagement with a mentee in accordance with an established schedule, clear objectives, reasonable expectations, a central focus, and accountability parameters that have been agreed upon in advance.

- Informal Mentoring   ————
  Informal mentoring involves impromptu meetings, which may be scheduled or unscheduled situational encounters initiated by someone seeking your advice or counsel in a specific area, or initiated by you when random opportunities present themselves.

- Nonformal Mentoring   ————
  Nonformal mentoring means inviting an interested observer to shadow you during certain activities or watch how you do something, or observing how the mentee does something and offering advice or insight on the spot.

Determining Parameters

Every mentor should determine acceptable parameters or boundaries for mentoring others. Two fundamental principles need to be stressed:

First, you have a responsibility *to* your mentee, but you must not assume responsibility *for* your mentee. This is a very important thing to grasp. The only person you can legitimately take responsibility for is yourself. You cannot take responsibility for how your mentee responds, accomplishes his or her objectives, or engages in the mentoring opportunity. The mentee is responsible for these matters. Now, if you fail to fulfill your obligations and responsibilities and as a result the mentee flounders through no fault of his or her own, that is your problem.

Second, you have to decide if the issue or issues being raised in the mentoring relationship are a knapsack the mentee should carry or a boulder you must help shoulder because he or she can't lift it alone. In scripture we are admonished to *"Carry each other's burdens,* and in this way you will fulfill the law of Christ. If anyone thinks he is something when he is nothing, he deceives himself. Each one should test his own actions. Then he can take pride in himself, without comparing himself to somebody else, for *each one should carry his own load."*[509]

At first reading, you might conclude there is a contradiction here: we are to carry each other's burdens, yet each one of us should carry his or her own load. There is no contradiction. Carrying others' loads when they should do it themselves simply enables them and possibly creates codependency. However, when a life situation is impossible to bear and the weight of the issue too heavy for a person to lift, a mentor should find ways to alleviate the burden and help support the load.

Other parameters you might set are insisting on a particular approach to mentoring and informing the mentee what your style of mentoring looks like. Candid discussion of these nonnegotiable parameters will help you manage expectations and set appropriate boundaries. When I am asked to mentor someone, I clarify my style of mentoring in the first interview, before a commitment to mentoring has been agreed upon. I tell the mentee what he or she can expect from me and what I expect in return.

I would encourage you to think through your nonnegotiable parameters and the boundaries that must be adhered to if mentoring is to take place. For instance, you may want to set boundaries regarding your availability, where and how you will conduct the mentoring meetings, what you expect in terms of compliance with tasks assigned to the mentee, what an appropriate response from a mentee looks like, whether you require written or verbal feedback or both, what constitutes healthy communication, what follow-through by the mentee should look like, how much time each meeting will require, what attitude and demeanor you expect from the mentee, what closure to the mentoring relationship will involve, whether there will be a probationary period before you make a final commitment to mentoring, what periodic evaluations of the mentoring experience will be required, and what final status report will be prepared to express the effectiveness of the mentoring engagement. There may be other parameters or boundaries you might add to this list; the point is to determine them beforehand so misunderstandings are few or avoided altogether.

---

509 Gal. 6:2–5.

Considering Mentees

You should consider several factors when deciding whether or not you will mentor a person. Is there a relational connection? Is what you have to offer what he or she needs? Are you the right person to mentor him or her, or is there someone else better equipped and qualified to do so? What attitude of cooperation does he or she convey? Is the person teachable? Can he or she follow direction? Will he or she submit to your authority? Will he or she abide by your nonnegotiable parameters and boundaries? Do you see untapped potential in him or her? Are you being led by the Lord to mentor him or her? Have you bathed the possibility in prayer? Do you have the time and interest to invest in him or her? Are his or her expectations reasonable? Is he or she willing to comply with your requests and complete the tasks you assign? You should consider all these factors as you contemplate mentoring another individual.

I recommend that you test the mentee before making a final decision. Give the candidate one or more assignments to complete and then evaluate the response. Set up a probationary period during which either of you can step away from the mentoring relationship if it seems expectations are not being met. Conduct an initial, exploratory interview to find out what led the candidate to you. Resist the temptation to correct his or her perceptions; just listen. Then follow up with more definitive requirements the candidate must satisfy before you conduct the follow-up meeting during which you'll decide whether to mentor him or her.

When you are face-to-face with the candidate initially, watch his or her body language and facial expressions to determine his or her readiness for mentoring. When I was an executive pastor for a church in California and had secured a mandate from the senior pastor to develop young leaders, I interviewed thirty-three potential candidates. It didn't matter to me what they said or whether their opinions coincided with those of the orthodoxy—I knew I could correct those later. I paid close attention to their posture and facial expressions to determine if they were teachable. If they sat back with folded arms, avoided eye contact, seemed distracted, or otherwise conveyed disinterest or apathy, they were out. If they leaned forward with eager anticipation, were alert and attentive, seemed excited about the opportunity, or conveyed a sense of "fire in the soul" and a willingness to learn, they were in.

While in the navy I was ordered to undergo instructor training as a preliminary step to becoming an instructor at a naval school. I thought I was going to learn about the subjects I would be teaching, but instead I was taught how to teach effectively using the acronym VEGA—Voice, Eyes, Gestures, and Attitude. I was taught how to emphasize what was important by inflecting my voice and managing the tempo of my delivery. I was taught to scan the entire room with my eyes, and if I was intimidated initially, to look just above the heads of the students. I was also taught how to read students' eyes to determine if I was connecting with them. I was taught not to use distracting gestures like continually adjusting my glasses or rattling change in my pocket, and to minimize nervous tics. Finally, I was taught how to convey different attitudes to complement the material I was teaching or engage students I was instructing.

The point of this illustration is to underscore the importance of nonverbal communication in determining whether you will mentor a particular individual. Considering these nonverbal clues coupled with the questions I posed earlier, testing the mentee before entering into a mentoring relationship, and conducting an exploratory first interview will help you decide whether or not you should mentor an individual. If you choose not to mentor a candidate, be prepared to recommend someone else who might help him or her.

Conducting Initial Meeting

When conducting your first meeting, establish the framework for ongoing mentoring meetings. You will be doing most of the talking during this first meeting.

- Ask the mentee if anything has changed since the exploratory interview was held.
- Restate your understanding of the goal or goals communicated to you in the exploratory meeting.
- Establish the objectives you both hope to obtain when mentoring is included.

- Explain the nonnegotiable parameters and boundaries that must be honored.
- Review the *mentoring contract* and revise as necessary. You may want to consider having the mentee sign the contract.
- Stress the importance of maintaining confidentiality and explain when confidentiality will be broken (e.g., the commitment of a crime or the indication of personal abuse).
- Request and insist upon openness, honesty, candor, and full disclosure.
- State what you expect of the mentee and what he or she can expect of you.
- Let him or her know when you will be available to respond to questions or address issues that may arise outside the scheduled meetings.
- Set the specifics of how accountability will be maintained.
- Provide any initial materials the mentee will need and describe any assignment he or she must complete before the next meeting.
- Verify the meeting schedule, how long each meeting will last, and when face-to-face meetings are required. Also, tell the mentee what is expected if he or she must cancel a meeting.
- Explain when and how often evaluations of the mentoring experience will be conducted. Explain that during an evaluation, either party can opt out of the relationship or agree to continue for another designated time period.
- Ask if the mentee has any questions or concerns.
- Ask for prayer requests and then close in prayer.

Conducting Follow-Up Meetings

Effective mentoring has more to do with the attitude you convey than the information you impart. While every meeting may be different from the one before, requiring a different attitude applicable to the circumstances, the following twenty recommendations will help you be a more effective mentor. Each mentor possesses unique wiring and will express the recommendations differently, but the information you convey and the resources you offer will be better received when you convey and offer them with a proper attitude.

- Be thoroughly prepared.
- Be ready and present.
- Be available.
- Believe in your mentee.
- Give him or her the benefit of the doubt.
- Be understanding.
- Be tolerant.
- Be relevant.
- Be encouraging.
- Be honest but tactful.
- Be a learner.
- Be flexible.
- Be a good listener.
- Be clear.
- Be clarifying.
- Be responsive.
- Be aware.
- Be biblical.
- Be committed to follow-up.
- Inspect what you expect.

Bringing Closure

Every mentoring relationship comes to a point of closure. When specifics regarding the inevitability of closure are not addressed at the beginning of the process, closure can become messy. Because the participants have established a deep relationship, they will feel and express some measure of grief at closure. That is to be expected.

Releasing a mentee at closure may happen for a number of reasons:

- The agreed-upon objectives have been met.
- New objectives have been uncovered, requiring a new mentoring start.

- The individual needs additional help the current mentor cannot provide.
- The individual is moving to another city or state.
- The demands of the individual's job interfere with the goals of mentoring.
- The mentee has not complied with the specifics of the mentoring contract.
- The mentor believes it is time to end the formal relationship.

When a mentoring experience has gone well and parting seems abrupt, you might want to consider shifting the formal relationship to an informal one. As I stated earlier, an informal mentoring relationship consists of impromptu meetings that may be scheduled or unscheduled—situational encounters initiated by a former mentee seeking your advice or counsel in a specific area, or initiated by you when a random opportunity presents itself.

Regardless of the reason for closure, the last meeting before closure is initiated should celebrate what was accomplished during the mentoring process. The perspectives of both the mentor and mentee should be expressed. The following questions might be explored in this final meeting:

What took place during mentoring that was especially helpful and should be celebrated?

What took place during mentoring that should be changed if mentoring were to continue?

What took place during mentoring that was not helpful at all and should not be repeated?

What did not take place during mentoring that should have been addressed?

What are the positive takeaways from the mentoring experience?

How has the mentee grown spiritually and personally during the mentoring experience?

The next steps in the process should be discussed. If informal mentoring is needed or requested, its specific nature and framework should be outlined. A brief report summarizing the answers to the questions above might be helpful for later review.

Personal Mentoring Strategy

When we take a journey, we can benefit from the services of a guide who is familiar with the terrain. In fact, depending on the nature of the trip, different guides may be required. If the nature of the journey is to build foundations for our faith and practice, we'll need an intensive guide. If the nature of the journey is to teach us life skills for a particular need, we'll need an occasional guide. If we want to learn on our own by exposure to the best resources around, we'll want a passive guide.

Being mentored, mentoring others, and forming peer-mentoring relationships will provide ample opportunities to fill up your tank so you can empty it into the tanks of others. So in effect, you need a guide, you are a guide, and you fellowship in the company of guides.

When developing your *Personal Mentoring Strategy*, you will need to think through the following questions and jot down your conclusions.

Personal Assessment
Why do you want to be mentored?

What type of mentor do you need?

Who within your sphere of relationships is the type of mentor you need?

What areas of your life require mentoring?

How much accountability will you require?

What objective(s) do you hope to attain?

What will a successful outcome of mentoring look like to you?

What mentoring format do you prefer?

How will the mentoring relationship be evaluated from time to time?

How long do you think you will need mentoring to meet your objectives?

In addition to answering the questions above, consider taking the following steps:

First, identify your mentoring goals for the next two years with regard to the spiritual, personal, intellectual, emotional, and relational dimensions of your life. Once these goals have been determined, decide what category of mentor you will need, what type of mentor you will require, what mentoring format you will need (i.e., formal, informal, or nonformal), and who may provide the kind of mentoring you will need.

Second, given the type of mentor you are, the category of mentoring you like to perform, and your perceived availability over the next two years, determine how many people you intend to mentor formally, informally, and nonformally.

Finally, form peer-mentoring relationships with at least one external mentor and one internal mentor. As a reminder, *internal co-mentors* are peers in the same ministry environment as you and with about the same level of spiritual maturity. They provide mutual growth and accountability, contextual insights within the organization, and friendship during difficulty. *External co-mentors* are also your peers, except they are from outside your ministry situation. They are at about your level of development and maturity. They provide an objective perspective and can challenge you to think through the way you act and apply the insights you have gained over time.

Appendix A: The Guide will provide guidelines for developing a Personal Mentoring Strategy. A form is also provided for your use.

Conclusion

*Human beings judge one another by their external
actions. God judges them by their moral choices.*

—C. S. Lewis

We've come to the end of our journey of conceptualization. Now we'll begin the journey of exploration. The *compass* has been oriented, and each cardinal and intercardinal point has been identified:

- north: Jesus Christ
- northeast: beliefs
- east: the Holy Spirit
- southeast: values
- south: the Bible
- southwest: worldview
- west: spiritual disciplines
- northwest: motives

Oriented and ready to go, you are now prepared for the journey ahead. No matter the terrain, the weather, the season, or the hazards, regardless of darkness or light, your compass will keep you on track. You will not be lost; you will find your way. The situation may be dire, the landscape seemingly impossible to discern, but you will know in which direction you need to head.

Your unique *map* indicating the topography you will traverse throughout the remainder of your life will not be daunting to you, because you have been equipped with the knowledge and tools to serve your single purpose: to make it to your God-ordained destiny. Your compass will help you maintain the proper bearing and make your way, because with it you can read the terrain. The terrain we are talking about includes:

- biblical purpose
- life purpose
- committed passion
- role characteristics
- unique methodologies
- ultimate contribution

With your compass in hand and your map before you, you need only a guide to help you complete the journey. In fact, you will need more than one guide; you will need intensive guides, occasional guides, and passive guides to help you manage the journey. As you learn the terrain, you will have opportunities to share your discoveries with other travelers with similar pursuits. You also will be able to pass on the lessons you've learned to beginning travelers who don't have the experience you do.

The journey will be so rewarding that you will make plans for additional journeys with your trusted compass and appropriate map. Other guides will be needed then, as well, to help you avoid pitfalls and hold you accountable to your objectives. Guides and guidance include:

- intensive mentors
- occasional mentors
- passive mentors
- formal mentoring
- informal mentoring

- nonformal mentoring
- internal co-mentors
- external co-mentors
- spiritual goals
- personal goals
- intellectual goals
- emotional goals
- relational goals

Appendix A: Focused Life Plan

Your Focused Life Plan is a strategy designed to help you realize your divinely intended purposes until you are called to your heavenly home. The plan is a description of the life you desire to live as you progress along your journey. The plan is your declaration that you intend to live in accordance with God's purposes for you. The plan will serve as a standard by which you can evaluate your progress toward a life of godliness and God-inspired focus. Such a plan will help you live a life that matters, model a life that is meaningful, provide a clear trajectory for your future, and help you leave an impactful and influential Kingdom legacy. Review the plan at least twice a year and evaluate your progress toward its objectives. As you mature both personally and spiritually, you will need to revise your plan accordingly. The plan is a living document until God calls you home.

Focused Life Plan Structure

The plan consists of three components: compass, map, and guide. The *compass* represents a plan that will align your heart to the heart of God, establish a solid core for advancing God's agenda for you, and provide a center of equilibrium that will help you manage the ups and downs of life. The *map* is unique to you alone and represents the topography of your life, establishes the boundaries of your engagement, and provides a trajectory for your journey ahead. The *guide* represents mentoring and mentors who will help you advance, give you guidance along the way, provide godly counsel, and hold you accountable.

These three components—compass, map, and guide—comprise a Focused Life Plan. The following worksheet is meant to help you record the various elements of this plan as you become aware of them. Once the worksheet is complete, it will serve as the primary resource from which you will develop a draft, using the form provided as a guideline. I have included individual examples of each component of the Focused Life Plan.

The Compass
Central Operational Beliefs

Operational beliefs are also absolute truths. The difference, however, is that they are actionable—they compel us to do something. They require a response and provide a general guideline for our behavior and actions. They provide the basis for our values—the filter through which we process our decisions, the hills we are prepared to die on, the principles we intend to live out in our daily lives. They have to do with our doingness.

Examples:

- I have a destiny to fulfill (Jer. 29:11).
- I have a contribution to make (1 Cor. 12:4–7).
- I have a ministry to complete (Eph. 4:11–16).
- I have a legacy to leave (2 Tim. 2:2; 1 Chron. 28:8).
- I am to live a sober, upright, and godly life (Titus 2:11–14).

Identify and select two or more operational beliefs with scripture to support them. Your selected beliefs will provide the foundation on which you will stand and from which you will intentionally and proactively engage the world around you. It represents the truth you will live going forward.

1. Belief:
   Scripture:

2. Belief:
   Scripture:

3. Belief:
   Scripture:

4. Belief:
   Scripture:

5. Belief:
   Scripture:

Core Values

In addition to the fruit of the Spirit (God's family values given in seed form to every believer), identify other values you believe should mark your life. Values are the hills you are prepared to die on, the primary principles you hope to live by, the filter through which your life decisions will be made. Values are qualities that you esteem and by which you intend to direct your behavior. Your values are personal commitments that propel you to act. Values govern your underlying thoughts, attitudes, and decisions that result in God-honoring behavior.

Select two or more personal values. Each value identified should include a phrase or sentence describing it, as well as one or two scriptural references that provide a focus for the value and help explain what the value means to you. Then select the context within your sphere of influence where you believe that value can be most effectively practiced. That setting could involve your eternal relationships with others, such as your spouse, children, relatives, friends, or work associates, or the people you serve. Or it could involve more personal, internal dimensions of your life, such as the spiritual, intellectual, emotional, or physical areas. Finally, select a time frame for each value—the time you will focus on a particular value in a given context. The time period should not exceed six months; three months is preferable. At the end of that time frame, evaluate your progress, noting your consistency (+), inconsistency (/), or failure (-) in practicing that value. Perhaps for the next six months, God will direct you to practice the value in a different sphere of influence.

Example:

Value: People First
Description: My capacity to influence requires maintaining
    relationships.
Focus: Gen. 1:27; John 13:34–35.
Context: My workplace.
Time Frame: Next 3 months.

1. Value:
    Description:
    Focus (Scripture):

    Context:

    Time Frame:

2. Value:

    Description:

    Focus (Scripture):

    Context:

    Time Frame:

3. Value:

    Description:

    Focus (Scripture):

    Context:

    Time Frame:

4. Value:

    Description:

    Focus (Scripture):

    Context:

    Time Frame:

5. Value:

    Description:

    Focus (Scripture):

    Context:

    Time Frame:

Worldview (Perceptual Attitudes)

Making sense of the world around us depends on our perceptual attitudes about how life works. This set of attitudes is our worldview—the lens through which we view the world and try to make sense of our observations. Every worldview comprises fundamental beliefs and values. Every worldview answers questions about ultimate reality, personhood, the basic human dilemma, the solution to the dilemma, and one's human destiny from that perspective.

Establishing a biblical worldview is paramount to understanding and comprehending the world around us from God's perspective. We must see the world as God sees it. We must understand its complexity from a foundation of truth—a biblical point of view—if we are to navigate its vagaries effectively and finish well. In your words, briefly describe your biblical worldview as it relates to each of the areas listed below. Remember, you are expressing an intention to view the world and evaluate it through this lens so you are not carried away by other philosophies and ideologies. Our beliefs, values, and perceptual attitudes, if they are biblical, provide an excellent backdrop for the exercise of godly wisdom.

Example: A Biblical Worldview

1. The nature of ultimate reality: God exists and is active in our lives.
2. The nature of human personhood: Humans bear the image of God.
3. The basic human dilemma: The image of God is marred by sin.
4. The solution to the human dilemma: The person and work of Christ.
5. Our human destiny: Eternal life or eternal damnation.

*   The nature of ultimate reality:
    Questions to consider: What is your belief about divine intelligence? Is the world we live in all there is to reality? Is there a higher intelligence out there? Does God exist? If so, how is He related to humans?

*   The nature of human personhood:
    Questions to consider: What is your understanding about humanity? What makes us human? What makes us distinct from other living things? Are humans animals of a higher order or the divine image of God?

*   The basic human dilemma:
    Questions to consider: What is the fundamental problem of mankind? What is the single most significant issue that prevents us from reaching our full potential? What holds us back from reaching perfection? What prevents us from rising above our situation or circumstances?

*   The solution to the human dilemma:
    Questions to consider: What is the solution to the basic human

dilemma? How can the problem of mankind be resolved? What force or forces can be brought to bear to solve our dilemma? What is the answer to our dilemma?

- Our human destiny:
  Questions to consider: Where will you go when you die? Is there existence after death? Is there more than one destination after death? If there is a place of bliss, how do we attain it?

Primary/Secondary Motives

God searches the motives of our hearts. Motives compel us to move from thought to action, stimulated by a situation, circumstance, or event. Motives imply an emotion or desire that operates on our will. God expects us to act based on godly motives.

The foremost godly motive is unconditional love—a love that is others-oriented, a love that is action not emotion, a love that seeks the best of the one loved, a love that desires another's well-being and welfare even if he or she is unlikable. The following passage describes what love is, what love is not, and what love is, regardless:

"Love is patient, love is kind. It does not envy, it does not boast, it is not proud. It is not rude, it is not self-seeking, it is not easily angered, it keeps no record of wrongs. Love does not delight in evil but rejoices with the truth. It always protects, always trusts, always hopes, always perseveres. Love never fails. But where there are prophecies, they will cease; where there are tongues, they will be stilled; where there is knowledge, it will pass away" (1 Cor. 13:4–8).

Examples of Primary Motives:
Unconditional love, Christ-likeness, godliness, holiness, Kingdom purposes, sacrifice.

Examples of Secondary Motives:
Commitment, discovery, equality, excellence, fairness, faithfulness, goodness, growth, improvement, justice, kindness, knowledge, meaning, mission, obedience, obligation, perfection, personal development, proficiency, purpose, responsibility, service, significance, spirituality, worship.

Select one or two *primary* motives and one or two *secondary* motives that you intend to act on to the exclusion of any other motive. Inform your choices by making sure they reflect biblical motivations.

Primary:

1.

2.

3.

Secondary:

1.

2.

3.

Implementation Strategy

Once you have recorded your beliefs, values, worldview, and motives, explain what you intend to do with the plan over the next *six months*.

- How do you intend to *engage* the plan to make it an observable reality in your life?
- Who will hold you *accountable* for its implementation?
- What *steps* do you intend to take to implement it?
- Consider *prioritizing* what you intend to do, focusing on what is most needed at this stage of your life.

What *elements* of the plan do you intend to implement over the next six months (e.g., operational belief, core value, worldview, motive)?

In what *context* (relational—wife, children, friends, relatives, coworkers, church members, organization members, ministry members, etc.; or dimensional—spiritual, intellectual, emotional, physical, etc.) will you implement your strategy?

What *dimension* of your life will serve as the center of your engagement (personal management, intellectual advancement, emotional development, relational dynamics, spiritual growth, and/or discipline)?

What *behavioral results* are you hoping to realize in six months? What *behaviors* might someone see in your life as a result of your plan?

Once the entire compass plan is complete, have someone you trust review it for clarity, completeness, and congruence. In other words, does the plan make sense? Does it include all components (beliefs, values, attitudes, motives)? Does it represent your personal journey to date and what you hope to see in the future? Does it hang together, or is it a gathering of loose, unassociated elements? Is it harmonious?

The Map
Biblical Purpose

Your *biblical purpose* answers the *why* of your life. It is a statement of *being*.

- It answers the question of *why* we do what we do.
- It should focus on *self*.
- It can be applied to *many people*.
- It is *general* in nature.

It should represent your commitment to the Great Commandment (Matt. 22:37–40) and the Great Commission (Matt. 28:19–20)—a love for God and others and a commitment to make disciples. It should represent a commitment to worship, spiritual growth, and service (Ps. 34:1–3; Col. 2:6–7; Isa. 58:6–12).

Living a focused life requires a solid foundation. Scripture reveals to each believer both why he or she exists, and gives guidance for the journey. A proper biblical foundation provides the "true north" for every believer. Clarifying biblical purpose helps a believer in three ways: It declares why you exist. It captures the heart of why you are on this planet and what it means to live in relationship with God. It defines your life not by what you think, but by what God thinks. It anchors your life in the character of your Creator. It clarifies the nonnegotiable. It tells what never changes about who you are, regardless of the circumstances. Take a moment and list the verses that God has used to guide your life. They are verses that remind you what is most important. Often, these are the verses that we turn to when we are confused, or when we feel like we are lost. List the verse, then summarize what is important from each verse.

Examples of a biblical purpose:

> My purpose is to bring glory to my Lord and Savior Jesus Christ through consistent worship of Him with my praise and my life, to cultivate a life of intimacy with Jesus that will reflect His love and the grace of God to my world.

> The purpose of my life is to know God and to hear His voice so clearly that I live a life of servanthood and obedience.

> I live to glorify my Lord and Savior Jesus Christ (Rom. 15:5–6).

> I seek to personally experience the grace and truth of the Gospel (John 1:14) in order to demonstrate an authentic walk with Christ to believers ensnared in religion and unbelievers trapped in darkness.

Draft a biblical purpose—a statement of beingness versus doingness. Consider the responsibilities and duties required of every disciple of Christ.

Biblical Purpose Statement:

Life Purpose

Your *life purpose* answers the *what* of your life. It is a statement of *doing*.

- It answers the question of *what* we are called to do for others.
- It should focus on *others.*
- It should apply only to *you.*
- It is *specific* in nature.
- It should include a hint of the *strategies* you will employ to make your life purpose a reality.
- It should include *action verbs* (e.g., to influence; to facilitate; to align; to encourage; to exhort; to teach; to counsel; to mentor).
- It does not have to include every dimension or role in your life. What we are all called to be is a given and should not be wrapped up in your life purpose statement.

A statement of personal calling (life purpose) is a (person's) best understanding to date of his or her unique, personal destiny. It is a holistic statement that integrates what a leader understands God has called him or her to be and to do for His glory. A (life purpose statement) is a dynamic statement reflecting your best understanding to date of what God is calling you to be and do in your future. Over time, as a believer refines his or her life purpose statement, it becomes a very unique document, reflecting the style, perspective, and growing insight of that leader. However, at the core it is a simple document that integrates the work you have now completed. Effective life purpose statements have three clear, yet integrated components: biblical purpose, life values and personal vision. Life purpose statements bring three roads together into one, future direction. A life purpose statement describes why you exist, who God has shaped you to be, and what God is calling you to accomplish.

Your life purpose is a magnet that pulls you into the future.

Helpful Questions to Consider:

1. How would you articulate the one thing you must do in alignment with your calling?
2. What has your unique wiring prepared you to do regarding Kingdom purposes?
3. Toward what destiny do you feel you are being pulled?
4. What do you feel you were born to do?
5. In what purpose do you feel compelled to engage?

Life Purpose Statement:

Committed Passion(s)

Psalm 37:3–5: "Trust in the Lord and do good; dwell in the land and enjoy safe pasture. Delight yourself in the Lord and he will give you the desires of your heart. Commit your way to the Lord; trust in him and he will do this."

Galatians 1:15–16: "But when God, who set me apart from birth and called me by his grace, was pleased to reveal his Son in me so that I might preach him among the Gentiles, I did not consult any man ..."

Committed passion is the focused, intentional, energized action defined by your inner drive to fulfill your revealed destiny and be all God has equipped and wired you to be. Life purpose without the follow-through of committed passion is merely a dream with little chance of becoming a reality. It's the magnetism that causes the needle of your internal compass to point to true north. It's dedication and devotion to realizing one's full created potential.

Passion is the God-given desire that compels us to make a difference in a particular ministry. Your passion will lead you to some compelling action. Passion addresses *which people* we most want to help and *which causes* we feel strongly about.

The following questions have been excerpted from the book *Network*:

1. If you could snap your fingers and know that you couldn't fail, what would you do?
2. At the end of your life, you'd love to be able to look back and know that you'd done something about:
3. If someone were to mention your name to a group of your friends, what would they say you were really interested in or passionate about?
4. What conversation would keep you talking late into the night?
5. What would you like to do for others?
6. Which people would you most like to help? Put a checkmark next to the people groups you feel called to serve:

Abused	Infants	Retired
Addicts	Infirmed	Seekers
Agnostics	Laborers	Service Providers
Atheists	Lay Leaders	Sick
Business Leaders	Leaders	Single Mothers
Children	Marketplace	Single Parents
Children in Foster Care	Married Couples	Singles
Church Leaders	Members of the Military	Social Workers
College Students	Men	Teachers
Disabled	Mentally Challenged	Teen Moms
Divorced	Missionaries	Unchurched
Doctors	Nurses	Unemployed
Educators	Orphans	Unsaved
Elderly	Parents	Veterans
Empty Nesters	Pastors	Widowed
Fatherless Children	Patients	Women
Foreigners	People in Midcareer	Young People in Careers
Government Workers	Police	Youth
Homeless	Politicians	Others:
Hospitalized	Poor	
Hungry	Prisoners	
Immigrants	Refugees	

7. Which issues or causes do you feel strongly about? Put a checkmark next to the issues you feel called to embrace:

Abortion	Evangelism	Missions
Abuse	Family	Politics
Addictions	Global Concerns	Poverty
Aids	Healthcare	Prisons
Childcare	Homosexuality	Racism
Church	Human Slavery	Secularism
Community Outreach	Human Trafficking	Sex Trade
Community Service	Hunger	Social Needs
Development	Immigration	Technology
Discipleship	Injustice	Violence
Economics	Intolerance	Women's Rights
Education	Justice	Others:
Employment	Literacy	
Environment	Marriage	

8. List the top five to seven positive experiences you've had in your life. Briefly describe them and why they were meaningful to you.

Committed Passion(s)

1.
2.
3.

Major Role Characteristics

A suitable major role is one that enhances giftedness and allows use of unique methodologies that will lead to ultimate contributions, a legacy. Five components combine to make up an effective major role: (1) a suitable sphere of influence for ministry; (2) a job description that covers the major thrusts needed; (3) ministry activity compatible with giftedness; (4) the freedom to proactively choose actions that enhance focus and to refuse those that do not; (5) a respected status that facilitates entrance to a ministry opportunity, bespeaks spiritual authority, and gives a good hearing.

Questions to Consider:
- What must the ministry environment look like so that your life purpose, committed passion, and giftedness (spiritual gifts, natural abilities, and acquired skills) can thrive?
- What are the nonnegotiables, the deal breakers, and the irreducible minimums that must be present if you are to be a faithful steward of God's embedded trust in you?
- What must be present in order for you to make your greatest contribution to God's redemptive purposes?
- What ministry settings have allowed your gifts to be unleashed and exercised?

Example:

The major role that will provide the platform for my life's purpose is one in which I'm allowed to focus my energies in investing in the lives of budding leaders who are in the process of becoming but haven't arrived, and malleable leaders who have the potential for greater purposes but do not know how to realize their full potential in Christ. This role will allow me to cultivate relationships with these leaders through networking, teaching, writing, and mentoring one-on-one, working in small groups and workshop settings, and exposing these leaders to leadership-development concepts, values, principles, and practices. My spiritual gifts exercised in these settings find their primary application in the word-cluster gifts, including teaching, exhortation, and leadership. Less dominant, but observable, are the spiritual gifts of words of wisdom, discernment of spirits, and gifts of governance.

If you could rewrite your present job/ministry description, what would it look like?

1.
2.
3.
4.
5.
6.
7.
8.

Draft a description of nonnegotiables that must exist in any role in order for your life purpose and committed passion to thrive. Some roles do not permit much room for adaptation, while others do. When considering a role, the questions you need to ask yourself are, "What are the minimum deal breakers given the position I am in or I've been offered? Will I be allowed to exercise my life purpose and committed passion, either implicitly or explicitly? Am I being asked to fulfill a role that will compromise my life purpose and committed passion? What freedom do I have to exercise my life purpose and committed passion?"

Draft a role characteristics statement that reflects the irreducible minimums that must exist in your role.

Role Characteristics Statement:

Unique Methodologies

Psalm 139:13–16: "For you created my inmost being; you knit me together in my mother's womb. I praise you because I am fearfully and wonderfully made; your works are wonderful, I know that full well. My frame was not hidden from you when I was made in the secret place. When I was woven together in the depths of the earth, your eyes saw my unformed body. All the days ordained for me were written in your book before one of them came to be."

Unique methodologies are the filters through which you express your ordained uniqueness. They might include *spiritual gifts*, *natural abilities* (StrengthsFinder; personality temperament; unique aptitudes such as math, languages, etc.), *acquired skills* (counseling, conflict resolution, strategic planning, organizational skill, prayer, intercession, etc.), *personality temperament*, *leadership style* (situational leadership: director, coach, partner, mentor), *core values* (the hills you're prepared to die on, the principles you intend to lead by, the filter by which you make your leadership decisions), and *operating principles* (those sure-fire principles you have accumulated over time that have proven to be effective in ministry and life).

Helpful Questions to Consider:
1. What unique tools are in your personal toolbox?
2. What can you do better than most other people?
3. What spiritual gifts have you exercised effectively?
4. What natural abilities and/or aptitudes were you born with that are evident today?
   (e.g., artistic ability, athleticism, clerical skills, communications, creativity, dexterity, emotional intelligence, empathy, helping others, innovation, intellect, language, leadership, logic, manual ability, mathematics, mechanical skill, medical expertise, musical ability, numerical skill, organization, physical skills, sales, science, singing, spatial perception, teaching, temperament, understanding others, verbal comprehension, visual acuity, writing, etc.).
5. How would you describe your unique operational style?
6. Who are your heroes? Why?

Fill in the following areas to identify the toolbox of resources you can apply to any situation. Your tools are your unique wiring, giftedness, values, and operating principles. Their totality represents *how* you will live and serve God's redemptive purposes.

Spiritual Gifts:
1.
2.
3.
4.
5.

Natural Abilities (use whatever test/scale you have taken or check whatever applies):

Personality Temperament Scale:

E/I _____; S/N _____; T/F _____; J/P _____ (Myers-Briggs)
A _____; B _____; C _____; D _____ (Bourgond Temperament Matrix)

Strengths (StrengthsFinder Results):
1.
2.
3.
4.
5.

Aptitudes (Innate Abilities):
1.
2.
3.
4.
5.

Acquired Skills:

What skills have you developed that can be applied to ministry settings and contexts?

1.
2.
3.
4.
5.

Leadership Style (pick the appropriate framework):

Director _____; Coach _____; Partner _____;
Mentor _____ (Situational Leadership)
Catalyst _____; Corporate _____; Causal _____ (McManus)
Vision _____; Passion _____; Mission _____ (McManus)
Strategic _____; Tactical _____; Logistical _____ (McManus)
Commander _____; Motivator _____; Participator _____;
Delegator _____ (Clinton)

Core Values:

Core values are the hills you are prepared to die on, the biblical principles you intend to live and lead by. Please identify from two to five values according to the following guidelines:

- Select at least two Bible verses to support the value you choose. These verses should help bring focus to the value.
- State the value in one word or a short phrase. If a sentence is required, please make it succinct.
- Identify the context in which you intend to live out the value. (For instance, let's assume you chose the value of truth. You might select John 8:31–32 as a supporting biblical text. As you examine your life, you realize that you have a tendency to stretch the truth when you teach or when you interact with others. So the context in which you will express the value of truth will be in your ministry setting or with those you teach.)

Focus	Value	Context
1.		
2.		
3.		

4.

5.

Operating Principles:

Operating principles are the lessons you have learned in life and ministry that serve as guidelines for your ministry efforts. Together they serve as a ministry philosophy, the foundation from which you lead and serve. These principles frame, inform, and condition what you do. Here is an example of operating principles:

- Character: Effective, godly leadership flows from being, is a matter of the heart, and is character-centered, not skill-centered. Skills are the tools of effective leadership; character is the power of effective leadership.

- Purpose: The ultimate purpose of the Church is to produce Christ-likeness in its followers—beginning with salvation, continuing with sanctification, and concluding with glorification.

- Authenticity: Authentic spirituality is a prerequisite for godly leadership and is produced when we tune our lives to God's standards of excellence. Its vitality comes from living our lives for an audience of One.

- Personal: Effective leaders know the capabilities, limitations, weaknesses, and potential of their followers. The leader is responsible for providing opportunities for people to realize their potential in Christ.

1.

2.

3.

4.

5.

6.

7.

8.

Example:

My spiritual gifts exercised within my sphere of influence find their primary application in the word-cluster gifts, including teaching, exhortation, and leadership. Less dominant, but observable, are the spiritual gifts of words of wisdom, the discernment of spirits, and gifts of governance.

- Core Values: devoted to God, keeper of promises, seeker of truth, loyal servant, man of integrity, faithful to family, lifelong learner, spiritually informed leadership, submission to biblical authority, responsible behavior, strength, and honor

- Natural Abilities: learner, activator, achiever, input, belief, relator, responsibility, command, focus, self-assurance, strategic

- Acquired Skills: leadership, organizational effectiveness, problem resolution, mentoring, teaching, preaching, character development, distance learning, leadership development, life mapping, focused living, men's ministry, ministry planning, operational effectiveness, spiritual formation, strategic planning, systems theory

- Personality Temperament: introverted (I), intuitive (N), thinking (T), judging (J); driver/analytical, choleric/melancholy, lion/beaver

- Leadership Style: primary—passion; secondary—corporate/ causal; team—tactical; situational leadership—director/coach

My unique methodologies are rooted in five major ministry insights which have played out repeatedly in my ministry experience. Effective, godly leadership flows from being, is a matter of the heart, and is primarily character-centered and secondarily skill-centered. Skills are the tools of effective leadership; character is the power of effective leadership. Lasting behavioral change that brings glory to God begins with the heart in general and a core belief system in particular. Satan's battlefield has always been the heart. What we store in our hearts will evidence itself in our behaviors. Our central beliefs establish our core values, our core values inform our worldview, our worldview conditions our motives, and our motives energize our behavior. Authentic spirituality is a prerequisite for godly leadership and is produced when we tune our lives to God's standards of excellence. Its vitality comes from living our lives for an audience of One. Effective, godly leadership is developed over a lifetime, is exercised through our God-given passion and giftedness, finds its source and authority in God, is built on biblical principles and values, and is practiced in culturally sensitive ways. The only legacy worth leaving is the godly legacy we live out daily and leave in the lives of others. Legacy is the sweet-smelling aroma that lingers in the lives of others long after we're gone from this earth. We make decisions and evaluate options by seeing situations, circumstances, and events through four frameworks: structural or systems (systems theory), human resources (personal needs), symbolic (mission, vision, and values), and political (stakeholder and constituency concerns).

These major ministry insights influence how I cultivate my network of relationships, how I teach, what I focus on in my writing, and what I emphasize in my mentoring activities. I intend to act faithfully by behaving in accordance with my core values, leveraging my natural strengths, finding appropriate expression for my temperament, and exercising leadership in appropriate, life-giving ways.

Draft a statement that reflects how you will carry out your life purpose and committed passion. This statement should include your giftedness (spiritual gifts, natural abilities, and acquired skills), personality temperament, leadership style, core values, and operating principles.

Unique Methodologies Statement:

Ultimate Contribution(s)

Your ultimate contribution is the legacy you hope to leave when God calls you home. It is the aroma left in the nostrils of those God has given you the opportunity to serve. It is the destiny toward which God is drawing you, the mark you will leave on this world when you are gone. Randy Reese, author and leadership developer, defines ultimate contribution as "a lasting legacy of a Christian for which he or she is remembered and which furthers the cause of Christianity." He offers the following questions for consideration:

1. What ministry dynamics continued to bear fruit after you left the scene?
2. What is the signature of your ministry?
3. How will you be remembered?
4. What would cause you disappointment or pain if you were ninety-four and reflecting upon your life?
5. What legacy do you want to leave in the lives of those God has called you to lead?
6. What legacy or legacies do you want to leave in the lives of your loved ones?
7. How does your current ministry reflect the legacy you would like to leave?

J. Robert Clinton has identified twelve possible legacies a leader might leave, as well as five categories of ultimate contributions:

Character:
   Saint: someone who leads a model life—not a perfect one, but a life others want to emulate. *Stylistic Practitioner*: someone with a model ministry style that sets the pace for others and which other ministries seek to emulate.

Ministry:
   Mentor: someone who leads a productive ministry with individuals, small groups, etc. *Public Rhetorician*: someone who leads a productive public ministry with large groups.

Catalytic:
   Pioneer: a person who starts apostolic ministries. *Change Person*: a person who rights wrongs and injustices in society and in church and mission organizations. *Artist*: a person who has creative breakthroughs in life and ministry and introduces innovations.

Organizational:
   Founder: a person who starts a new organization to meet a need or capture

the essence of some movement or the like. *Stabilizer*: a person who can help a fledgling organization develop or help an older organization move toward efficiency and effectiveness in order to solidify it.

Ideation:

Researcher: someone who develops new ideas by studying various things. *Writer*: someone who captures ideas and reproduces them in writing to help and inform others. *Promoter*: someone who effectively distributes new ideas and/or other ministry-related things.

What ultimate contribution(s) do you hope to make to facilitate God's redemptive purposes? What legacy do you hope to leave that will further His Kingdom? What will remain as a positive, lingering aroma in the lives of others once God calls you home?

1.
2.
3.
4.
5.
6.
7.
8.

Ultimate Contribution Statement:

The Guide

The journey that leads to finishing well requires guides to help you reach your destination. You will need many mentors of various kinds throughout your journey. Mentors share their God-given resources, experiences, expertise, spiritual maturity, and networks to help in your lifelong development. Intensive mentors (disciplers, spiritual guides, or coaches) may be needed to help develop strong faith foundations. Occasional mentors (counselors, teachers, or sponsors) may be required to help you with a specific need or in a particular area. Passive mentors (exemplary models, historical people of faith, or divine contacts) may be required to help you build expertise or acquire new skills or to feed your soul.

The resources shared in a mentoring relationship could include wisdom and discernment; life and ministry experience; timely advice; new methods and skills; principles, important values, and lessons; organizational influence; sponsorship and networking; and, on occasion, financial resources. Finding the appropriate mentor for a situation or circumstance requires prayer and thoughtful consideration.

There are five dynamics involved in cultivating mentoring relationships; these dynamics define five aspects of mentoring: (1) Attraction—like attracts like. People naturally move toward those who seem helpful. Mentees may be attracted by a mentor's personality, spirituality, ministry skills, or experience. (2) Relationship—the best exchanges of empowerment resources happen when mentors and mentees trust each other. (3) Responsiveness— the mentee's willingness to respond to the mentor's information is vital for learning empowerment. (4) Accountability—mentees must answer to someone for their growth and spiritual development. Often there is mutual accountability between mentors and mentees. (5) Empowerment—this is the actual exchange of resources and encouragement between mentor and mentee in areas of life and ministry.[510]

When you are seeking a mentor, consider the following ten questions:

1. Why do you want to be mentored?

2. What category and type of mentor do you need?

3. Who within your sphere of relationships is the type of mentor you need?

4. What areas of your life require mentoring (e.g., spiritual disciplines, family skills, self-management, life management, relationships, leadership development, spiritual development)?

5. What accountability will you require?

6. What objectives do you hope to attain?

---

510 Walling, *Mentoring: Focused Living*, 18.

7. What will a successful outcome of mentoring look like to you?

8. What mentoring format do you prefer (i.e., weekly, biweekly, monthly, quarterly; phone, e-mail, in person, etc.)?

9. How will the mentoring relationship be evaluated from time to time?

10. How long do you think you will require mentoring to meet your objectives?

Once you have carefully prayed over and thought through answers to the questions above, set up a meeting with your potential mentor to explore the possibility of a mentoring relationship. Share your answers to the questions, and then ask if he or she would be willing to mentor you initially for three months. After that initial period, both of you should evaluate the relationship and decide whether to end it with gratefulness or extend it for another three months. Maybe the mentoring fit is wrong. Maybe your objectives are not being met. Maybe circumstances may preclude either of you from continuing. Setting three-month mentoring periods followed by honest and open evaluation will prevent unease about terminating the relationship. Once mentoring has been completed, celebrate what God has accomplished in you.

Establishing a Mentoring Contract

1. Jointly agree on the purpose of the relationship.
Consider the objective(s) of the mentoring relationship. Determine the type of mentor needed. Identify the area(s) needing to be addressed.

2. Set the criteria for evaluation.
What will a successful outcome look like? How will you know the objectives have been accomplished? Have the mentee describe what he or she hopes to accomplish.

3. Determine the regularity of interaction.
Interaction should happen at least twice a month, but it could be more often, depending on the needs of the mentee and the availability of the mentor.

4. Determine accountability parameters.

Parameters involve honesty, vulnerability, accountability, and whatever else is required by the mentor and agreed upon by the mentee. What accountability parameters will be applied?

5. Set up communication mechanisms.

E-mail, phone, face-to-face—choose whichever means of communication is the most convenient. At least one face-to-face meeting is required per month in addition to second or additional meetings by phone and/or e-mail.

6. Clarify the level of confidentiality.

What is shared on a personal level must remain confidential unless it is of a legal nature, such as abuse of any kind, a crime, etc.

7. Set the life cycle of the relationship.

A good starting point is a three-month preliminary period, at the end of which each of you should evaluate the relationship. If you agree to continue, set an end date not to exceed six additional months, for a total of nine months.

8. Evaluate the relationship from time to time.

I recommend an evaluation every two to three months. Keep a journal of lessons learned, insights gained, progress made, objectives met, etc.

9. Modify expectations to fit the real-life mentoring situation.

If an issue or concern arises that needs more focused attention, the mentor and mentee should decide whether the parameters of mentoring need to be changed.

10. Bring the mentoring relationship to a close.

Celebrate the completion of the journey.

Follow-Up Strategy

In addition to answering the questions above, I recommend you consider doing the following:

First, identify your mentoring goals for the next two years with regard to the spiritual, personal, intellectual, emotional, and relational dimensions of your life. Then decide what category and type of mentor you will need, what mentoring format will be required (i.e., formal, informal, or nonformal), and who may provide the kind of mentoring you will need.

- Spiritual Goals:

- Personal Goals:

- Intellectual Goals:

- Emotional Goals:

- Relational Goals:

Second, given the type of mentor you are, the category of mentoring you like to perform, and your perceived availability over the next two years, determine how many people you intend to mentor formally, informally, and nonformally.

- Formal Mentoring:

- Informal Mentoring:

- Nonformal Mentoring:

Finally, form peer-mentoring relationships with at least one external and one internal mentor. Remember, *internal co-mentors* are peers in the same ministry environment and with about the same level of spiritual maturity as yours. They provide mutual growth and accountability, contextual insight within the organization, and friendship during difficulty. *External co-mentors* are peers like internal co-mentors, except they are outside the ministry situation. They share your level of development and maturity. They provide objective perspective and can challenge you to think through the way you act and apply insights you have gained over time.

- Internal Co-mentors:

- External Co-mentors:

Focused Life Plan Form

The following form will help you compile the information you gather as you identify your unique compass, map, and guide. From this form you can prepare your entire plan. The format is not as important as completeness.

Name: Date:

My Compass

Central Operational Beliefs:

Belief –
Scripture –

Belief –
Scripture –

Belief –
Scripture –

Belief –
Scripture –

Belief –
Scripture –

Personal Core Values:

Value –
Description –
Scripture Focus –
Context –
Time Frame –

Value –
Description –
Scripture Focus –
Context –
Time Frame –

Value –
Description –
Scripture Focus –
Context –
Time Frame –

Value –
Description –
Scripture Focus –
Context –
Time Frame –

Value –
Description –
Scripture Focus –
Context –
Time Frame –

Biblical Worldview:

The nature of ultimate reality –

The nature of human personhood –

The basic human dilemma –

The solution to the human dilemma –

The nature of ultimate reality –

Additional worldview considerations –

Activating Motives:

Primary Motives –

Secondary Motives –

Implementation Strategy:

My Map

Biblical Purpose (Statement of Being—*Why*):

Life Purpose (Statement of Doing—*What*):

Committed Passion (People to Serve, Cause to Embrace—*Where*):

Role Characteristics (Contextual Nonnegotiables—*When*):

Unique Methodologies (Your Toolbox—*How*):

- Spiritual Gifts:

- Natural Abilities (StrengthsFinder; other aptitudes):

- Acquired Skills (competencies; learned expertise):

- Personality Temperament (Myers-Briggs or Matrix type):

- Leadership Style (situational leadership or primary/secondary team categories):

- Core Values (value, description, focus, context, time frame):

- Operational Principles (philosophy of engagement, axiomatic truths for you):

Ultimate Contributions (Legacy, Aroma, Epitaph—*So What*):
Examples: Saint, Stylistic Practitioner, Mentor, Public Rhetorician, Pioneer, Change Person, Artist, Founder, Stabilizer, Researcher, Writer, Promoter, etc.

The contributions to God's redemptive purposes I desire to make include …

When all is said and done, the legacy I hope will linger long after I am gone is …

The following Kingdom-serving epitaph will mark my journey:

My Guide

Being Mentored by Others …

- Mentoring Purpose(s):

- Mentor Category and Type(s):

- Mentor Candidate(s):

- Mentoring Area(s):

- Accountability Parameters:

- Mentoring Objective(s):

- Expected Outcome(s):

- Preferred Format(s):

- Evaluation Criteria:

- Time Period:

Mentoring Contract Guidelines

1. Purpose of the mentoring relationship:

2. Criteria for evaluation:

3. Regularity of interaction:

4. Accountability parameters:

5. Communication options:

6. Level of confidentiality required:

7. Life cycle of the relationship:

8. Periodic evaluation time frame:

9. Declaration of expectations and responsibilities:

10. Closure details:

Mentoring Strategy—Long-Range Mentoring Goals (Two Years)

- Spiritual Goals:

- Personal Goals:

- Intellectual Goals:

- Emotional Goals:

- Relational Goals:

Mentoring Others ...

- Formal Mentoring (Number or Persons):

- Informal Mentoring (Number or Persons):

- Nonformal Mentoring (Venue or Resource):

Co-mentoring with Others ...

- Internal Co-mentors:

- External Co-mentors:

Compass Examples

Example A: Stefan

Central Operational Beliefs

1. The Bible is my sole authority in faith and practice (2 Tim. 3:16–17; Heb. 4:12).
2. I am to love the Lord my God with all my heart, soul, and mind. Also, I am to love my neighbor as myself (Matt. 22:37–39).
3. My highest purpose is to bring glory to God (1 Cor. 10:31; 1 Pet. 2:9).
4. I must put on the whole armor of God (Eph. 6:10–18).
5. I will love my wife as Christ loves the Church (Eph. 5:25).
6. I am to walk by the Holy Spirit and not by my flesh (Gal. 5:16–26).
7. I am to live in harmony with others (Rom. 12:18).

Core Values (P = Personal, S = Spiritual, R = Relational)

Value: Centeredness (P)
Description: proactive living, vision, and direction
Focus (Scripture): Acts 4:29
Context: looking to the future with a proactive, not reactive, mind-set
Time Frame: 6 months

Value: Hard Work (P)
Description: doing my best in everything
Focus (Scripture): Heb. 12:11; Phil. 2:14
Context: holding myself to a higher standard in my work; working for God, not men
Time Frame: 6 months

Value: Spiritual Devotion (S)
Description: prayer, Bible reading
Focus (Scripture): Isa. 1:18–20; 1 Tim. 4:8
Context: understanding God's heart and who He wants me to be
Time Frame: 6 months

Value: Servanthood (S)
Description: service to others
Focus (Scripture): Phil. 2:5–11

Context: being a servant for Jesus's glory in my work and family life
Time Frame: 6 months

Value: Compassion (R)
Description: having a heart that cares for others
Focus (Scripture): John 13:34
Context: seeing people who are in need and helping them
Time Frame: 6 months

Value: Forgiveness (R)
Description: never withholding what I have been given
Focus (Scripture): Col. 3:13
Context: being quick to forgive when I am wronged
Time Frame: 6 months

Value: Honesty (R)
Description: telling the truth
Focus (Scripture): Ps. 15:1–3
Context: being a man of my word whom people can trust
Time Frame: 6 months

Value: Unselfishness (R)
Description: considering others to be better than me
Focus (Scripture): Phil. 2:3–4
Context: setting my priorities aside to do things for my wife and son
Time Frame: 6 months

Worldview (Perceptual Attitudes)

• the nature of ultimate reality
God is the Creator of all things. He sustains everything according to His will. He loves all people no matter what they have done and proved this by sending His only Son, Jesus Christ, to die on a cross so we could be put back into right standing with God.

• the nature of human personhood
Since we are created by God, we bear His image. The chief purpose of man is to bring glory to God and enjoy Him forever.

- the basic human dilemma

All people are sinners. The image of God in us has been tainted by our wrongdoing. Our wrongdoing makes it impossible for us to stand before a perfect God and claim we are sinless.

- the solution to the human dilemma

God sent His Son to die in our place so we would not have to be punished for the wrongs we have committed. Jesus Christ is the only way to God. The sacrifice of Jesus allows God to view us as perfect once again.

- our human destiny

Belief in the life, death, and resurrection of Jesus Christ secures our future once we die. Salvation is found only in Jesus, and we must receive this gift in order to be assured of our destiny. We can also choose to reject this gift, a choice that leads to a life eternally apart from God.

Primary/Secondary Motives

1. Obedience/Christ-likeness (P)
2. Unconditional Love (S)
3. Excellence (S)

Implementation Plan

- Who will hold me accountable for acting on this plan?

I will be held to this plan of action by a man who has gone through Phase I with me, along with my wife and best friend, who has been at my side experiencing the changes in my life during this journey. First, my brother will hold me accountable for putting this plan into action. Second, my wife, Rebecca, will help me put these values into action through our everyday interactions. Just as soldiers in battle cannot be victorious fighting alone, Christians cannot battle the enemy alone and expect to experience victory (Prov. 27:17).

- What behaviors will others see as a result?

I have selected my four values in the relational category to put into action: compassion, forgiveness, honesty, unselfishness. This battle plan is intentional about producing a change of heart followed by a change of behavior. Some of these behaviors are more evident in my life than others right now, and it is my goal that all these behaviors will continue to become more obvious to those around me. In a more tangible sense, my goal is to grow each behavior in a specific way throughout the next six months.

First, I want my lens to be prescribed by the Holy Spirit, so that when I am in contact with pre-Christians they may see the compassion of Christ flowing out of me.

Second, as we are commanded in the Bible to forgive "seventy times seven," so I want to extend forgiveness to others in my life when I am wronged.

Third, my prayer is that my life will be an example of "let your yes be yes and your no be no." I will be a man of my word; others will know that I mean what I say and that they can count on me to be honest at all times.

Fourth, the behavior of unselfishness will be apparent in my actions toward my wife and how I raise my son. The leadership in my home will be an example of the unselfish, servant's leadership demonstrated by Jesus Christ, who gave of Himself for those He loved.

Example B: Brian

Central Operational Beliefs

1. My family is my highest priority (1 Tim. 5:8).
2. I should love my neighbors as myself (Matt. 22:39).
3. I am to live in harmony with others (Rom. 12:14–21).

Core Values

Value: Unconditional Love
Description: I will love my family unconditionally.
Focus (Scripture): 1 Cor. 13:4–8
Context: Family Setting
Time Frame: Evaluate in 3 to 6 months

Value: Honesty
Description: If I expect it from others, I must first model it.
Focus (Scripture): John 8:31–32

Context: Family Setting
Time Frame: Evaluate in 3 to 6 months

Value: Kindness
Description: I am to show kindness to my neighbors.
Focus (Scripture): Acts 28:2
Context: Neighbors
Time Frame: Evaluate in 3 to 6 months

Value: Forgiveness
Description: I am to forgive the wrongs of the past.
Focus (Scripture): Eph. 4:31–32
Context: Ex-Wife
Time Frame: Evaluate in 3 to 6 months

Worldview (Perceptual Attitudes)

The nature of ultimate reality: God exists and cares about us.
The nature of human personhood: Every person is created in the image of God.
The basic human dilemma: sin
The solution to the human dilemma: the cross and Christ
Our human destiny: heaven or hell

Primary/Secondary Motives

1. Unconditional Love
2. Success
3. Personal Development

Implementation Plan:

1. For the next six months I will show unconditional love to my family to show them they are my number-one priority.

2. As I expect honesty, I will model honesty in both my work and home environments.

3. I will show kindness to those in my neighborhood as well as other individuals I may encounter.

4. I will be more intentional in my prayers, asking for God's guidance in order to show more forgiveness. I will try to do the right thing, whether or not my behavior is reciprocated.

Example C: Jeff

Central Operational Beliefs

1. I will love my wife as Christ loved the Church (Heb. 13:4–7; Eph. 5:25).

2. I will raise my children up in faith in Christ Jesus (Eph. 6:4; Prov. 22:6; Titus 1:6).

3. I will keep God's commandments (Eccles. 12:13; 1 John 5:2–5).

4. I have a contribution to make (2 Tim. 2:2; Eph. 4:11–16; Jer. 29:11).

5. I will treat my body as a temple to the Holy Spirit (1 Cor. 6:19–20; Eph. 2:3–5; Eccles. 11:10).

Core Values

1. Family
Description: I will make choices that value my family as a priority in my life.
Focus (Scripture): 1 Tim. 3:4, 12
Context: Work and Home

2. Courage
Description: I will lean into the inconvenient moments to make an impact.
Focus (Scripture): Jer. 1:9; Matt. 8:23–26
Context: Work

3. The local church as the hope of the world
Description: I will use my gift of leadership to help grow the church.
Focus (Scripture): Eph. 4:11–13
Context: Church

4. Wisdom

Description: Continued growth + continued investment in others = more impact.

Focus (Scripture): Prov. 10:23; Jer. 9:23–24; James 3:13–18

Context: continue to develop my spiritual growth

5. Strength and Honor

Description: I will cultivate strong convictions and beliefs, and respect for myself and others.

Focus (Scripture): 2 Tim. 1:6–7; Mark 10:42–45

Worldview (Perceptual Attitudes)

- The nature of ultimate reality: God exists, created us, and loves us.
- The nature of human personhood: We are created in God's image.
- The basic human dilemma: We are saints who sin.
- The solution to the human dilemma: Jesus died on a cross in our place in order to pay for our sins.
- Our human destiny: Those who receive Christ will go to heaven.

Primary/Secondary Motives

1. Multigenerational impact
2. Spiritual growth and development

Implementation Strategy

1. Element: Treat my body as a temple
   a. Context: watch what I eat at work; exercise more at home
   b. Dimension: my health
   c. Behavioral Results: better eating and exercise habits

2. Family
   a. Context: better investment of my time (home versus work), being intentional at home with Carrie and the kids
   b. Dimension: family dynamics
   c. Behavioral Results: time with Carrie and the kids, giving up work agenda (like MP)

3. Spiritual Growth
    a. Context: personal, men's group, church
    b. Dimension: spiritual growth
    c. Behavioral Results: personal devotion time, Heart of a Warrior Phase 2, bringing what I've learned into my interactions with others (wringing the sponge out)

Map Examples

Example A: Greg

Biblical Purpose

My biblical purpose is to live with abandon, fulfilling the mandate God has given me. My mandate is to live in such a way as to exemplify and model Christ-likeness in all I think, say, and do. The hills I will die on include fidelity to my personal relationship with Christ and my loyalty and faithfulness to Him; faith as the saving grace of the Gospel in all its implications, even if it takes me to uncomfortable places; my family, as I strive to be and do what serves their best interests; and a focus on God's purposes for my life in alignment with what He has called me to be and do. I seek to tune my heart to the heart of God and live accordingly. The Bible is my sole foundation, and I submit to its authority for faith and practice. My objective is to model the character of Christ and leave a pleasing aroma in the nostrils of all who come within my sphere of influence.

Life Purpose

My life purpose is to influence leaders and intentional followers, directly and indirectly, to live all-out for Christ; to help them determine how God has wired them; to help them align their lives according to God's plans; to encourage them to become proactive partners in God's purposes and redemptive activity; and to exhort them to live a legacy worth leaving in the lives of others.

Committed Passion

My committed passion is to help men and women realize their God-given potential in Christ and develop to the fullest their God-given gifts, abilities, and capacities for godly leadership from the inside out and within legitimate limitations, such as temperament, aptitude, and maturity. My primary sphere of influence will be leaders. My secondary context will be men and women who are searching for clarity regarding the purpose, focus, and foundation of their lives.

Major Role Characteristics

The major role that will provide the platform for my life's purpose is one in which I'm allowed to focus my energies on investing in the lives of budding leaders who are in the process of becoming but have yet not arrived, and malleable leaders who have the potential for greater purposes but do not know how to realize their full potential in Christ. This role will allow me to cultivate relationships with them through networking, teaching, writing, and mentoring one-on-one or in small groups and workshop settings, exposing them to leadership-development concepts, values, principles, and practices. My spiritual gifts exercised in these settings find their primary application in the word-cluster gifts, including teaching, exhortation, and leadership. Less dominant, but observable, are the spiritual gifts of words of wisdom, discernment of spirits, and gifts of governance.

Unique Methodologies

My unique methodologies are rooted in five major ministry insights that have played out repeatedly over time in my ministry experience:

- Effective, godly leadership flows from being, is a matter of the heart, and is primarily character-centered and secondarily skill-centered. Skills are the tools of effective leadership; character is the power of effective leadership.

- Lasting behavioral change that brings glory to God begins with the heart in general and our core belief system in particular. Satan's battlefield has always been the heart. What we store in our hearts will evidence itself in our behavior. Our central beliefs establish our core values, our core values inform our worldview, our worldview conditions our motives, and our motives energize our behavior.

- Authentic spirituality is a prerequisite for godly leadership and is produced when we tune our lives to God's standards of excellence. Its vitality comes from living our lives for an audience of One.

- Effective, godly leadership is developed over a lifetime, is exercised through our God-given passion and giftedness, finds its source and authority in God, is built on biblical principles and values, and is practiced in culturally sensitive ways.

- The only legacy worth leaving is the godly legacy we live out daily and leave in the lives of others. Legacy is the sweet-smelling aroma that lingers in the lives of others long after we're gone from this earth.

These major ministry insights influence the cultivation of my network of relationships, the style of my teaching, the foci of my writing, and the emphases of my mentoring activities.

I intend to act faithfully by behaving in accordance with my core values, leveraging my natural strengths, finding appropriate expression for my personality, and exercising leadership in appropriate and life-giving ways.

I will exercise my mandate through my strengths, which include learning, activating, achieving, giving input, believing, relating, being responsible, commanding, focusing, self-assurance, and strategic thinking.

I will also leverage my mandate through my personality temperament (introverted, intuitive, thinking, judging: INTJ) and my primary leadership style of passionate and mission-oriented, my secondary leadership style of corporate and causal, and my team leadership style of tactical.

I will seek to live by my core values of being devoted to God, a keeper of my promises, a seeker of biblical truth, a loyal servant, a man of integrity, faithful to my family, a lifelong learner, a biblically centered leader, submissive to the authority of the Bible, committed to responsible behavior, and a man of strength and honor.

Finally, I desire to use my acquired skills of biblical understanding, strategic planning, organization, implementation, leadership, development, mentoring, discipling, communication, focused intensity, and spiritual guidance to further God's redemptive purposes in the world.

Ultimate Contributions

Although I am in the process of becoming, having not yet arrived, I believe at this time that my ultimate contributions could coalesce around the roles of mentor, saint, researcher, writer, and stabilizer. I am beginning to see significant results as a mentor (with a productive ministry with individuals and small groups); saint (leading a model life focused on leaving a godly legacy in the lives of others within my sphere of influence); researcher (discovering new ideas regarding spiritual formation and leadership development); writer (capturing and recording ideas relevant to spiritual and leadership development); and stabilizer (stabilizing and maximizing organizational objectives that coincide with my life's purpose and passion). My "end game" is to live a legacy worth leaving in the lives of my family and the leaders I've had the privilege to influence for the glory of God.

Example B: Mike

Biblical Purpose:
I am God's adopted son. My primary purpose is to connect with my Father and His teachings, values, and wisdom so that I know and reflect the heart of God. Out of this connection I will bear good fruit: love, joy, peace, patience, kindness, goodness, faithfulness, gentleness, and self-control.

Life Purpose:
My primary life purpose is to be an effective husband, father, and spiritual leader in my family. Outside my family, my life purpose is to support others by being an open, genuine, nonjudgmental listener and counselor. God has gifted me with the ability to create research and analytical tools and to communicate the findings of my research to couples and counselors. The goal of these analytical tools is to reduce the rate of divorce by using context-sensitive interventions specific to the couple's marriage and point in life. I naturally view the world as a puzzle to be analyzed and solved. The cause I am embracing is to reduce the divorce rate in the United States.

Committed Passion:
My committed passion is to support couples and individuals dealing with the stresses of life, especially those concerning mental illness, marriage, divorce, and stepfamilies.

Major Role:
My major role is one in which I am allowed to research, discover, and communicate meaningful concepts about relationships and marriage to those who would benefit from and are ready to receive the information. The role needs to involve both the ability to discover and the ability to lovingly communicate to those who are in need. The communication side may include some personal communication in small groups, support groups, one-on-one and individuals counseling, large-group presentations, and automated assessments from information provided to me. Some of the information will empower counselors, pastors, and leaders who wish to communicate to couples. That is, there needs to be a population-level intervention on top of direct communication. My ability to analyze observational data to uncover and predict important patterns will be a key to the ministry. Through data analysis, I could potentially create predictive models of marriage to help discover what will benefit a given couple (in the current context, based on information from many other couples in the same context).

Unique Methodologies:

- Spiritual Gifts: mercy, pastoring, giving, teaching, exhortation, helping
- Natural Abilities: analytical skills, connectedness, strategic skills, intellection, learning
- Acquired Skills: scientific methods, statistical analysis, predictive models, observational data, psychotherapy, group therapy, writing
- Personality Temperament: Myers-Briggs—introvert, intuitive, thinking, perceiving; Five-Factor Model—social/introversion (very introverted), change/openness (mid), organized/ conscientiousness (mid-low), pleasing/agreeableness (high), emotional/neuroticism (mid)

- Leadership Style (situational leadership; primary/secondary/team): participating and then selling with moderate-to-high adaptability
- Core Values: spiritual growth (Scott Peck Sense); discovering truth (learning through data); family and marriage; open, honest, genuine connecting; wisdom, discernment, and critical thinking; "Whatever you do for one of the least of these brothers, you did for me."
- Operational Principles (philosophy of engagement, axiomatic truths for you):
  1. Marriage is the primary relationship God uses to mold us. His relationship to the Church is described by analogy to marriage.
  2. Divorce is not God's plan, and the ripples from this single negative event carry into our later relationships and the marriages of our children.
  3. If we forgive each other instead of walking away when things are difficult, we will grow, move closer to one another, and better understand how God forgives and loves us.
  4. God's love has tremendous depth and patience.
  5. The power of forgiveness is revealed in marriage.
  6. You can't put God in a box.
  7. Pain is a gift from God (2 Cor. 7:10).
  8. All models are wrong, but some are useful.
  9. Think before you act.
  10. Money is a tool that comes and goes; it does not create happiness or self-worth.
  11. Actions speak louder than words.

Operating Framework

I have been given a gift for analytical thinking, research, data analysis, conceptual understanding, and strategic thinking. My innate gifts have been developed over the past twenty years in health-outcomes research, through which I have learned more about techniques for identifying and communicating meaningful findings from observational (noninterventional) data. Studies of marriage largely need to be observational in nature, and research is not strongly emphasized in marriage- and family-therapy training. I have experience using secondary databases (administrative claims, government data), prospective observational studies, and predictive modeling, all of which can be easily adapted to use in marriage studies. I find myself in the unique position of being passionate about preventing divorce and having the ability to apply advanced statistical methods to identify the risk of divorce for a given marriage in a given situation at a given time. I will need to identify and collect data to develop the models; smartphones and the Internet will allow me to communicate the predictions after a couple has answered a few of my questions over the Web (or provided them through their marriage counselor). Such research results are most often reported in peer-reviewed scientific literature and are not proactively communicated to the study's subjects in an accessible manner.

In addition, I have gifts of counseling, comforting, and giving that can be used to assist others in dealing with life's challenges (including mental health issues, physical difficulties, divorce recovery, and marital problems).

Ultimate Contributions:

My ultimate contribution will be a nonprofit organization dedicated to enriching marriages and preventing divorce, particularly in the United States. This process will involve being a researcher, writer, and founder. My ultimate contribution will be to positively influence marriages so that they remain intact and grow rather than dissolving and creating a chain-reaction of challenges. The nonprofit will continue after I have gone. God willing, my ultimate contributions will be reduced divorce rates and enhanced marriages.

Example C: Larry

Biblical Purpose (Statement of Being—*Why*)
God created me in His own image (Gen. 1:27), He saved and sealed me to bring Him glory (Eph. 1:13–14), and He has called me to fulfill His purpose for my life (Rom. 8:28).

Life Purpose (Statement of Doing—*What*)
My life purpose is to evangelize and disciple whomever God would like to put in my path—from those who are skeptics to those who are already

Christians. In essence, I am to help anyone progress down the Engle scale to the point of salvation (Justification) and then down through the steps of Sanctification.

Committed Passion (People to Serve, Cause to Embrace—*Where*)
I particularly enjoy engaging nonbelievers who have never been accepting of the truths or facts of the Bible, by making them aware of archaeological proof. Arguments of biblical creationism are also effective. I also enjoy teaching new believers, because they have the indwelling of the Holy Spirit and are open to biblical truths; thus, the Bible can make sense to them. Seeing the expression on their faces when they understand a biblical truth for the first time is awe-inspiring. Also, hearing a man express how his marriage improved after he implemented a few scriptural principles is tremendously rewarding.

Role Characteristics (Environmental Nonnegotiables—*When*)
God typically brings to my attention individual men who are either seeking or are in need of discipling and are brought to my attention by pastoral staff, everyday circumstances, or chance meetings. Sometimes they come to my attention as an answer to prayer or directly by request of the person himself. Depending on the person, I usually start with one-on-one mentoring for a period of time and then get him involved in a small group (sometimes one I am leading at the time). If he is married, I get my wife to do the same with his wife, or sometimes we mentor as a couple, especially if they are working through marital issues.

On a larger scale, I have a passion to teach scriptural principles in a classroom environment, out of which individual mentees or even the nucleus for a small group can emerge. Also, I have been able to enlist more than a few members for multiple small groups of mine by inviting couples that I have interviewed for membership in my role as an elder.

Unique Methodologies (Your Toolbox—*How*)
• Spiritual Gifts:
   A primary gift of teaching will enable me to communicate truth so that people will understand what is conveyed in God's Word and will gain biblical insight into life situations. Secondary gifts of prophecy, discernment, and administration will help in the following areas:

prophecy will enable me to proclaim the scriptures with authority; discernment will give me insight into the spiritual source of people's problems; and administration will enable me to help people put together an efficient plan of action.

- Natural Abilities (StrengthsFinder, Other Aptitudes):

  My strength as a learner will help me understand why individuals behave the way they do; it will help me make recommendations for a possible course of action; and it will be a significant aid as I learn more about the Bible and how it can be applied in people's lives.

  My strength as an achiever will give me the work ethic to prepare and teach Bible classes as clearly as possible in classroom and one-on-one situations.

  My analytical strength will enhance my biblical understanding, helping me prove that science and the Bible can be correlated and that archeological evidence continually supports biblical accuracy.

  My strength of focus will help me stay on track when I'm teaching a group or class or giving counsel in a one-on-one situation.

  My strength of individualization will help me observe people's behavior and determine what they are thinking or feeling as they deal with life's challenges.

- Acquired Skills (Competencies, Learned Expertise):

  Effective writing is one of my acquired skills. By putting Bible teachings in writing and accompanying them with discussion questions, I can hand a whole series of teachings to any small group or individual to be used as a stand-alone study, with only a Bible needed for reference. Biblical understanding, discipling, and mentoring are also among my acquired skills.

- Personality Temperament (Myers-Briggs, Matrix Type):

  Being an ENTP (a driven, choleric doer) enables me to prepare and write weekly studies for adult classes, small groups, and multiple one-on-ones. It also drives me to seek out those who have gifts and talents to accomplish the ministry tasks I am striving to enhance.

- Leadership Style (Situational Leadership, Primary/Secondary/ Team):

  My total score of 30 indicates a high degree of adaptability in accurately diagnosing the ability and willingness of followers. My primary leadership style is S2 (which enables me to clarify biblical truth for those who don't understand it); the secondary is S3 (which enables me to encourage those who may be unwilling to accept biblical truth); the remainder is S1 (which enables me to talk to and guide those who are unwilling and unable to accept and understand biblical truth).

- Core Values (Value, Description, Focus, Context, Time Frame):
  - continually striving to understand more of Christ and His Word
  - striving to serve Christ according to His Word
  - loving my wife, kids (and their spouses), and grandkids
  - being a Christ-like role model for my family and church family
  - teaching and recording biblical truths for skeptics, seekers, and young Christians
- Operational Principles (Philosophy of Engagement, Axiomatic Truths for You):
  - We exist to bring honor and glory to God. Biblical truth is the only door we can bring it through.

Ultimate Contribution(s) (Legacy, Aroma, Epitaph—*So What*)
Within six weeks of receiving Christ (thirty-eight years ago), I became involved with mentoring (ministering to individuals and organizing small groups) for the sake of spreading the Gospel. I have also been a founder of small-group ministries in two churches and am currently helping stabilize a small-group ministry at CCC. Over the last twelve years, I have been a writer of Bible studies (capturing ideas and reproducing them in written form) to inform others of the Gospel.

Guide Examples

Example A: Debby

Being mentored by others …

Mentoring Purpose(s): to establish my faith by building a biblical foundation

Mentor Category and Type(s): Intensive—Discipler

Mentor Candidate(s): female ministry leader; Sunday school teacher; female mentor

Mentoring Area(s): basic discipleship

Accountability Parameters: Follow recommended accountability guidelines. Meet monthly to assess progress and determine faithfulness. Evaluate commitment to discipleship process related to completion of assignments.

Mentoring Objective(s):

1. Establish biblical foundations including an understanding of fundamental Christian doctrines.

2. Establish biblical foundations including an understanding of salvation through Christ.

3. Establish biblical foundations including an understanding of the Bible, prayer, worship, fellowship, and stewardship.

4. Establish biblical foundations including an understanding of living by faith, obedience, and godliness.

Expected Outcome(s):

- knowledge about the Bible
- deeper personal relationship with God
- guidelines for how to live by faith
- development of spiritual disciplines

Preferred Format(s): one-on-one engagement with a mentor; meetings at least twice a month

Evaluation Criteria: completion of assignments

Time Period: 6 months

Mentoring Contract Guidelines

1. Purpose of the mentoring relationship, criteria for evaluation, regularity of interaction, and accountability parameters: see above.

2. Communication options: in person; by phone, text messaging, and e-mail.

3. Level of confidentiality required: complete confidentiality unless specified otherwise.

4. Life cycle of the relationship: 6 months.

5. Periodic evaluation time frame: monthly.

6. Declaration of expectations and responsibilities: to be determined.

7. Closure details: celebration when discipleship is completed.

Long-Range Mentoring Goals (Two Years)

- **Spiritual Goals:** to grow in knowledge about and knowledge of my faith
- **Personal Goals:** to learn the books of the Bible and their major themes; to learn how to memorize scripture; to learn how to study the Bible
- **Intellectual Goals:** development of a broad, comprehensive knowledge of the Bible and establishment of procedures for growing in my faith
- **Relational Goals:** to develop a deeper relationship with Christ

Personal mentoring of others …

Formal Mentoring (Number or Persons): Once I have completed discipleship, I intend to disciple two people over the next year.

Informal Mentoring (Number or Persons): I want to be available to help others build a strong faith foundation.

Nonformal Mentoring (Venue or Resource): I plan to read four Christian biographies in the next year.

Co-mentoring with others …

Internal Co-mentors: I plan to meet with other mentors who are discipling others.

External Co-mentors: I'm not sure.

Example B: Tony

Being mentored by others …

Mentoring Purpose(s): to develop leadership competency and assume a ministry leadership role

Mentor Category and Type(s): Occasional—Counselor and/or Sponsor

Mentor Candidate(s): mature ministry leader; retired leader; marketplace leader; pastor

Mentoring Area(s): I would like to develop competencies in basic ministry leadership, form my character as a biblical leader, and clarify my giftedness.

Accountability Parameters:

1. Evaluate my effectiveness in the practice of basic competencies.

2. Assess my character to ensure it honors God.

3. Determine my spiritual gifts, abilities, and skills.

Mentoring Objective(s):

1. Learn basic leadership competencies.

2. Tune my heart to God's heart so that my character brings honor to Him.

3. Understand my unique wiring and how I can leverage it for Kingdom purposes.

4. Get recommendations for ministry opportunities related to my skill set.

Expected Outcome(s):

- Effectively implement basic ministry competency.
- Establish evidence that my character reflects the heart of God.
- Establish my toolbox of skills I can use for ministry purposes.
- Determine what type of leader I am.

Preferred Format(s): one-on-one meetings with an accomplished leader; assignments that will help me develop as a leader

Evaluation Criteria: knowledge and practice of leadership competencies based on my wiring and my character

Time Period: 9 months

Mentoring Contract Guidelines

1. Purpose of the mentoring relationship, criteria for evaluation, regularity of interaction, and accountability parameters: see above.

2. Communication options: in person and by e-mail.

3. Level of confidentiality required: complete confidentiality unless specified otherwise.

4. Life cycle of the relationship: 9 months.

5. Periodic evaluation time frame: monthly.

6. Declaration of expectations and responsibilities: to be honest and candid with me; to hold me accountable; to provide a candid assessment of my leadership capacity; to make recommendations about where I best fit.

7. Closure details: celebration when mentorship is completed.

Long-Range Mentoring Goals (Two Years)

- **Spiritual Goals:** to grow in Christ-like character
- **Personal Goals:** to develop as a leader, with increasing responsibility and scope of ministry activity
- **Intellectual Goals:** to understand leadership from a biblical perspective and apply what I have learned from that foundation

Personal mentoring of others …

Formal Mentoring (Number or Persons): Once I have completed mentorship, I intend to mentor two people over the next year and three people the following year.

Informal Mentoring (Number or Persons): I will seek opportunities to teach leadership principles and practices whenever I am given an opportunity to do so.

Nonformal Mentoring (Venue or Resource): I plan to attend two leadership development conferences a year. I also intend to read a leadership book every quarter for the next two years.

Co-mentoring with others ...

Internal Co-mentors: I plan to meet with other leaders who are on a similar journey as mine.

External Co-mentors: I plan to seek out external mentors who have a similar desire to invest in other leaders.

Example C: Nancy

Being mentored by others ...

Mentoring Purpose(s): I seek to develop an ongoing personal and spiritual development program consisting of exposure to historical saints who have left an indelible and positive legacy worth emulating.

Mentor Category and Type(s): Passive—Historical

Mentor Candidate(s): female leaders in the Bible; Henreitta Mears; Joyce Myers; Ann Graham Lotts

Mentoring Area(s): I would like to establish principles and practices for becoming a woman who will finish well and make significant contributions to facilitating God's redemptive purposes in the world.

Accountability Parameters:

1. the establishment of an ongoing journal that will serve as a repository for lessons learned

2. a record of books read from key female authors

3. the development of lessons for passing on to other women

4. the mentoring of other women who have a similar interest

5. attendance at conferences that will satisfy my mentoring purposes

Mentoring Objective(s):

1. Learn timeless principles that will expedite my spiritual and personal formation.

2. Learn how to develop my inner life so I can effectively engage external circumstances.

3. Learn principles I can share with other women.

Expected Outcome(s):

- establishment of principles and practices leading to spiritual and personal maturation
- writing of lessons learned so they can be passed on to others
- development of passive mentoring resources

Preferred Format(s): reading the classics; reviewing case studies; attending conferences and workshops taught by passive mentors; listening to recorded messages on subjects germane to my developmental interests.

Evaluation Criteria: evidence of spiritual and personal maturation that can be observed by others

Time Period: 12 months

Mentoring Contract Guidelines

1. Purpose of the mentoring relationship, criteria for evaluation, regularity of interaction, and accountability parameters: see above.

2. Communication options: NA.

3. Level of confidentiality required: NA.

4. Life cycle of the relationship: 12 months.

5. Periodic evaluation time frame: quarterly.

6. Declaration of expectations and responsibilities: I want to notice positive changes and growth in my life.

7. Closure details: NA.

Long-Range Mentoring Goals (Two Years)

- **Spiritual Goals:** to mature as a believer and follower of Christ
- **Personal Goals:** to develop emotional intelligence in terms of self-awareness, social awareness, relationship management, and self-management

Personal mentoring of others ...

Formal Mentoring (Number or Persons): Once I have established a workable pattern for spiritual and personal development, I intend to share my findings with others seeking the same.

Informal Mentoring (Number or Persons): I will seek opportunities to put into written form the lessons I have learned from others who have gone before me.

Nonformal Mentoring (Venue or Resource): I will mentor at least two others in practices that will help them mature spiritually and personally.

Co-mentoring with others ...

Internal Co-mentors: I plan to meet with others who have similar interests.

External Co-mentors: I plan to seek out external mentors who have a similar desire to grow spiritually and personally through passive means.

Appendix B: Bible Study

Observation

What does the Bible say?

In this first step of Bible study, you are a detective. You are simply making an unemotional observation. Resist the temptation to jump to application. The basic idea of observation is awareness—it is training the eye to see and the mind to grasp what is there.

You are seeking to answer the following questions:

What do I see? What are the clues? What are the facts?

Techniques

1. Five *W*s and an *H*
- *Who* is involved?
    - Who is the author?
    - Who are the major figures?
    - Who are the key people involved?
    - Who was the book (chapter, passage) written for?
- *What* is (are) the event(s)?
    - Write a summary sentence.
    - What are key words?
    - What are the key events?
    - What are the key ideas?
    - What particular problems are addressed?
- *When* did it happen?
    - Describe the times.
    - Describe the historical background.
    - When was it written?
    - What is the historical setting?

- *Where* does it take place?
    - What major places are cited?
    - What specific locations are cited?
- *Why* did it happen?
    - Explain the general significance of the passage.
- *How* did it transpire?
    - Explain the personal significance of the passage.

2. What to Look For ...
- things that are *emphasized* ...
- things that are *repeated* ...
- things that are *related* ...
- things that are *alike* ...
- things that are *unalike* ...
- things that are *true to life* ...

3. Look for Relationships ...
- comparisons and contrasts (i.e., *but, like*)
- repetition (e.g., John 15:1–8)
- connectives (e.g., *therefore, if, because, and, or, then*)
- progression (i.e., progression of an idea; e.g., Eph. 4:17–24; 2 Pet. 1:5–7)
- major ideas (i.e., themes, etc.)
- minor ideas (i.e., subthemes, etc.)
- cause and effect (i.e., *if ... then*)

Scripture Observation Passages

You might want to select a single passage and use it through all three steps of observation, interpretation, and application.

- Genesis 3:1–7
- Psalm 1:1–6
- Psalm 15:1–5
- Psalm 139:1–18
- Matthew 4:1–11
- Matthew 5:1–12
- John 4:46–54

- John 14:23–27, 16:5–15
- John 15:1–8
- Romans 1:1–18
- 1 Corinthians 3:10–15
- Galatians 5:16–26
- Ephesians 4:1–16
- Ephesians 4:17–24
- Philippians 2:5–11
- 2 Timothy 3:16–17
- Titus 2:11–14
- Hebrews 4:12
- James 2:14–26
- 1 John 2:15–17

Interpretation

What does the passage mean?

When you're interpreting a passage, your objective is to determine what the original author meant at the time of its writing. Here the interpreter bombards the text with questions such as, "What did these details mean to the people to whom they were given? Why did the author say this? What is the major idea the author is seeking to communicate?" Interpretation answers the following general questions:

What is the context? What did it mean then? What does it mean today?

Procedure

1. **Use a literal Bible** (i.e., NIV, NRSV, or NASV). Work from the assumption that the Bible is authoritative. Its primary purpose is to change our lives, not increase our knowledge.

2. **Read the verse or passage in context.**

3. **Review cross-references.**

4. **Apply the seven basic rules of interpretation,** adapted from *Understand* by Walter A. Henrichsen:

Interpret the Bible in light of its language, history, and culture. Use the common meaning of the words. Be careful to note the type of language used (e.g., narration, poetry, prophesy) and figures of speech (e.g., hyperbole, metaphor, simile, analogy). When an inanimate object is used to describe a living being, the statement may be considered figurative. When an expression is out of character with the thing described, the statement may be considered figurative.

Allow scripture to interpret scripture. Consider the whole counsel of God's word to shed light on the passage being analyzed. Consult cross-references. This rule answers the question, How does this relate to the rest of what the Bible says?

Individual verses of the Bible must be understood in the context of other verses in that passage. Interpret a word in relation to its sentence and context. Interpret a passage in harmony with its context.

Each passage of scripture has one interpretation; however, there may be more than one application. Interpret personal experience in light of scripture, not scripture in light of personal experience.

Do not build major doctrines or positions on isolated or unclear verses of the Bible. Biblical examples are authoritative only when supported by a command (e.g., John 3:34–35). A doctrine cannot be considered biblical unless it sums up and includes all that the scriptures may say about it. When two doctrines taught in the Bible appear to be contradictory, accept both as scriptural in the confident belief that they resolve themselves into a higher unity.

In most cases, as with the rest of the Bible, parables have one basic meaning.

There are two guardrails along the highway of correct biblical interpretation: the Holy Spirit and the Christian community. Saving faith and the Holy Spirit are necessary for us to understand and properly interpret the scriptures.

5. **Use common biblical resources.** You might consider purchasing Bible study software containing all the resources you need (PC Biblesoft, Logos Software).
    *   an exhaustive concordance
    *   a Bible dictionary or encyclopedia

- a Bible handbook
- a Bible atlas
- a topical Bible
- a Bible introduction or survey
- a book of biblical customs and traditions
- a good (and current) commentary

6. Summarize findings.

7. Derive timeless truths.

Keys to Interpretation

- Content
- Context
- Comparison
- Culture
- Consultation

Scripture Interpretation Passages

You might want to select a single passage and use it through all three steps of observation, interpretation, and application.

- Genesis 3:1–7
- Psalm 1:1–6
- Psalm 15:1–5
- Psalm 139:1–18
- Matthew 4:1–11
- Matthew 5:1–12
- John 4:46–54
- John 14:23–27, 16:5–15
- John 15:1–8
- Romans 1:1–18
- 1 Corinthians 3:10–15
- Galatians 5:16–26
- Ephesians 4:1–16
- Ephesians 4:17–24
- Philippians 2:5–11

- 2 Timothy 3:16–17
- Titus 2:11–14
- Hebrews 4:12
- James 2:14–26
- 1 John 2:15–17

Application

How does this passage apply in general? How does this passage apply to me specifically? I recommend keeping a journal to record what God is saying to everyone in general and to you specifically.

Techniques

1. Questions to ask …
   - Is there an *example* for me to follow?
   - Is there a *sin* to avoid?
   - Is there a *promise* to claim?
   - Is there a *prayer* to repeat?
   - Is there a *command* to obey?
   - Is there a *condition* to meet?
   - Is there a *verse* to memorize?
   - Is there an *error* to observe or avoid?
   - Is there a *challenge* to face?
   - Is there a *lesson* I should learn?
   - Is there a *principle* I should comprehend?
   - Is there a *belief* I should act on?
   - Is there a *value* I should consider?

2. "SPECKS"
   - **S**ins to forsake!
   - **P**romises to claim!
   - **E**xamples to follow!
   - **C**ommands to obey!
   - **K**nowledge to acquire about God, Christ, or myself!
   - **S**tumbling blocks to avoid!

3. 2 Timothy 3:16
   - Teaching
   - Reproof
   - Correction
   - Instruction in Righteousness
   - Steps to Make This Part of My Life
     1. things to do today …
     2. things to do in one week …
     3. things to do by the end of the month …

Scripture Application Passages

You might want to select a single passage and use it through all three steps of observation, interpretation, and application.

- Genesis 3:1–7
- Psalm 1:1–6
- Psalm 15:1–5
- Psalm 139:1–18
- Matthew 4:1–11
- Matthew 5:1–12
- John 4:46–54
- John 14:23–27, 16:5–15
- John 15:1–8
- Romans 1:1–18
- 1 Corinthians 3:10–15
- Galatians 5:16–26
- Ephesians 4:1–16
- Ephesians 4:17–24
- Philippians 2:5–11
- 2 Timothy 3:16–17
- Titus 2:11–14
- Hebrews 4:12
- James 2:14–26
- 1 John 2:15–17

Appendix C: Operational Beliefs

The following operational beliefs originally appeared in *Victory Over the Darkness* by Neil T. Anderson. I have excerpted many of them. For a complete list, please refer to the book.[511]

I am the salt of the earth (Matt. 5:13).

I am the light of the world (Matt. 5:14).

I am a child of God (John 1:12).

I am part of the true vine, a channel of Christ's life (John 15:1, 5).

I am Christ's friend (John 15:15).

I am chosen and appointed by Christ to bear his fruit (John 15:16).

I am a slave of righteousness (Rom. 6:18).

I am enslaved to God (Rom. 6:22).

I am a son of God; God is spiritually my father (Rom. 8:14–15; Gal. 3:26).

I am a joint heir with Christ, sharing his inheritance with Him (Rom. 8:17).

I am a temple—a dwelling place—of God. His Spirit and life dwell in me (1 Cor. 3:16, 6:19).

I am united to the Lord and am one spirit with Him (1 Cor. 6:17).

I am a member of Christ's body (1 Cor. 12:27; Eph. 5:30).

I am a new creation (2 Cor. 5:17).

I am reconciled to God and am a minister of reconciliation (2 Cor. 5:18–19).

I am a son of God and one in Christ (Gal. 3:26, 28).

I am an heir of God since I am a son of God (Gal. 4:6–7).

I am a saint (Eph. 1:1; 1 Cor. 1:2).

I am God's workmanship—His handiwork—born anew in Christ to do His work (Eph. 2:10).

---

511 Anderson, *Victory Over the Darkness*, 38–39.

I am a fellow citizen with the rest of God's family (Eph. 2:19).

I am a prisoner of Christ (Eph. 3:1, 4:1).

I am righteous and holy in Christ (Eph. 4:24).

I am a citizen of heaven, seated in heaven right now (Phil. 3:20; Eph. 2:6).

I am hidden with Christ in God (Col. 3:3).

I am an expression of the life of Christ because He is my life (Col. 3:4).

I am chosen of God, holy and dearly loved (Col. 3:12; 1 Thess.1:4).

I am a son of light and not of darkness (1 Thess. 5:5).

I am a holy partaker of a heavenly calling (Heb. 3:1).

I am a partaker of Christ; I share in His life (Heb. 3:14).

I am one of God's living stones, being built up in Christ as a spiritual house (1 Pet. 2:5).

I am a member of a chosen race, a royal priesthood, a holy nation, a people for God's own possession (1 Pet. 2:9–10).

I am an alien and stranger to this world in which I temporarily live (1 Pet. 2:11).

I am an enemy of the devil (1 Pet. 5:8).

I am a child of God, and I will resemble Christ when He returns (1 John 3:1–2).

I am born of God, and the evil one—the devil—cannot touch me (1 John 5:18).

I am not the great "I am," but by the grace of God, I am what I am (1 Cor. 15:10).

Appendix D: Core Values

The list that follows is not exhaustive. There may be other values God will lay on your heart. The key is to make sure it is a biblical value. That is why you should select a verse or two to frame the values. You might also want to look at the Book of Proverbs; in that book are the values that matter to God.

Abundance	Consciousness	Expressiveness	Intelligence	Precision
Acceptance	Consistency	Fairness	Intensity	Preparedness
Accomplishment	Content over Fluff	Faith	Intimacy	Presence
Accountability	Contentment	Faithfulness	Intuitiveness	Preservation
Accuracy	Continuity	Fame	Inventiveness	Privacy
Achievement	Continuousness	Family	Investing	Proactivity
Acknowledgement	Contribution	Fidelity	Joy	Progress
Adaptability	Control	Flexibility	Justice	Prosperity
Adventure	Conviction	Flow	Kindness	Punctuality
Aggressiveness	Convincing	Focus	Knowledge	Quality
Agility	Cooperation	Forgiveness	Leadership	Quiet
Alertness	Courage	Fortitude	Learning	Rationality
Ambition	Courtesy	Freedom	Liberty	Recognition
Anticipation	Creativity	Friendship	Logic	Relationships
Appreciation	Curiosity	Frugality	Longevity	Reliability
Assertiveness	Daring	Fun	Love	Religion
Attentiveness	Decisiveness	Generosity	Loyalty	Resourcefulness
Audacity	Delight	Gentleness	Making a Difference	Respect
Awareness	Dependability	Giving	Mastery	Responsibility
Balance	Desire	Going Beyond	Maturity	Righteousness
Beauty	Determination	Goodness	Meaning	Risk Taking
Belonging	Devotion	Grace	Merit	Romance
Blissfulness	Dignity	Gratitude	Mindfulness	Safety
Boldness	Diligence	Growth	Modesty	Security
Bravery	Discipline	Guidance	Money	Self-Control
Brilliance	Discovery	Happiness	Motivation	Self-Esteem
Calm	Discretion	Hard Work	Nonviolence	Selflessness
Candor	Diversity	Harmony	Openness	Seriousness
Carefulness	Drive	Health	Opportunity	Service
Caring	Duty	Helpfulness	Optimism	Simplicity
Certainty	Eagerness	Heroism	Order	Sincerity
Challenge	Education	Holiness	Organization	Skill
Change	Effectiveness	Honesty	Orientation	Speed
Charity	Efficiency	Honor	Originality	Spirit
Cheerfulness	Elation	Hopefulness	Outcome	Stability
Clarity	Elegance	Hospitality	Outstanding Service	Strength
Cleanliness	Empathy	Humility	Passion	Style
Collaboration	Encouragement	Humor	Patience	Teamwork
Comfort	Endurance	Imagination	Peace	Timeliness
Commitment	Energy	Improvement	Perceptiveness	Tolerance
Communication	Enjoyment	Independence	Perseverance	Tradition
Community	Enthusiasm	Influence	Persistence	Tranquility
Compassion	Equality	Ingenuity	Personal Growth	Trust
Competence	Excellence	Inner Peace	Pleasure	Truth
Competition	Excitement	Innovation	Poise	Unity
Concentration	Experience	Insightfulness	Positive Attitude	Variety
Confidence	Expertise	Inspiration	Power	Well-Being
Connection	Exploration	Integrity	Practicality	Wisdom

Appendix E: Confessional Prayers

The following prayers are adapted from Neil T. Anderson's work and are suggested for removing sinful motives, values, and beliefs from our lives.[512]

1. **Ask God to reveal the corrupted motives, values and beliefs that are producing ungodly behavior in your life** (John 16:13, 24; Ps. 139:23–24). Spend time in reflection and prayer.

Dear heavenly Father, You have told us to put on the Lord Jesus Christ and make no provision for the flesh in regard to its lusts (Rom. 13:14). I acknowledge that I have given in to fleshly lusts that wage war against my soul (1 Pet. 2:11). I thank You that in Christ Jesus my sins are forgiven, but I have transgressed Your holy law and given the enemy an opportunity to wage war in my members (Rom. 6:12–13; James 4:1; 1 Pet. 5:8). I come before Your presence to acknowledge these sins and false beliefs and to seek Your cleansing (1 John 1:9) that I may be freed from the bondage of sin and falsehood. I now ask You to reveal to my mind the ways that I have transgressed Your moral law and grieved the Holy Spirit. In Jesus's precious name, I pray, Amen.

2. **Name them before the Lord and renounce them in the power of His Holy Spirit** (Eph. 4:15, 25).

Dear heavenly Father, I know that You desire truth in the inner self and that facing this truth is the way of liberation (John 8:32). I acknowledge that I have been deceived by the father of lies (John 8:44) and that I have deceived myself (1 John 1:8). I pray in the name of the Lord Jesus Christ that You, heavenly Father, will rebuke all deceiving spirits by virtue of the shed blood and resurrection of the Lord Jesus Christ. By faith I have

---

512 Adapted from Anderson, *Resolving Spiritual Conflicts* (Freedom in Christ Ministries, 1992).

received You into my life, and I am now seated with Christ in the most heavenly (Eph. 2:6). I acknowledge that I have the responsibility and authority to resist the devil, and when I do he will flee from me. I now ask the Holy Spirit to guide me into all truth (John 16:13). I ask You to "search me, O God, and know my heart; try me and know my anxious thoughts; and see if there be any hurtful way in me, and lead me in the everlasting way" (Ps. 139:23–24). In Jesus's name, I pray. Amen.

3. **If it is repeated sin in a specific area, confess it before God** (1 John 1:8–9).

Dear heavenly Father, You have said that rebellion is as the sin of witchcraft, and insubordination is as iniquity and idolatry (1 Sam. 15:23). I know that in action and attitude I have sinned against You with a rebellious heart. I ask Your forgiveness for my rebellion and pray that by the shed blood of the Lord Jesus Christ, all ground gained by the evil one and his spirits because of my rebelliousness be canceled. I pray that You will shed light on all my ways that I may know the full extent of my rebelliousness, and I now choose to adopt a submissive attitude and a servant's heart. I now confess these sins to You and claim through the blood of the Lord Jesus Christ my forgiveness and cleansing. I ask this in the wonderful name of my Lord and Savior, Jesus Christ. Remind me of this commitment and give me the courage to follow through with obedience. Amen.

4. **Replace the corrupted belief(s) with a biblically based belief (system)** (John 8:31–32). Read aloud the following affirmation of faith, and do so again as often as necessary to remind yourself of God's truth.

- I recognize there is only one true and living God (Exod. 20:2–3) who exists as the Father, Son, and Holy Spirit, and that He is worthy of all honor, praise, and glory as the Creator, sustainer, and beginning and end of all things (Rev. 4:11, 5:9–10; Isa. 43:1, 7, 21).

- I recognize Jesus Christ as the Messiah, the Word who became flesh and dwelt among us (John 1:1, 14). I believe that He came to destroy the works of Satan (1 John 3:8) and that He disarmed the rulers and authorities and made a public display of them, having triumphed over them (Col. 2:15).

- I believe that God has proven His love for me because when I was still a sinner, Christ died for me (Rom. 5:8). I believe that He delivered me from the domain of darkness and transferred me to His Kingdom, and in Him I have redemption, the forgiveness of sins (Col. 1:13–14).

- I believe that I am now a child of God (1 John 3:1–3) and that I am seated with Christ in the heavens (Eph. 2:6). I believe that I was saved by the grace of God through faith, and that my salvation was a gift and not the result of any works on my part (Eph. 2:8).

- I choose to be strong in the Lord and in the strength of His might (Eph. 6:10). I put no confidence in the flesh (Phil. 3:3), for the weapons of warfare are not of the flesh (2 Cor. 10:4). I put on the whole armor of God (Eph. 6:10–20), and I resolve to stand firm in my faith and resist the evil one.

- I believe that apart from Christ I can do nothing (John 15:5), and so I declare myself dependent upon Him. I choose to abide in Christ in order to bear much fruit and glorify the Lord (John 15:8). I announce to Satan that Jesus is my Lord (1 Cor. 12:3), and I reject any counterfeit gifts or works of Satan in my life.

- I believe that the truth will set me free (John 8:32) and that walking in the light is the only path of fellowship (1 John 1:7). Therefore I stand against Satan's deception by taking every thought captive in obedience to Christ (2 Cor. 10:5). I declare that the Bible is the only authoritative standard (2 Tim. 3:15–16). I choose to speak the truth in love (Eph. 4:15).

- I choose to present my body as an instrument of righteousness, a living and holy sacrifice, and I renew my mind and heart by the living Word of God in order to prove that the will of God is good, acceptable, and perfect (Rom. 6:13, 12:1–2). I have put off the old self with its evil practices and put on the new self (Col. 3:9–10), and I declare myself to be a new creature in Christ (2 Cor. 5:17).

- I ask my heavenly Father to fill me with the Holy Spirit (Eph. 5:18), lead me into all truth (John 16:13), and empower my life that I may live above sin and not carry out the desires of the flesh (Gal. 5:16).

- I crucify the flesh (Gal. 5:24) and choose to walk by the Spirit. I renounce all selfish goals and choose the ultimate goal of love (1 Tim. 1:5). I choose to obey the two greatest commandments: to love the Lord my God with all my heart, soul, and mind; and to love my neighbor as myself (Matt. 22:37–39).

- I believe that Jesus has all authority in heaven and earth (Matt. 28:18) and that He is the head over all rule and authority (Col. 2:10). I believe that Satan and his demons are subject to me in Christ since I am a member of Christ's body (Eph. 1:19–23). Therefore I obey the command to resist the devil (James 4:17) and command him in the name of Christ to leave my presence.

5. **Commit to acting on your new beliefs and values at every opportunity. Your worldview and motives will change as a direct result. Your behavior will follow** (James 2:14–26).

Appendix F: Process Items

J. Robert Clinton and his team of researchers have identified fifty-one process items God uses to shape believers in general and leaders in particular. The process items occur at different stages of a believer's development and may be repeated. The response of a believer to God's processing will determine how he or she advances along the continuum of spiritual maturity. God already knows our response to process items; processing is for the benefit of the follower of Christ.

authority insights P(AI): Those instances in ministry when a leader learns important lessons, via positive or negative experiences, about submission to authority, authority structures, authenticity or power bases underlying authority, authority conflict, or how to exercise authority.

basic skills P(BS): Skills acquired during the foundational phase, and/or the values learned in acquiring those skills, that will later affect leadership skills, attitudes, and styles.

conflict P(C): Incidents in a leader's life in which God uses conflict, whether personal or ministerial, to develop his or her dependence upon faith in God and inner-life growth.

contextual P(CXT): Providential factors arising in local, regional, national, and international situations during a leader's life that affect spiritual, ministerial, and strategic formations and frequently are a venue for God's strategic guidance for the leader.

crisis P(CR): Special, intense situations of pressure that God uses to test us and teach us dependence.

destiny fulfillment P(DF): A grouping of process items—significant acts, people, providential circumstances, or timing—that represents the completion of destiny processing that has gone on previously.

destiny preparation P(DP): A grouping of process items—significant acts, people, providential circumstances, or timing—that hints at some future or special significance and, when studied in retrospect, reinforces a sense of destiny in a leader's life.

destiny revelation P(DR): A grouping of incidents or process items with an unusual sense of God's presence working in them—significant acts, people, providential circumstances, or timing that confirm a future destiny and perhaps begin to clarify its nature.

divine affirmation P(DA): A special kind of destiny experience in which God gives approval to a leader so that he or she has a renewed sense of ultimate purpose and a refreshed desire to continue serving God.

divine contact P(DC): A person whom God brings in contact with a leader at a crucial moment in that leader's development in order to affirm potential, encouragement, specific guidance, protection from error, a challenge, a ministry opportunity, or some other blessing.

double confirmation P(DBLC): An instance when God makes clear His will by giving guidance directly to a leader and then reinforcing it through some other person who is totally independent and unaware of that guidance.

entry context P(EC): Items that are related to the cultural and historical settings of the local, regional, national, and international situation into which a leader is born and in which he or she will minister, and that God will use to process the leader in terms of strategic guidance, long-term convergence, and sense of destiny.

faith challenge P(FCHG): Those instances in ministry when a leader is challenged to take a leap of faith in regard to ministry and sees God meet that leap of faith with divine affirmation and ministry achievement that increase the leader's capacity to trust God in future ministry.

faith check P(FCHK): A process item God uses to shape a leader so that he or she can learn to trust God, by faith, to intervene in his or her life or ministry; refers to an early challenge God gives to a potential leader concerning some issue in which God's reality and faithfulness can be tested and seen to be true, and that builds the leader's confidence to trust God with bigger issues later.

family influence P(FI): Significant situations, events, and personalities that occurred in a leader's early family life and helped mold his or her character, perspectives, abilities, etc., and that will play a significant part in God's later leadership intentions.

flesh act P(FLESH): A decision made hastily or without proper discernment of God's choice; involves the leader using some human manipulation or other means, bringing ramifications that later negatively affect his or her ministry and life.

gifted power P(GP): A specific instance of the use of a spiritual gift in which it is clear that the Holy Spirit is channeling power through the use of the gift.

giftedness discovery P(GD): Any significant advancement along the giftedness development pattern, and the event, person, or reflection process that was instrumental in bringing about the discovery giftedness.

ideal influence-mix discovery P(IMD): Any significant discovery or use of the influence mix that results from the harmonizing of major and minor convergence factors.

ideal role discovery P(IRD): Any significant discovery or use of a role that enhances a leader's giftedness and maximizes influence-mix effectiveness.

influence challenge P(ICHG): An instance when a leader is prompted by God to take steps to expand leadership capacity in terms of sphere of influence.

integrity check P(IC): The special kind of process that God uses to evaluate heart (intent; consistency between inner convictions and outward actions) and that is a foundation from which God expands a leader's capacity to influence. The word *check* is used in the sense of *test*, meaning a check or checkup. See also *testing patterns*.

isolation P(I): The setting aside of a leader from normal ministry involvement in its natural context, usually for an extended time, so the leader will experience God in a new or deeper way. The isolation is God's work, not necessarily the result of the circumstances at hand.

leadership backlash P(LB): The reaction of followers, other leaders within a group, and/or Christians outside the group to a course of action taken by a leader because of its various ramifications. The situation is used to test the leader's perseverance, clarity of vision, and faith.

leadership committal P(LCOM): A special shaping activity of God observed in leadership emergence theory that is usually a spiritual benchmark and produces a sense of destiny in a leader. It is the call to leadership by God and the wholehearted response by the leader to accept and abide by that call. Paul's "road to Damascus" experience, the destiny revelation given by Ananias, and Paul's response to it as a life calling are classic New Testament examples of leadership committal.

life crisis P(LC): A high-pressure crisis situation in which a leader searches out the meaning and purpose of life and, as a result, experiences God in a new way as the source, sustainer, and focus of life.

literary (P/LI): The means by which God teaches leaders lessons for their own lives through the writing of others.

mentoring (P/M): The process through which a person with a serving, giving, encouraging attitude (the mentor) sees leadership potential in a still-to-be-developed person (the protégé) and promotes or otherwise significantly influences the realization of that potential.

ministry affirmation P(MAF): A special kind of destiny experience in which God gives approval to a leader in terms of some ministry assignment in particular or some ministry experience in general, resulting in the leader's renewed sense of purpose.

ministry assignment P(MASG): A ministry experience that is more permanent than a ministry task but has the same basic pattern of entry, ministry, closure, and transition out of the ministry situation, and through which God gives new insights to the leader in order to expand his or her influence capacity and responsibility for future leadership.

ministry challenge P(MCHG): The means by which a leader or potential leader is prompted to accept a new ministry assignment and sense God guiding him or her into service.

ministry conflict P(MCONF): Those instances in ministry in which a leader learns lessons, via the positive and negative aspects of conflict, about the nature of the conflict and possible ways to resolve it, possible ways to avoid or creatively use conflict, and God's personal shaping through conflict.

ministry skill P(MS): The acquisition of one or more identifiable skills that aid one in a ministry assignment.

ministry structure insights P(MSI): Discoveries about the various organizational units through which ministry is channeled, and the effects of those discoveries on leadership capacity.

ministry task P(MT): An assignment from God that primarily tests a person's faithfulness and obedience but often also allows use of ministry gifts in the context of a task that has closure, accountability, and evaluation.

negative preparation P(NEG): The special processing during which God uses events, people, conflict, persecution, or experiences, all focusing on the negative, to free someone from a situation so he or she can enter the next phase of development.

networking power P(NP): God's unusual use of mentors, divine contacts, or other related leaders to channel power in order to open doors or accomplish influence goals for a leader so that the leader senses the importance of relationships with other leaders and knows the touch of God through personal networks.

obedience check P(OC): That special category of process items through which God tests someone's personal response to revealed truth in his or her life.

paradigm shift P(PS): God's use of an incident or series of incidents to impress upon a leader a major new perspective for use in ministry.

power P(PI): Demonstrations of God's intervention that convince followers that God is indeed supporting the leader in his or her ministry.

power encounter P(PE): A crisis ministry situation in which there is confrontation between people representing God and people representing other supernatural forces, and in which power is the determining issue, God's credibility is at stake, and vindication is made by an unusual demonstration of God's power.

prayer challenge P(PC): Those instances in ministry when God impresses a leader in an unusual way with the essential spiritual dynamic lesson of ministry (a leader in ministry must pray for that ministry) and during which there is positive growth that affects later ministry.

prayer power P(PP): The use of specific prayer in a specific situation in such a way that it is clear that God has answered the prayer and demonstrated the authenticity of the leader's spiritual authority.

relationship insights P(RI): Those instances in ministry when a leader learns lessons, via positive or negative experiences, about relating to other Christians or non-Christians in light of ministry decisions or other means of influence. These lessons are intended to significantly affect future leadership.

social base P(SB): Incidents in which God gives guidance concerning one's social base; teaches lessons concerning the priority or importance of the social base to ministry; or teaches lessons concerning any of the three formations (spiritual, ministerial, strategic) from the members of the social base. These can occur during any developmental phase.

Social base includes emotional, economic, strategic, and social support:

> *Emotional support* involves the "soul mate" qualities of a trusted relationship which foster intimacy, freedom, support, safety, and renewal. It includes a listening support system which provides empathy, encouragement, and affirmation.

> *Economic support* is the financial base that covers cost of living, medical needs, retirement, recreation, and professional/ ministry goals.

> *Strategic support* provides guidance and support for the fulfillment of a leader's professional and ministerial calling and goals. It provides an outlet through which the leader can express his or her deepest concerns and dreams regarding life purpose.
>
> *Social support* is concerned with the question of how support is provided for basic needs, desires, and drives, such as issues of financial management, child care, sexuality, family crises, and addiction support systems.

sovereign guidance P(SG): God's guiding intervention in the life and ministry of a leader through the unique alignment of circumstances that point toward God's development of the emerging leader.

spiritual authority discovery P(SAD): Any significant discovery, insight, or experience that advances a leader along the spiritual authority development pattern.

spiritual warfare P(SW): Those instances in ministry when the leader discerns that ministry conflict is primarily supernatural in its source and essence, and resorts to various power items to solve the problem in such a way that leadership capacity, notably spiritual authority, is expanded.

training progress P(TP): A closure experience through which a leader's identifiable progress is noted in terms of influence capacity, responsibility, or self-confidence. It occurs during or after a period of training—formal, nonformal, or informal.

word check P(WC): A process item that tests a leader's ability to understand or receive a word from God personally and see it worked out in life with a view toward enhancing the authority of God's truth and the desire to know it.

word P(WI): An instance when a leader receives a word from God that significantly affects his or her guidance, committal, decision making, personal value system, spiritual formation, spiritual authority, or ministry philosophy.

Appendix G: Personality Temperament

I have included two instruments of my design. The first is a matrix that represents a composite of many personality theories and structures. Review the listed characteristics of Types A, B, C, and D and identify the style truest of you.

The second instrument will help you determine your temperament using Myers-Briggs categories. Explanations of your findings can be found on the Internet; simply type in the letters (e.g., INTJ, ESFP). Other instruments for determining your personality temperament are widely available on the Internet, as well.

TEMPERAMENT MATRIX
A Composite View from Many Sources
Dr. Greg Bourgond

CATEGORY	TYPE 'A'	TYPE 'B'	TYPE 'C'	TYPE 'D'
PERSONALITY STYLE	Driver, Lion, Choleric, Doer, "D"	Expressive, Otter, Sanguine, Influencer, "I"	Amiable, Golden Retriever, Phlegmatic, Relater, "S"	Analytical, Beaver, Melancholy, Thinker, "C"
	INTP-ENTP-INTJ-ENTJ	ISTP-ESTP-ISFP-ESFP	ISFJ-ESFJ-ISTJ-ESTJ	INFJ-ENFJ-INFP-ENFP
LEADERSHIP STRENGTH	Doing the Difficult	Influencing Others	Implementing Teamwork	Insuring Quality
PERSONAL MOTIVATION	Challenge Results	Recognition Desire to Help Others	Appreciation Relationships	To Be Right Quality
LEADS THROUGH	Forcefulness Persistence	Verbal Skills Motivational Skills	Building Relationships Group Interaction	Structure Methodology
LEADERSHIP WEAKNESS	Insensitive Impatient Inflexible Demanding Taking On Too Much	Impulsive Too Optimistic Lack of Follow Through Talking Too Much Jumping To Conclusions	Non-Initiating Resists Change Avoids Conflict Being Indecisive Meeting Deadlines	Overly Cautious Too Detailed Pessimistic Rigidness Resisting Responsibility
UNDER TENSION	Autocratic	Attacks	Acquiesces	Avoids
NEEDS TO TRUST GOD FOR	Unconditional Love Patience With Others Being More Flexible	Better Control of Time Discipline Discernment	More Goal Orientation Facing Confrontation Initiating More	Being More Optimistic Self-Confidence Being More Open
NEEDS OTHERS TO PROVIDE	Sensitivity to Others Caution Details and Facts	To Handle Details A Logical Approach Concentration on Task	Stretch To Challenge Help Solving Problems Initiative and Change	Quick Decision Making Reassurance Stretching of Capabilities
IDEAL LEADERSHIP SITUATION	Challenge Change Freedom Authority	New and Exciting Freedom from Detail Opportunity to Motivate Social Interaction	Area of Specialization Working with a Group Consistency Opportunity to Help	Clearly Defined Requires Precision Limited Risk Methodology & Structure
IMPROVEMENT AREA	Listening	Pausing	Initiating More	Declaring
BIBLICAL MODELS	Paul & Martha	Peter & Ruth	Barnabas & Mary	Moses & Mary (Jesus)

Dr. Greg Bourgond

Determining Personality Temperament

	Where, primarily, do you prefer to direct your energy? *How do you recharge your batteries?*		
E	People, things, situations, "The Outer World"… Around people.	I	Ideas, information, explanations, beliefs, "The Inner World"… Away from people.
	How do you prefer to process information? *Do you generally focus on the present or the future?*		
S	Prefer to deal with facts, what you know…(concrete) Focus on the <u>present</u>.	N	Prefer to deal with ideas, look into the unknown…(abstract) Focus on the <u>future</u>.
	How do you prefer to make decisions? *Where do your decisions come from?*		
T	Primarily on logic and an <u>objective</u> analysis of cause and effect. The head.	F	Primarily on values and on <u>subjective</u> evaluation of personal concerns. The heart.
	How do you prefer to organize your life? *When considering an issue how do you prefer to respond?*		
J	Prefer plans, stability, and organization. Prefer to <u>have things settled</u>.	P	Prefer to go with the flow, flexibility, react to situations. Prefer to <u>keep my options open</u>.
	Online Instrument: Keirsey Temperament Sorter (KTS-II) - http://www.keirsey.com/ Our **personality temperament** is our *expression of being*. Our **leadership style** is our *method of influence*.		

Gregory W. Bourgond, DMin, EdD (2010)

340

Appendix H: Giftedness Venn Diagram[513]

A Venn diagram is a pictorial diagram that uses symbols, spacing, and sizes to communicate information. By the end of this chapter, you should be able to draw a Venn diagram to display your giftedness set. The diagram uses three elements to communicate information.

Symbols

Three different symbols are used to display giftedness:

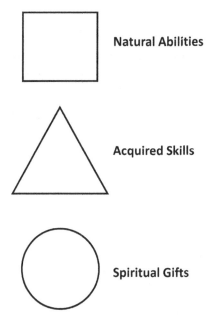

Natural Abilities

Acquired Skills

Spiritual Gifts

---

513 These guidelines are the original creation of Bobby Clinton. I have adapted them for the purposes of this book. The original guidelines were first outlined in a reader used in a course Clinton taught, ML530 Romans Series.

Size

The size of the symbols is important. Bigger denotes more importance; smaller denotes less importance.

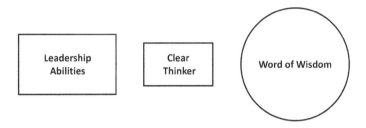

In this example, there are two natural abilities and one spiritual gift shown. The leadership abilities are shown as more important than the ability of clear thinking. The spiritual gift of word of wisdom is larger than the natural abilities of leadership and clear thinking; therefore the spiritual gift is more important than the natural abilities.

Spacing

Spacing is the most complex feature of a Venn diagram. The way you place two symbols on the diagram shows the relationship between them. If two elements of the giftedness set are seen as working together, they would be placed in a way that demonstrates that relationship. Overlap means that some of both elements occur simultaneously. Where there is no overlap, the elements also occur alone.

The most important elements are the largest ones; they are placed in the center of the diagram.

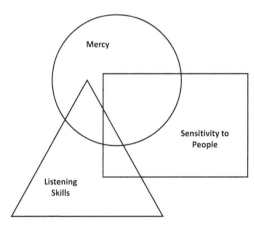

In this example, this person is demonstrating a relationship between three elements of the giftedness set. The dominant feature is the natural ability of sensitivity to people. Its symbol is the largest one, placed in the center of the diagram. The spiritual gift of mercy enhances the operation of this natural ability in a ministry situation; God takes the person's natural sensitivity and empowers it with His Holy Spirit and releases the love of God in the situation. This person also has acquired some skills in the area of listening. One would summarize this diagram by saying that this person uses his/her natural ability to release a spiritual gift, usually through listening to others.

Diagram Development Steps

Step 1: Gather Your Data

At this point you should have identified the most important elements of your giftedness set. List them here.

Your Natural Abilities:
Your Acquired Skills:
Your Spiritual Gifts (primary gifts only):

Step 2: Determine the Focal Element

Before you can start drawing your giftedness diagram, you'll need to decide which is the focal element, the element that dominates your giftedness. You will make that symbol the biggest. Occasionally there will be two elements that are equally important, but that's not common.

Step 3: Determine Relationships and Importance

Begin with the focal element and determine how dominant each of its components is. For example, if spiritual gifts are the focal element, then look at your list of gifts and determine which one of those is dominant and make it the biggest. Then decide how the other gifts relate to that gift. When you overlap symbols, the overlap area indicates that all the overlapping items operate together. Then move to the other two elements of the giftedness set and repeat the process.

Step 4: Draw Your Diagram

By now you should have assigned some degree of importance to and some degree of relationship among the various components of your giftedness set. Begin drawing, starting with your focal element. Make the dominant component the largest and place it in the center. Then add the other components, placing them according to their importance and relationships as you see them. It will probably take you two or three tries, so do the first few in pencil.

Step 5: Get Feedback

Once you have drawn a rough draft, contact some people who know you and have observed you closely. Share your diagram with them. Talk through the relationships of the various components, describing how you see the importance of each one. Get feedback. As you share the diagram and talk about it, you will learn more. You may want to modify your diagram based on what you have learned.

Step 6: Prepare Your Final Draft

Once you have gotten some feedback, you can draw your final draft. Recognize that giftedness development is not static; your giftedness set will change over the years as you grow and mature. From time to time, review your giftedness set and modify it as you see fit.

Example

In the diagram below, the spiritual gift of teaching is the focal element. Other gifts of exhortation, wisdom, and knowledge either orbit around teaching or are central to teaching, as is the case of wisdom. The natural intellectual abilities used in teaching always have elements of exhortation, wisdom, and knowledge embedded whenever teaching takes place.

When the acquired skills of motivation, mentoring, and communication come into play, they always have a teaching dimension.

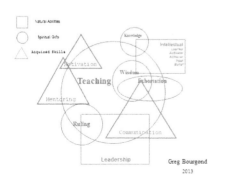

Notice that leadership, ruling, and communication are close to each other and always include some teaching when they are exercised. The acquired skill of communication, in my case, includes speaking and writing.

344

Appendix I: Leadership Style

The situational leadership model is described in chapter 9. Two additional models, McManus and Clinton, are also mentioned. The specific characteristics and features of the latter two are described below. You are encouraged to review the specifics and identify your primary leadership style using any or all of the models discussed.

Erwin McManus Model

Primary Leadership Styles

Vision: Envisions clearly God's future—*Clarity*. Defines the *focus* (purpose, aim) of what we do and answers the question of *why*. Responsible for commission. Sees possibilities and solves problems. Sees two years or more out. Visionary leaders (theorists) draw strategic personnel who may be catalytic or corporate leaders. *Solomon & John (NT)*

Passion: Experiences deeply God's concerns—*Intensity*. Defines the *form* (style, pattern) of what we do and answers the question of *how*. Responsible for community. Coaches and counsels. Sees thirty days out. Passionate leaders (zealots) draw tactical personnel who may be catalytic or causal leaders. *Elisha & Peter (ESP/NF)*

Mission: Embraces personally God's appointment—*Destiny*. Defines the *scope* (task, ministry) of what we do and answers the question of *what*. Responsible for communication. Coordinates and organizes. Sees one day out. Mission leaders (specialists) draw logistical personnel who may be corporate or causal leaders. *Noah & Luke (SJ/ISP)*

Secondary Leadership Styles

Corporate Leader: Brings together the powerful focus and intentionality of *vision* and *mission*. A *visionary strategist* best suited to working with systems and structures. Through their ability to invest in long-term goals and use organizational structures to accomplish them, corporate leaders often emerge as both *entrepreneurs* and *executive leaders. Nehemiah & James (ENTJ/INTJ)*

> Must ensure that he is constantly in touch with people's emotional transition and not simply the restructuring of the organization. The lack of a "human factor" is often the Achilles heel of his leadership. He must surround himself with counselors who have their fingers on the pulse of the people. He will increase his effectiveness by remembering that people are motivated by passion.

Catalytic Leader: Brings together the dynamic and catalytic combination of *vision* and *passion*. An *entrepreneurial initiator* who works best in an environment where he or she can generate new ideas and actions. Catalytic leaders are natural risk takers who test boundaries and barriers and often emerge as *new paradigm pioneers. David & Apollos (ENFP/ENTP)*

> Must ensure that he continually identifies and develops emerging leadership, since he rarely remains in whatever endeavor he has initiated. He must either choose to establish a long-term base of ministry or unify his ministry through a common purpose or mission. Without a commitment to reproduce and restrict himself, his efforts may be diluted and fail to result in a multigenerational impact.

Causal Leader: Brings together the persuasive and focused intensity of *passion* and *mission*. A *compelling flag bearer* for the cause he or she cares deeply about. Causal leaders work best on short-term assignments that require rapid mobilization and response. Excelling under pressure, they often emerge as exceptional *cause and crisis leadership. Elijah & Stephen (ESTP/ENFJ)*

> Must ensure he is continually connected to a visionary or he might focus on short-term issues or problems that are disconnected from the long-range goals and direction of the ministry. Driven by values and issues, he leads others

through hands-on activism. He will increase his effectiveness in decision making by beginning with the end in mind.

Team Leadership Styles

Dream team excellence needs *strategic*, *tactical*, and *logistical* personnel.

Strategic Leader: Skillfully develops, coordinates, and employs goals and tactics. Sets challenging visionary goals that often seem impossible to achieve. Strategic leaders are analytical and systematic in their thinking and are gifted in the ability to foresee the implications of present decisions on future effectiveness. Strategic leaders are *two-year visionaries*.

> Gift Mix: Faith, Leadership, Apostleship, Discernment, Word of Wisdom
> Style Mix: INTJ, INTP, ENTP, ENTJ

Tactical Leader: Expeditiously implements tasks and develops objectives to accomplish goals. Tactical leaders are powerful motivators with the uncanny ability to mobilize others to accomplish a specific task. They will ensure the implementation and application of theory and will drive impersonal concepts to the meeting of human needs. They are players/coaches who believe deeply in their cause and care deeply for their team. They are hands-on leaders who are highly focused on the task at hand. Tactical leaders are *thirty-day visionaries*. They excel in short-term projects.

> Gift Mix: Exhortation, Helps, Mercy, Hospitality, Prophecy
> Style Mix: ENFJ, ENFP, INFJ, ISTP, INFP

Logistical Leader: Streamlines organization and administration related to the mobilization of resources, materials, and information. Logistical leaders will ensure the simplification of abstract concepts, validate intuitive leaps with facts and data, and manage the organization of material. Logistical leaders are *one-day visionaries*. They administer the immediate next step in the overall strategy.

> Gift Mix: Administration, Serving, Giving, Word of Knowledge, Teaching
> Style Mix: ISTJ, ESTJ, ISFJ, ISTP, ESFJ

Bobby Clinton Model

Leadership Styles

At the heart of leadership style theory is the way the leader operates towards followers in all that he/she does. These behaviors are usually located upon a continuum characterized by four basic positions: highly directive, directive, nondirective, and highly nondirective.

Commander—*Highly Directive.* Makes decisions, gives specific instructions, closely supervises carrying out of instructions, and feels a necessity for being personally controlling.

> **Apostolic Style:** The leader with this style assumes the role of delegated authority over those for whom he or she is responsible, receives revelations from God concerning decisions, and commands obedience based on the role of delegated authority and revelation concerning God's will. *1 Thess. 5:12–13; 1 Tim. 5:17; Heb. 13:17; 1 Thess. 2:6*

> **Confrontation Style:** This approach to problem solving brings the problem out into the open with all parties concerned, analyzes it in light of revelational truth, and brings force to bear upon the parties to get them to accept recommended solutions. *1 and 2 Corinthians Letters, Jude*

> **Father-Initiator Style:** This is similar to the apostolic style, and it uses the leverage that comes to those who have founded the work to gain acceptance of influence. Obligation is used as a power base. *1 Cor. 4:14–15*

Motivator—*Directive.* Makes decisions, may dialogue, and may explain. Demands feedback, intervenes frequently to ensure results, feels responsible for implementation, and has a need to control.

> **Obligation-Persuasion Style:** An appeal to followers to obey some recommended directives that uses persuasion, not commands, leaving the decision to do so in the hands of the followers but forcing them to recognize their obligations to the

leader due to the leader's past service to the follower. Strongly implies that the follower owes the leader some debt and should follow the recommended advice as part of paying back the obligation. Reflects the leader's strong expectation that the follower will conform to the persuasive advice. *Philemon, 1 and 2 Corinthians*

Father-Guardian Style: A style primarily concerned with protecting and encouraging followers. Expresses a mutually caring relationship between the leader and the follower. Often used when the leader is spiritually mature and followers are spiritually immature. *1 Thess. 2:10–11*

Participator—*Nondirective.* Leader and followers decide, leader shares ideas, and leader facilitates and encourages follower-made decisions with guidance and encouragement. Leader monitors and gives guidance only when needed; follower gives frequent feedback and feels responsible for implementing results.

Maturity Appeal Style: A *form* of leadership influence that relies on godly experience, usually gained over a long period of time; empathetic identification based on shared experience; and recognition of the influential power of modeling to convince people to accept the leader's ideas. *1 Pet. 5:1–4; 2 and 3 John; 2 Cor. 11:16–33, 12:1–10*

Nurse Style: A style characterized by gentleness, sacrificial service, and loving care that indicates that a leader has given up rights in order to nurture those following him or her. *1 Thess. 2:7; 2 Tim. 2:24–25*

Delegator—*Highly Nondirective.* Follower makes decisions, is responsible for the decision, and may keep leader informed. Leader observes, intervening only for corrective feedback, while follower feels responsible for implementing the results.

Imitator Style: The conscious use of modeling to influence followers. The leader models appropriate thought or behavior with the expectation that followers will be encouraged to follow his or her example. *Phil. 4:9; 2 Tim. 3:10–11*

Consensus Style: Leadership that involves group participation in decision making and finding solutions acceptable to the whole group. The leader must be skilled at bringing diverse thoughts together to meet the whole group's needs. *Acts 5, 13, 15*

Indirect Conflict Style: An approach to problem solving that requires discerning the spiritual motivation behind the problem and usually results in spiritual warfare without direct confrontation with the parties involved. *1 Cor. 5: 3–5; Matt. 16:21–23; Mark 3: 20–30; Eph. 6:10–20*

Appendix J: Five Habits Checklist

There are five habits that help enhance a believer's capacity to finish well. They are one result of the research of Dr. J. Robert Clinton, professor of leadership at Fuller Seminary in Pasadena, California. Clinton has studied more than four thousand biblical, historical, and contemporary servants of God.

1. Effective believers maintain a learning posture throughout their entire lives. They never stop learning—informally (reading, personal growth, projects, personal research); nonformally (workshops, seminars, conferences); or sometimes formally (continuing education, degree programs).

2. Effective believers recognize mentoring as a priority. They are committed to being mentored and mentoring others God brings their way.

3. Effective believers have dynamic statements of personal calling. They allow God to continually shape their unique and ultimate contributions. A believer's calling typically emerges in one's late thirties and the ability to articulate it in one's forties and fifties.

4. Effective believers experience repeated times of renewal. Effective, godly servants develop intimacy with God which, in turn, overflows into all parts of their lives and ministries.

5. Effective believers increasingly perceive their lives in terms of a big-picture, lifetime perspective. They manifest a growing awareness of their sense of destiny. This habit is the focus of this workbook and exercise.

The Five Habits Checklist[514]

Read each statement and check the number on the continuum that most accurately describes you. Check 0 if the statement on the left represents you; check 5 if you feel you are described best by the statement on the right. Numbers 1 through 4 reflect various positions between the two extremes.

I have a desire to do some personal growth projects, but I seldom have the time or discipline necessary to do so.	|—|—|—|—|—| 0 1 2 3 4 5	I view my personal development as a lifelong learning process and am regularly involved in study projects.
I hear of various workshops and seminars that others find helpful, but I seldom attend.	|—|—|—|—|—| 0 1 2 3 4 5	I regularly attend workshops and seminars that help enhance my personal growth and development as a leader.
I am simply too busy or have little desire for continuing formal education.	|—|—|—|—|—| 0 1 2 3 4 5	I enjoy my continuing education classes and am currently enrolled in an education program.
I do some things for myself, but I don't feel fulfilled or that I am growing as a person or leader.	|—|—|—|—|—| 0 1 2 3 4 5	I work to develop the "whole" person and set improvement goals for wide areas of personal growth development.

Section One Total _____

I feel overwhelmed by the needs of the ministry and seldom, if ever, spend time developing new leaders.	|—|—|—|—|—| 0 1 2 3 4 5	I am always in the process of developing a pool of new leaders to release into ministry.
It is often hard for me to imagine that I have something to offer in a mentoring relationship to others.	|—|—|—|—|—| 0 1 2 3 4 5	I generally have a good estimation of the strengths and abilities I can offer to other leaders.
I feel "alone" in the ministry and feel there are few who are helping me grow.	|—|—|—|—|—| 0 1 2 3 4 5	I deeply value others and have a regular series of relationships that help me grow and develop.
I don't know what my actual developmental needs are or how a mentor could help.	|—|—|—|—|—| 0 1 2 3 4 5	I view my development as a high priority and have obtained mentors to help ensure my ongoing growth.

Section Two Total _____

I often feel frustrated, wondering if I am doing what God really intends for me.	|—|—|—|—|—| 0 1 2 3 4 5	I feel the things I do every day are meaningful and part of my biblical purpose and reason for existence.
I sometimes get glimpses of what I should do with my life, but somehow these visionary moments get lost in busy activity.	|—|—|—|—|—| 0 1 2 3 4 5	I have thought deeply about why I exist as a person and have clarified my personal vision and what God is calling me to accomplish.
I often work based upon the need of the moment as opposed to a clear philosophy of engagement.	|—|—|—|—|—| 0 1 2 3 4 5	I am able to decide what is important for me to do, basing my decisions upon a clear ministry philosophy.
I am easily frustrated by changes in the direction of ministry or in my life situation.	|—|—|—|—|—| 0 1 2 3 4 5	I feel like I have a clear direction, but I allow God to teach me new things and alter how I should act.

Section Three Total _____

I nearly always feel "buried," having more to do than I can handle. Getting away for me seems impossible.	|—|—|—|—|—| 0 1 2 3 4 5	I regularly schedule times away for personal retreat and reflection.
I feel that "personal" time is selfish, especially when I am called to help minister to others.	|—|—|—|—|—| 0 1 2 3 4 5	I feel an investment in my personal walk with Christ will cause me to experience deeper intimacy with Christ and greater effectiveness.
If someone were to ask me how long has it been since I have felt the presence of God, I'd have to respond, "Quite some time."	|—|—|—|—|—| 0 1 2 3 4 5	I regularly experience times of renewal and freshness in my walk and intimacy with Christ.

---

514 Used by permission of Terry B. Walling, *Leader Breakthru* (2013).

Although I know the spiritual disciplines are important to real growth, I seldom have time to focus on them.	0 1 2 3 4 5	My walk with Christ is greatly enhanced through regular usage of a variety of spiritual disciplines.

Section Four Total _____

I have trouble rising above the current circumstances to get a big-picture perspective on my life.	0 1 2 3 4 5	I earnestly try to understand my current circumstance in light of what God has been doing over my lifetime.
I realize that God is shaping my life, but I seldom am able to understand how He is at work in my life.	0 1 2 3 4 5	I feel that the things that happen to me every day are part of God's development of my life, and I can recognize patterns of His work.
I have trouble trying to keep track of the many areas of my life: home, office, etc.	0 1 2 3 4 5	I feel a sense of order in my life because I am able to regularly gain perspective on my life.
I hear other leaders talk about their calling and vision, but I rarely feel I have a sense of destiny.	0 1 2 3 4 5	In my times with Christ, I continue to sense a unique, personal destiny that He has for my life.

Section Five Total _____

Go back and total your score in each section. Record your totals in the boxes. Review your scores. Where are you strong? Weak? Look at your scores in relationship to each other.

Habit #1 (lifelong learning) and Habit #4 (repeated times of renewal) are attitudes that a believer must commit to maintain if they are to finish well.

Habit #5 (perspective), Habit #3 (personal calling) and Habit #2 (mentoring) are the three steps that comprise the Focused Living process.

1. Maintains a learning posture throughout life.   Section One Total _____
2. Commitment to being mentored and mentoring.   Section Two Total _____
3. Dynamic personal mission and calling.   Section Three Total _____
4. Repeated times of personal renewal.   Section Four Total _____
5. Lifetime, big-picture perspective   Section Five Total _____

Any section 12 or below should signal a serious need to make some major changes. Any section between 13 and 16 should signal a need for improvement.

Appendix K: Accountability Guidelines

The following accountability guidelines are provided to help you finish well. Following these suggestions will safeguard the trustworthiness of the mentoring experience.

When you meet with your accountability partner, every exchange should start with two questions: "How has God blessed you this week?" and "What problem has consumed you this week?" Regarding your spiritual life, I recommend that the accountability partner ask the following questions:

1. **Regarding God's Word:** Have you read it consistently? If so, for how many days, and for how long? If not, why not, and will you next week?
2. **Regarding Prayer:** Describe your prayers—for yourself and others; for praise, confession, or gratitude. How is your relationship with Christ evolving?
3. **Regarding Temptation:** How have you been tempted since we last checked in? How did you respond?
4. **Regarding Confession:** Do you have any unconfessed sin in your life?
5. **Regarding Worship:** Did you worship in church this week? Was your faith strengthened? Was God honored?
6. **Regarding Witness:** Have you shared your faith? If so, in what ways? How can you improve?

Home life is a telling context for faithfulness and therefore should be included in the accountability realm.

1. **Regarding Your Spouse:** How is it going with your spouse in terms of time spent with him or her, meaningful conversation between you, attitudes conveyed, intimacy enjoyed, irritations

encountered, disappointments experienced, and his or her relationship with Christ?

2. **Regarding Your Children:** How are your children? Have you given them encouragement and quantity and quality time, imparted biblical values, and discussed educational pursuits and spiritual warfare issues and concerns?

3. **Regarding Finances:** How are your finances doing in terms of debt, sharing, saving, spending, and stewardship?

4. **Regarding Time:** How have you invested your time around the house? Have you fulfilled your household responsibilities?

The work environment is also a place where accountability questions should be asked.

1. **Regarding Your Job:** How are things going in terms of your career progress, relationships, temptations, workload, and stress? Are you working too much or too little?

2. **Regarding Your Testimony:** How have you lived out your faith? How have you honored or dishonored God since the last time we met? What impressions have you left with your coworkers?

Some critical concerns should also be raised during your accountability meetings.

1. **Regarding God's Will:** Do you feel you are in the center of God's will? Do you sense His peace?

2. **Regarding Thought Life:** What are you wrestling with in secret? What are you viewing that is causing you to stumble?

3. **Regarding Service:** What have you done for someone else since the last time we met that can't be repaid? Have you done anything for the poor? Have you encouraged anyone, extended mercy, or provided unconditional service to others?

4. **Regarding Priorities:** Are your priorities in the right order? Are you living a centered life or striving for balance? Are you living by the clock or the compass?

5. **Regarding Integrity:** Is your moral and ethical behavior as it should be? Are you truthful? Are you sexually pure?

6. **Regarding High-Risk Areas:** How are you doing in your personal high-risk areas?
7. **Regarding Transparency:** Are the "visible" you and the real you consistent in our relationship and your relationship with others? Did you just lie to me? If so, in what ways?

The accountability appointment should always conclude with ten to fifteen minutes of shared prayers focusing on concerns raised during the checkup.

Appendix L: Additional Resources

Anderson, Keith, and Randy D. Reese. *Spiritual Mentoring: A Guide for Seeking and Giving Direction*. Downers Grove: Inter Varsity Press, 1999.

Anderson, Leith. *Winning the Values War in a Changing Culture: Thirteen Distinct Values That Mark a Follower of Jesus Christ*. Minneapolis: Bethany House, 1994.

Anderson, Neil T. *The Bondage Breaker*. Eugene: Harvest House, 1990.

———. *The Core of Christianity*. Eugene: Harvest House, 2010.

———. *Victory Over the Darkness*. Ventura: Regal, 2000.

———. *Winning the Battle Within*. Eugene: Harvest House, 2008.

———. *Winning Spiritual Warfare*. Eugene: Harvest House, 1990.

Arterburn, Stephen, Fred Stoeker, and Mike Yorkey. *Every Man's Battle: Winning the War on Sexual Temptation: One Victory at a Time*. Colorado Springs: WaterBrook, 2000.

Arthur, Kay. *How to Study Your Bible*. Eugene: Harvest House, 1994.

Arthur, Kay, David Lawson, and B. J. Lawson. *Understanding Spiritual Gifts*. Colorado Springs: Waterbrook, 2010.

Barna, George. *Growing True Disciples: New Strategies for Producing Genuine Followers of Christ*. Colorado Springs: WaterBrook, 2001.

———. *Think Like Jesus: Make the Right Decision Every Time*. Nashville: Integrity, 2003.

———. *Transforming Children into Spiritual Champions*. Ventura: Regal, 2003.

Bertrand, J. Mark. *Rethinking Worldview: Learning to Think, Live, and Speak in This World*. Wheaton: Crossway Books, 2007.

Bevere, John. *Driven by Eternity: Making Life Count Today and Forever.* New York: Warner Faith, 2006.

Biehl, Bobb. *Mentoring.* Nashville: Broadman & Holman Publishers, 1997.

Blackaby, Henry T., and Claude V. King. *Experiencing God: How to Live the Full Adventure of Knowing and Doing the Will of God.* Nashville: Broadman & Holman, 1998.

Bonhoeffer, Dietrich. *The Cost of Discipleship.* New York: Touchstone, 1995.

Bourgond, Greg. *Papa's Blessings: The Gifts That Keep Giving.* Bloomington: iUniverse, 2011.

———. *A Rattling of Sabers: Preparing Your Heart for Life's Battles.* Bloomington: iUniverse, 2012.

———. *Reader: Ministry Competencies.* Minneapolis: Self-Published, 2003.

Boyd, Gregory A., and Edward K. Boyd. *Letters from a Skeptic.* Wheaton: Victor Books, 1994.

Bradberry, Travis, and Jean Greaves. *Emotional Intelligence 2.0.* San Diego: TalentSmart, 2009.

Brand, Paul W., and Philip Yancey. *Fearfully and Wonderfully Made.* Grand Rapids: Zondervan, 1980.

Bridges, Jerry. *The Discipline of Grace.* Wheaton: Tyndale House Publishers, 2006.

Briscoe, Stuart D. *Discipleship for Ordinary People.* Wheaton: Harold Shaw, 1995.

Briscoe, Stuart D., and Jill Briscoe. *The Family Book of Christian Values: Timeless Stories for Today's Family.* Elgin: Christian Parenting Books, 1995.

Buford, Bob. *Finishing Well: What People Who Really Live Do Differently!* Nashville: Integrity, 2004.

———. *Game Plan: Winning Strategies for the Second Half of Your Life.* Grand Rapids: Zondervan, 1997.

———. *Halftime: Changing Your Game Plan from Success to Significance.* Grand Rapids: Zondervan, 1994.

Bugbee, Bruce. *Discover Your Spiritual Gifts the Network Way: Four Assessments for Determining Your Spiritual Gifts.* Grand Rapids: Zondervan, 2005.

Bunyan, John, and James Henderson Thomas. *Pilgrim's Progress in Today's English.* Chicago: Moody, 1964.

Carpenter, Gary. *What the Bible Says about the Heart.* Joplin: College Press, 1990.

Cionca, John R. *Before You Move: A Guide to Making Transitions in Ministry.* Grand Rapids: Kregel Academic & Professional, 2004.

Clark, David K., and Robert Vincent Rakestraw. *Readings in Christian Ethics.* Grand Rapids: Baker Books, 1994.

Clifton, Donald O., and Edward "Chip" Anderson. *StrengthsQuest: Discover and Develop Your Strengths in Academics, Career, and Beyond.* Washington, DC: Gallup Organization, 2004.

———. *Finishing Well—Six Characteristics.* Altadena: Barnabas Publishers, 2007.

Clinton, J. Robert. *Having a Ministry That Lasts: Becoming a Bible Centered Leader.* Altadena: Barnabas, 1997.

———. *Leaders, Leadership and the Bible.* Altadena: Barnabas Publishers, 1993.

———. *Leadership Emergence Theory: A Self-Study Manual for Analyzing the Development of a Christian Leader.* Altadena: Barnabas Resources, 1989.

———. *The Leadership Emergence Theory Reader: Finishing Well—The Challenge of a Lifetime.* Altadena: Barnabas Publishers, 2005.

———. *The Making of a Leader: Recognizing the Lessons and Stages of Leadership Development.* Colorado Springs: NavPress, 2012.

———. *Strategic Concepts.* Altadena: Barnabas, 1995.

Clinton, Richard, and Paul Leavenworth. *Living and Leading Well.* CreateSpace, 2012.

———. *Starting Well: Building a Strong Foundation for a Lifetime of Ministry.* Altadena: Barnabas, 1998.

Cloud, Henry. *Integrity: The Courage to Meet the Demands of Reality.* New York: Collins, 2006.

Cloud, Henry, and John Sims Townsend. *Boundaries: When to Say Yes, When to Say No to Take Control of Your Life.* Grand Rapids: Zondervan, 1992.

Colson, Charles W. *Loving God.* Grand Rapids: Zondervan, 1983.

Colson, Charles W., and Harold Fickett. *The Faith: What Christians Believe, Why They Believe It, and Why It Matters.* Grand Rapids: Zondervan, 2008.

Colson, Charles W., and Nancy Pearcey. *How Now Shall We Live?* Wheaton: Tyndale House, 1999.

Damazio, Frank. *The Making of a Leader.* Portland: City Christian Publishing, 1996.

Eggerichs, Emerson. *Love & Respect: The Love She Most Desires; The Respect He Desperately Needs.* Nashville: Integrity, 2004.

Engstrom, Ted W., and Ron Jenson. *The Making of a Mentor: Nine Essential Characteristics of Influential Christian Leaders.* Waynesboro: Authentic Media, 2005.

Erickson, Millard J. *Concise Dictionary of Christian Theology.* Grand Rapids: Baker Book House, 1986.

Fee, Gordon D., and Douglas K. Stuart. *How to Read the Bible for All It's Worth: A Guide to Understanding the Bible.* Grand Rapids: Zondervan, 1993.

Foster, Richard J. *Celebration of Discipline.* Hodder & Stoughton, 1989.

————. *Sanctuary of the Soul: Journey into Meditative Prayer.* Downers Grove: Inter Varsity Press, 2011.

Friesen, Garry, and J. Robin Maxson. *Decision Making and the Will of God.* Sisters: Multnomah, 2004.

Grenz, Stanley J. *The Moral Quest: Foundations of Christian Ethics.* Downers Grove: Inter Varsity Press, 1997.

Hagberg, Janet, and Robert A. Guelich. *The Critical Journey: Stages in the Life of Faith.* Salem: Sheffield, 2005.

Harris, Joshua. *Dug Down Deep: Unearthing What I Believe and Why It Matters*. Colorado Springs: Multnomah Books, 2010.

Henrichsen, Walter A., and Gayle Jackson. *Studying, Interpreting, and Applying the Bible*. Grand Rapids: Lamplighter Books, 1990.

Hersey, Paul. *The Situational Leader*. Escondido: Center for Leadership Studies, 2008.

Hettinga, Jan David. *Follow Me: Experience the Loving Leadership of Jesus*. Colorado Springs: NavPress, 1996.

Holmes, Arthur F. *Contours of a World View*. Grand Rapids: Eerdmans, 1983.

Huckabee, Mike, and John Perry. *Character Is the Issue: How People with Integrity Can Revolutionize America*. Nashville: Broadman & Holman, 1997.

Hunter, James Davison. *The Death of Character: Moral Education in an Age without Good or Evil*. New York: Basic Books, 2000.

Hybels, Bill, Dale Larsen, Sandy Larsen, and Bill Hybels. *Character—Who You Are When No One's Looking: Six Studies for Individuals or Groups, with Guidelines for Leaders & Study Notes, NIV Text Included*. Downers Grove: Inter Varsity Press, 1994.

Hybels, Bill, Kevin Harney, and Sherry Harney. *Character: Reclaiming Six Endangered Qualities*. Grand Rapids: Zondervan, 1997.

Kaiser, Walter C., and Moisés Silva. *Introduction to Biblical Hermeneutics: The Search for Meaning*. Grand Rapids: Zondervan, 2007.

Keirsey, David. *Please Understand Me II: Temperament, Character, Intelligence*. Del Mar: Prometheus Nemesis Book Company, 1998.

Keirsey, David, and Marilyn M. Bates. *Please Understand Me: Character & Temperament Types*. Del Mar: Prometheus Nemesis Book Company, 2000.

Keller, Timothy J. *King's Cross: The Story of the World in the Life of Jesus*. New York: Dutton Redeemer, 2011.

———. *The Reason for God: Belief in an Age of Skepticism*. New York: Dutton, 2008.

Keller, Timothy J., and Katherine Leary Alsdorf. *Every Good Endeavor: Connecting Your Work to God's Work*. New York: Dutton, 2012.

Kise, Jane A. G., David Stark, and Sandra Krebs Hirsh. *Lifekeys: Discovering Who You Are, Why You're Here, What You Do Best*. Minneapolis: Bethany House, 1996.

Kreeft, Peter. *Back to Virtue: Traditional Moral Wisdom for Modern Moral Confusion*. San Francisco: Ignatius, 1992.

Kroeger, Otto, and Janet M. Thuesen. *Type Talk: The Sixteen Personality Types That Determine How We Live, Love, and Work*. New York: Dell, 1989.

LaHaye, Tim. *Spirit-Controlled Temperament*. Wheaton: Tyndale House Publishers, 1994.

Lawrence, Brother. *The Practice of the Presence of God: The Best Rule of a Holy Life*. Radford: Wilder, 2008.

Lewis, C. S. *The Abolition of Man,* San Francisco: Harper, 2009.

———. *The Great Divorce: A Dream*. San Francisco: Harper, 2001.

———. *Mere Christianity*. San Francisco: Harper, 2009.

———. *The Screwtape Letters, with Screwtape Proposes a Toast*. San Francisco: Harper, 2001.

Little, Paul E. *Know Who You Believe*. Downers Grove: Inter Varsity Press, 2008.

Little, Paul E., and Marie Little. *Know What You Believe*. Colorado Springs: Chariot Victor, 1999.

———. *Know Why You Believe*. Colorado Springs: Chariot Victor, 1999.

MacArthur, John. *Found: God's Will*. Colorado Springs: Chariot Victor, 1977.

———. *Glory of Heaven*. Wheaton: Crossway, 2013.

———. *The Pillars of Christian Character: The Basic Essentials of a Living Faith*. Wheaton: Crossway Books, 1998.

———. *The Power of Integrity: Building a Life without Compromise*. Wheaton: Crossway Books, 1997.

MacDonald, Gordon. *Building below the Waterline: Shoring Up the Foundations of Leadership*. Peabody: Hendrickson Pub, 2011.

———. *Mid-Course Correction*. Nashville: Nelson, 2000.

MacIntyre, Alasdair C. *After Virtue: A Study in Moral Theory*. South Bend: University of Notre Dame Press, 2003.

Malphurs, Aubrey. *Maximizing Your Effectiveness: How to Discover and Develop Your Divine Design*. Grand Rapids: Baker Books, 2006.

———. *Values-Driven Leadership: Discovering and Developing Your Core Values for Ministry*. Grand Rapids: Baker Books, 1996.

Marks, Darren C. *Bringing Theology to Life: Key Doctrines for Christian Faith and Mission*. Downers Grove: Inter Varsity Press Academic, 2009.

McCallum, Dennis. *The Death of Truth*. Minneapolis: Bethany House, 1996.

McDowell, Josh. *Evidence That Demands a Verdict*. Nashville: Nelson, 1999.

———. *Guide to Understanding Your Bible: A Simple, Step-by-Step Method for Effective Bible Study and Life Application*. Holiday: Green Key Books, 2006.

McGrath, Alister E. *Understanding Doctrine: Its Relevance and Purpose for Today*. Grand Rapids: Zondervan, 1992.

McIntosh, Gary, and Samuel D. Rima. *Overcoming the Dark Side of Leadership: How to Become an Effective Leader by Confronting Potential Failures*. Grand Rapids: Baker Books, 2007.

McManus, Erwin Raphael. *The Barbarian Way: Unleash the Untamed Faith Within*. Nashville: Nelson, 2005.

———. *Chasing Daylight: Dare to Live a Life of Adventure*. Nashville: Nelson, 2006.

———. *Seizing Your Divine Moment: Dare to Live a Life of Adventure*. Nashville: Nelson, 2002.

———. *Uprising: A Revolution of the Soul*. Nashville: Nelson, 2003.

———. *Wide Awake*. Nashville: Nelson, 2008.

McKnight, Scot. *King Jesus Gospel*. Grand Rapids: Zondervan, 2011.

Merritt, Bob. *When Life's Not Working: Seven Simple Choices for a Better Tomorrow*. Grand Rapids: Baker Books, 2011.

Murrow, David. *The Map: The Way of All Great Men*. Nashville: Nelson, 2010.

Myers, Isabel Briggs., and Peter B. Myers. *Gifts Differing: Understanding Personality Type*. Palo Alto: Davies-Black, 1995.

Nash, Ronald H. *Worldviews in Conflict: Choosing Christianity in a World of Ideas*. Grand Rapids: Zondervan, 1992.

Naugle, David K. *Worldview: The History of a Concept*. Grand Rapids: Eerdmans, 2002.

Nelson, Thomas. *Nelson's Complete Book of Bible Maps and Charts, 3rd Edition*. Nashville: Nelson, 2010.

Ortberg, John. *The Life You've Always Wanted: Spiritual Disciplines for Ordinary People*. Grand Rapids: Zondervan, 1997.

———. *Who Is This Man? The Unpredictable Impact of the Inescapable Jesus*. Grand Rapids: Zondervan, 2012.

Packer, J. I. *Affirming the Apostles' Creed*. Wheaton: Crossway Books, 2008.

———. *Keeping the Ten Commandments*. Wheaton: Crossway Books, 2007.

———. *Knowing God*. Downers Grove: Inter Varsity Press, 1973.

Packer, J. I., and Gary A. Parrett. *Grounded in the Gospel: Building Believers the Old-Fashioned Way*. Grand Rapids: Baker Books, 2010.

Patterson, Ben. *Serving God: The Grand Essentials of Work & Worship*. Downers Grove: Inter Varsity Press, 1994.

Peel, William Carr, and Kathy Peel. *Discover Your Destiny: Finding the Courage to Follow Your Dreams*. Colorado Springs: NavPress, 1996.

Piper, John. *The Passion of Jesus Christ: Fifty Reasons Why He Came to Die*. Wheaton: Crossway Books, 2004.

Rath, Tom, and Marcus Buckingham. *StrengthsFinder 2.0*. New York: Gallup Press, 2007.

Reese, Randy D., and Robert Loane. *Deep Mentoring: Guiding Others on Their Leadership Journey*. Downers Grove: Inter Varsity Press, 2012.

Rima, Samuel D. *Leading from the Inside Out: The Art of Self-Leadership*. Grand Rapids: Baker Books, 2000.

Scazzero, Peter. *Emotionally Healthy Spirituality: Unleash a Revolution in Your Life in Christ*. Nashville: Integrity, 2006.

Schwarz, Christian A. *The Three Colors of Ministry: A Trinitarian Approach to Identifying and Developing Your Spiritual Gifts*. St. Charles: ChurchSmart Resources, 2001.

Simon, Sidney B., Leland W. Howe, and Howard Kirschenbaum. *Values Clarification*. New York: Warner Books, 1995.

Sire, James W. *Naming the Elephant: Worldview as a Concept*. Downers Grove: Inter Varsity Press, 2004.

———. *The Universe Next Door: A Basic Worldview Catalog*. Downers Grove: Inter Varsity Press, 2009.

Smart, Ninian. *Worldviews: Cross-Cultural Explorations of Human Beliefs*. Upper Saddle River: Prentice Hall, 2000.

Smith, Gordon T. *Courage & Calling: Embracing Your God-Given Potential*. Downers Grove: Inter Varsity Press, 1999.

Stanley, Paul D., and J. Robert Clinton. *Connecting: The Mentoring Relationships You Need to Succeed in Life*. Colorado Springs: NavPress, 1992.

Stein, Robert H. *A Basic Guide to Interpreting the Bible: Playing by the Rules*. Grand Rapids: Baker Academic, 2011.

Stott, John R. W., and Lance Pierson. *Christian Basics: Beginnings, Belief, and Behavior*. Grand Rapids: Baker Book House, 1999.

Strauss, Mark L. *Four Portraits, One Jesus: An Introduction to Jesus and the Gospels*. Grand Rapids: Zondervan, 2007.

———. *How to Read the Bible in Changing Times: Understanding and Applying God's Word Today*. Grand Rapids: Baker Books, 2011.

Strobel, Lee. *The Case for a Creator: A Journalist Investigates Scientific Evidence That Points toward God*. Grand Rapids, MI: Zondervan, 2004.

Taylor, Daniel. *Is God Intolerant? Christian Thinking about the Call for Tolerance*. Wheaton: Tyndale House, 2003.

Tozer, A. W., and Jonathan L. Graf. *The Pursuit of God, with Study Guide.* Camp Hill: WingSpread, 2006.

Trent, John, Rodney Cox, and Eric Tooker. *Leading from Your Strengths: Building Intimacy in Your Small Group.* Nashville: Broadman & Holman, 2005.

Tripp, Paul David. *Dangerous Calling: Confronting the Unique Challenges of Pastoral Ministry.* Wheaton: Crossway, 2012.

Walling, Terry B. Focus *Workbook.* Chico: Leader Breakthru, 2013.

———. Mentoring *Workbook.* Chico: Leader Breakthru, 2013.

———. Perspective *Workbook.* Chico: Leader Breakthru, 2013.

———. *Stuck! Navigating the Transitions of Life and Leadership.* St. Charles: ChurchSmart Resources, 2008.

Warren, Richard. *The Purpose-Driven Life: What on Earth Am I Here For?* Grand Rapids: Zondervan, 2002.

Wells, David. *Losing Our Virtue.* Grand Rapids: Eerdmans Publishing Company, 1999.

Willard, Dallas. *Renovation of the Heart: Putting on the Character of Christ.* Colorado Springs: NavPress, 2002.

———. *The Spirit of the Disciplines.* London: Hodder & Stoughton, 1996.

Willard, Dallas, and Don Simpson. *Revolution of Character: Discovering Christ's Pattern for Spiritual Transformation.* Colorado Springs: NavPress, 2005.

Winseman, Albert L., Donald O. Clifton, and Curt Liesveld. *Living Your Strengths: Discover Your God-Given Talents and Inspire Your Community.* New York: Gallup Press, 2004.

Online Resources

The Clinton Institute (J. Robert Clinton)
BobbyClinton.com

- Getting Perspective: Using Your Unique Timeline
- Getting Perspective on Sense of Destiny
- Social Base Issues
- The Timeline: What It Is and How to Construct It
- Timelines of Thirteen Important Bible Leaders
- The Ministry Timeline
- Afterglow Perspective: Looking toward Finishing Well after a Lifetime of Ministry
- Isolation Processing: Learning Deep Lessons from God
- Lifelong Development Case Studies Reader
- Mentor Reader: Clinton Articles on Mentoring
- Focused Lives
- Leadership Values
- Unlocking Your Giftedness
- Conclusions on Leadership Style
- Lifelong Development Reader

Leader Breakthru (Terry Walling)
LeaderBreakthru.com

- APEX Online
- Your Life and the Generalized Timeline
- Focused Living Online
- Focusing Your Leadership
- Focusing Your Leadership Reader
- Perspectives Workbook
- Focus Workbook
- "Strategic Concepts" by J. Robert Clinton
- "Unlocking Your Giftedness" by J. Robert Clinton
- "Having a Ministry That Lasts" by J. Robert Clinton
- Mentoring Workbook
- Barnabas: A Study in Mentoring
- Finding Mentors: Building a Mentoring Constellation

The Convergence Group (Paul Leavenworth)
TheConvergenceGroup.org

- The Discipleship and Mentoring Workbook
- The Bible-Centered Leader Workbook
- The Spirit-Empowered Leader Workbook
- Finishing Well
- Deep Processing
- The Extraordinary Power of a Focused Life
- Focused Life Workshop (DVD)
- Finishing Well (DVD)

StrengthsFinder (Gallup Inc.)
GallupStrengthsCenter.com/

- Strengths Discovery Package
- Strengths Development Package
- Strengths Coaching Starter Kit
- Coaching Managers and Teams Kit

Ministry Insights (Rodney Cox)
MinistryInsights.com

- Profile: Leading from Your Strengths
- Profile: Marriage Insights
- Profile: Family Insights
- Parenting from Your Strengths
- Different By Design

Vantage Point 3 (Randy Reese)
VantagePoint3.org/

- The Journey
- A Way of Life

Bible Study Software

- PC Study Bible
  BibleSoft.com

- Logos Bible software
  Logos.com

Personality Inventories

- Keirsey Temperament Sorter
  www.keirsey.com/sorter/register.aspx
  www.keirsey.com/4temps/overview_temperaments.asp

- Jung Typology Test
  www.humanmetrics.com/cgi-win/jtypes2.asp

- Myers-Briggs Test – Personality Pathways
  www.personalitypathways.com/type_inventory.html

- Personality Inventory
  www.test.personality-project.org/

- Fullerton Personality Inventory
  www.psych.fullerton.edu/mbirnbaum/web/personalityb.htm

- Personality Test – Tim LaHaye
  www.goingthedistance.org/pages.asp?pageid=18151

Spiritual Gifts Inventories

- Gifted 2 Serve
  http://buildingchurch.net/g2s.htm

- Spiritual Breakthroughs
  www.elmertowns.com/spiritual_gifts_test/

- Church Growth
  www.churchgrowth.org/cgi-cg/gifts.cgi?intro=1

Situational Leadership
The Center for Leadership Studies
Situational.com

- Situational Leadership: The Model Online with LEAD Self and
  LEAD Others Assessments
- Situational Leadership: The Model Online with LEAD
  Self-Assessment

Index

N

narrative, as component of story, 172–174

nationalism, 75

natural abilities, 142, 150, 186, 189, 194, 206, 208

needs assessment (in mentoring), 238–241

negative preparation, 153–154, 178, 183, 336

negative shaping incidents, 175

Network (Bugbee, Cousins, and Hybels), 203

New Age, 75

new Dark Age, 66–67

nonformal mentoring, 250, 288, 293

nonformal ministry assignments, 150

Nooma Rhythm 011, 36

north cardinal point, 10–11, 63

North Star, truths of, 9

northeast intercardinal point, beliefs as, 63, 69–71

northwest intercardinal point, motives as, 64, 75–76

O

obedience check, 58, 149–150, 178, 336

occasional and needs-based mentors, 231, 249

Odysseus (Ulysses), 232

1 Corinthians
  4:5, 75
  12:4–7, 140, 144
  12:8–10, 144, 186
  13:4, 117
  13:4–8, 268

1 Peter, xxiii, 144

1 Timothy 4:16, 67

Onesimus, 246

one-thought method, 32

operating principles, 277, 280

operational beliefs, 72, 264, 294, 297, 299, 325–326

operational principles, 208

ordinal directions (of compass), 63

organizational, as category of ultimate contribution, 282–283

organizational influence, 46, 159, 235, 285

orientation
  Jesus Christ as source of, 23
  positioning and, 64–69

P

paradigm values, 30, 34–35

partner, as one of four styles of leadership, 191

passion, committed, 152, 197, 202–203, 205, 208, 215, 261, 272–274

passive and indirect mentor, 249

passive mentoring, 243–244

passive mentors, 232

pathway
  brain, 86
  character, 95–98
  conscience as faculty of, 85, 89–91
  heart as faculty of, 85, 92–95
  mind as faculty of, 85, 87–88
  soul as faculty of, 85, 91–92

Paul
  on discipline, 227
  as example of finishing well, 221
  on heart, 94
  as lifelong learner, 228
  as mentee, 246
  on the mind, 87

people, as part of your story, 173–174

perceptual attitudes, 20, 54, 57, 58, 64, 71, 74, 106, 112–114, 126, 162. *See also* attitudes (worldview)

V

values
as component of worldview, 74
core values. *See* core values
as domain of heart, 51, 53, 57–58, 60, 61
as related to and interdependent with beliefs, 73
as southeast intercardinal point, 64, 72–73
VEGA (Voice, Eyes, Gestures, and Attitude), 253
Venn diagram, 194, 341
Victory Over the Darkness (Anderson), 325
virtue, as level of resolve, 103
vocation, 143, 145

W

west cardinal point, 19–21, 63
wide-awake dream, xxxii–xli
wiring, 141, 142–143, 152
word, as process item, 156, 338
word check, 57, 149, 150, 177, 334, 338
the world, as magnetic influence, 77–78, 100
worldview (attitudes)
as domain of heart, 51, 54–55, 57–58, 60, 61
examples of, 295–296, 298, 300
list of corrupt worldviews, 75
as part of Focused Life Plan, 266–268
perceptual attitudes, 112–114
as southwest direction, 64
as southwest intercardinal point, 73–75
worship, as spiritual discipline, 19
woundedness (victim mentality), as one of six legacy barriers, 225
writer, as legacy, 213, 283

About the Author

Gregory W. Bourgond, DMin, EdD
Shoreview, Minnesota
E-mail: GWBourgond@aol.com
LinkedIn: Dr_Greg_Bourgond

Dr. Greg Bourgond earned a bachelor's degree in psychology from Chapman University (1979), a master of divinity degree (MDiv) from Bethel Seminary in San Diego (1983), a doctor of ministry degree (DMin) in church leadership from Bethel (1997), and a doctor of education degree (EdD) in instructional technology and distance education (2001) from Nova Southeastern University. He completed postgraduate studies at the Institute for Educational Management at Harvard Graduate School of Education (2003). He is the author of award-winning books such as *A Rattling of Sabers: Preparing Your Heart for Life's Battles*, published in 2010 and 2012, and *Papa's Blessings: The Gift That Keeps Giving*, published in 2011.

His previous experience includes ten years in the defense industry and commercial business and more than eighteen years in various ministry positions. He has held positions as a principal analyst and project manager for Analysis & Technology, Inc., senior project engineer for Hughes Aircraft Company, unit training manager for General Electric, and general manager for Burdick Companies. In ministry he has been a deacon, elder, ministry director, associate pastor, and executive pastor in San Diego, California, and Rochester, Minnesota. He completed twenty-nine years of active and reserve duty in enlisted and officer ranks in the US Navy.

He is currently executive pastor of Christ Community Church in Rochester and the director of online coaching certification for Ministry Advantage in Houston, Texas. He serves in several consulting roles with other ministry organizations. He served as assistant to the provost of Bethel University and director of strategy for online education, providing direction for advancement of online education across Bethel University's four academic units. He provided operational support to Bethel Seminary in the areas of distributed learning, budget development, and future strategic operations. He has also served as vice president for operations and strategic initiatives, dean of the Center of Transformational Leadership, and dean of academic affairs and instructional technology at Bethel Seminary.

Greg serves as a consultant and teacher in the areas of leadership formation and development, spiritual and personal formation, legacy, life mapping and focused living, organizational systems theory and applications, operational effectiveness, ministry planning, strategic planning, distance learning and technology-mediated course delivery, men's ministry, small-group dynamics, and mentoring. He is the president and founder of Heart of a Warrior Ministries, dedicated to helping men live lives of integrity and honor under the authority of God. He has taught in graduate and postgraduate schools and ministry organizations, and spoken and preached in many churches and ministry contexts around the world. He has also twice been C. S. Lewis visiting scholar-in-residence at the Kilns in Headington, England. He has been happily married for forty-five years and enjoys seeing his grandchildren every chance he gets.

Other books by Dr. Bourgond ...